THE NAME GAME

Hate nicknames? Choose a name that can't be shortened, like **Brooke** or **Brett**.

Are you a young urban professional? Names like **Emma** and **Jackson** are favored among yuppie parents.

Expecting a dramatic child? Give her or him a soap opera name, like **Lexie** or **Damian**.

Want your kid to stand out from the crowd? Choose a creative name, such as **Tallulah** or **Tarquin**.

A classy kid needs a classic name. How about **Grace** or **Henry**?

Are you a nature lover? Consider naming your child **Ocean** or **Spruce**.

WHAT'S IN A NAME? FIND OUT IN . . .

*Beyond
Jennifer & Jason,
Madison & Montana*

Beyond
Jennifer
& Jason,
Madison &
Montana

Linda Rosenkrantz
&
Pamela Redmond Satran

St. Martin's Paperbacks

BEYOND JENNIFER & JASON, MADISON & MONTANA

Copyright © 1999 by Linda Rosenkrantz and Pamela Redmond Satran.

Library of Congress Catalog Card Number: 99-22073

ISBN: 0-312-97462-0

Printed in the United States of America

St. Martin's Griffin Edition / July 1999
St. Martin's Paperbacks edition / March 2000

10 9 8 7 6 5 4 3 2 1

For our wonderful daughters

Chloe Samantha Finch
&
Rory Elizabeth Margaret Satran

CONTENTS

ACKNOWLEDGMENTS

Once again, our first and foremost thanks go to our peerless editor, Hope Dellon, for her unflagging support and enthusiasm. Special thanks also for their help in putting together this new edition of our book to Regan Graves, Leah Fletcher, Marcella Vanwinden, Michael Shackleford, Dr. Stanley Lieberson, the family Barbot, Rory Satran, Emily Shapiro, Ailsa Gray, Ada Hets-Ohana, Anja Toepper, Mitzi Oppenheim, Rita DiMatteo, Sara Bethell. Representatives of various State Departments of Health who were particularly helpful in compiling statistics on most popular names included Joseph J. Aldorisio, Brenda Corkum, Mike Dare, Melvin De Suza, Debbie Draghia, Sandy Ficenec, Mark Gildemaster, Darrin Goldman, Jean Gunter, Bonnie Harrah, Robin Jones, Brian King, Kryn Krautheim, David Mayer, Mark A. Miller, Carol Nilles, Patricia W. Potrzebowski, Calvin Reynolds, Nancy Rice, Christine Romalewski, Wayne Schramm, Kerri Shipman, Joe Shively, Karen J. Sommer, Pat Starzyk, Stephanie Waldren, Jo Warren, and Jan Wick. And finally, of course, loving thanks to our always helpful husbands, Christopher Finch and Dick Satran.

INTRODUCTION

In the decade since we've begun writing about names, the world of baby-naming has mushroomed from a sleepy little enterprise, with parents naming their children Jennifer and Jason and wondering whether there might be anything more exciting out there, to an adventurous and intelligent and style-conscious activity in which parents investigate everything from their family trees to names from their ancestors' native lands to atlases and even dictionaries for names that are ever more inventive, individual, and enlightened.

We think we had something to do with that. But it's not a one-way street. Through the original publication of *Beyond Jennifer & Jason* in 1988, through two smaller revisions and now with this thorough renovation of this book, our work and the ever-more-creative name choices of parents have influenced each other. We offer new ideas about names, parents adopt them and add some twists of their own, and soon we're back reporting on the hottest trends we've heard, which an increasing number of parents pick up on. And next thing we know, we need to write another name book.

If you're a first-time *Beyond Jennifer & Jason, Madison & Montana* baby-namer, let us introduce you to how this book works. Our aim here is to help parents figure out how names fit into the real world their children will be entering. We try to provide a yardstick for measuring the effects of an unusual name, a unisex name, or a fashionable name on a child, as well as an easy way to figure out which names are which. All the other name books will tell you that Cameron means "crooked nose" in Scottish Gaelic; we're the only ones who will advise you that while Cameron's moving up on the popularity list for boys, it's quietly being coopted by the girls—and why that means you should think three times before giving it to your son.

Rather than the conventional dictionary format used by most other name books, ours organizes names by subjective categories—trendy names and saints' names, royal names and feminine names and place names. And we support those categories with text that tells you which trendy names are threatened with overuse, for instance, or why feminine names are beginning to sound stronger in these gender-bending times.

In this all-new edition, we keep the familiar subjective format but with many major changes. We've gone to six sections now instead of four. Style and Popularity have each grown so large, encompassing so many new subjects, that we split them into separate sections. And Family is no longer a subsection of Tradition but an entity unto itself.

Style, as always, is completely updated, with many names making the climb up from So Far Out They're In to What's Hot. In fact, more names than ever made that leap this time around, as an ever-growing number of parents embraced more categories of names designating hundreds of new names as fashionable rather than fringe. Names that are deemed far out are *really* far out this time around, and parents wishing to venture to the edge will find some wild and woolly territory. Mythological names like Andromeda and Zeus? Word names such as Seven and Cinnamon? We swear: it's coming.

A lot of people questioned our sanity when, in the original edition of this book in 1988, we predicted that Place Names like Dakota and Savannah would become fashionable, when we foresaw that former "old lady" names such as Madeleine and Natalie would come back into style, that Americans would adopt Irish names like Riley and Liam, that such old-fashioned favorites as Felicity and Rose, Stella and Julian and Trevor would return to vogue. All those names were in the So Far Out They're In section back then; now they're among the top one hundred.

In this edition, we rethink the Image and Sex sections, exploring the kinds of questions parents in search of a name grapple with themselves. How important is your choice of a name, anyway? Do names really have images and if so, what do they convey? Is there such a thing as a name that's too unusual? In these days of ever-shifting gender identities, what's the best kind of name for a girl, a boy? We turn to hard research, as well as common sense, to come up with these answers.

For our section on Tradition, we delve more deeply into the history of names, including all new chapters on pre-twentieth-century American naming history and on African-American naming traditions. And we go farther afield, adding hundreds of new listings of foreign names from Europe, Africa, and Israel. We also offer information and names from the Jewish, Christian, and Muslim religions.

And in the new section called Family, we include advice on name wrestling with your spouse and your in-laws, on choosing a family name, on naming siblings and twins, and on living with your ultimate name choice.

All the best parts of the earlier editions, all the elements that make this book different from any other name book, are still here, with the addition of new features. We include the most comprehensive up-to-date listing of celebrity baby names—and then regroup those names to illustrate specific chapters of the book, offering lists of starbabies with ethnic names, for instance, and a list of starbaby girls with boys' names. And we still tell you the whole truth: which names are becoming overexposed, which are becoming too girlish for boys, why you shouldn't spell Brianna "Briyana" no matter how adventurous your sense of style.

You can read this book straight through—the best way, we think—or you can choose a category that interests you and use that as a jumping-off point to the rest of the book, or you can find a name you like in the index and start from there. Whichever method you use, once you've finished you'll have the pleasure of knowing you have made a thoughtful and enlightened choice, whether you choose to move beyond Jennifer and Jason, Madison and Montana or not.

STYLE

We used to have to explain what we meant by style and names. No more. Now most parents are aware of how style affects names, and have a good idea what kind of style they want their own child's name to reflect.

In this section, we separate the fashionable from the trendy, the names that are coming in from those that are heading out of style. The major style categories are:

WHAT'S HOT   Names that are in fashion right now, and why.

SO FAR OUT THEY'RE IN   Cutting-edge names for style pioneers, these are the names that will set the fashions for the next decade and beyond.

SO FAR IN THEY'RE OUT   Trendy names threatened by overexposure, as well as fresher-sounding alternatives for old favorites.

FASHION LIMBO   Names retired from use, temporarily or, in a few cases, permanently.

WHAT'S HOT

There are lots of hot names these days, and that's news in itself. We have twice as many categories of What's Hot names now as we did in past editions. Not only are more parents aware of fashionable names, they want to choose names with real style for their children.

Most parents today are unwilling to settle for the stock favorites everybody else is choosing. They're looking farther afield for names that evidence personal style and individual meaning, that lend individual distinction to their child. And to find them, they're looking into family histories and foreign name rosters, to the Bible and the World Atlas.

Gone from the lineup of hot names are the Yuppie favorites of the eighties, the Carolines and Jameses, Philips and Parkers that sustained us through that status-conscious era. Here instead are quirkier, more adventurous names. Surname-names are still in, but instead of Cooper and Morgan we're turning to O'Brien and Maguire—ethnic family names as first names. Place names have moved beyond the overexplored Dakota and Savannah to the more exotic Sahara and Dublin. Exotic names have jumped the boundary from cutting-edge to hot, with once-foreign choices ranging from Flavia to Raoul, Maeve to Malachy, entering the American mainstream. And historical favorites from the turn of the last century, our grandparents' and great-grandparents' names, are appreciated again.

One of the best things about this selection is that it's so diverse and capacious that there are no individual names that are really in danger of rocketing from interesting to overused in two seconds flat. With hundreds of choices of different kinds, there are more than enough to go around.

Here is the wide range of names that are hot right now.

THE CENTURY NAMES

As we round the corner into the new millennium, we can't help but examine the last turn of the century, the period right around 1900. Some of those names that were well used during that time are rising on the popularity charts again today—most notably Abigail, Emma, Isabel, Laura, Madeleine, Sophia, Henry, Jack, and Julian—while many others are ripe for revival. If names with a gently old-fashioned feel appeal to you, survey this list for choices that seem fresh again a hundred years later.

GIRLS

ABIGAIL	ELIZA
ADELAIDE	ELLA
ADELINE	EMMA
ALICE	
AMELIA	FLORA
ANNA	FLORENCE
	FRANCES
BEATRICE	
BELLE	GRACE
BLANCHE	
	HAZEL
CECILIA	
CECILY	ISABEL
CELIA	IVY
CHARLOTTE	
CLAIRE	JOSEPHINE
CLARA	JULIA
CLARISSA	
CLEMENTINE	KITTY
DAISY	LAURA
DOROTHEA	LIBBY
	LILLIAN
EDITH	LILLIE
ELEANOR	LOUISA

LOUISE	PAULINE
LUCY	PHOEBE
LULU	POLLY
LYDIA	PRISCILLA
MABEL	
MADELEINE	ROSE
MARGARET	RUBY
MATILDA	
MAUD	SADIE
MAY	SOPHIA
MILLICENT	STELLA
MINNIE	
	VIOLET
NELLIE	VIRGINIA
NORA	
OLIVE	WINIFRED/WINNIE

BOYS

ABRAHAM	ELIAS
AMBROSE	EZRA
AMOS	
AUGUSTUS	
	FRANCIS
	FRANK
CHARLES	FREDERICK
CHESTER	
CORNELIUS	
	GEORGE
EDMUND	HARRY
EDWARD	HENRY

HOMER	MOSES
HUGH	
	OSCAR
	OTTO
ISAAC	
	PATRICK
JACK	PHILIP
JASPER	
JULIAN	REUBEN
	RUSSELL
LIONEL	
LOUIS	THEODORE

THE SURNAME NAMES

The Surname Names have become a group as wide as surnames themselves. Today, any last name is fair game for use as a first name—the more unusual, the more ethnic, the better. Sure, Waspy standards such as Cooper and Parker are still fashionable, but parents are moving far beyond these old standards to real family names or simply surname names that catch their fancy. If you can name a child Morgan, after all, why not Malloy? Why not O'Hara, Navarro, Willoughby?

Why not indeed. Look to your own family tree for inspiration, for use as a first name or a middle, or consider the options outlined here, for girls and boys alike.

AHERNE	BOONE
AILEY	BOWIE
ALCOTT	BRADY
ARCHER	BRANIGAN
	BRANSON
BAIO	BRENNAN
BARBEAU	BREWSTER
BECK	BRILL
BECKETT	BRODY
BELLAMY	

BRONTË

BROWN

CABOT

CABRERA

CALDER

CALHOUN

CALLAHAN

CALLOWAY

CAMPBELL

CARNEY

CARUSO

CARVER

CASSIDY

CHAN

CHANDLER

CHASE

CLAUDEL

CLAYTON

COLE

COLTON

CONNOLLY

CORTEZ

CROSBY

CRUZ

CUEVA

CULLUM

DALTON

DARWIN

DAVIS

DAWSON

DECKER

DELANEY

DEMPSEY

DENNISON

DEVEREUX

DIAZ

DIX

DIXON

DONAHUE

DONOVAN

DUARTE

DUFF

DUGAN

DURAN

DYSON

EDISON

EMERSON

FALLON

FARRELL

FINN

FITZGERALD

FLANNERY

FLETCHER

FLORES

FLYNN

FORREST

FRASER

FUENTES

GALLAGHER

GARCIA

GRADY

GRIFFIN

GULLIVER

GUTHRIE

HANSEN
HARDY
HARPER
HART
HAYDEN
HAYES
HUNTER

INGRAM
ISABEY

JACKSON
JAGGER
JAMESON
JARREAU
JARRETT
JELLICOE
JENNER
JENNISON
JENSON
JESSUP

KAHLO
KENNEDY
KENYON
KIERNAN

LALO
LANZO
LARSON
LAVISSE
LENNON
LENNOX
LENO
LINCOLN
LIOTTA

LORCA
LORIA
LOWRY
LUNDY
LURIE

MACY
MADIGAN
MAGUIRE
MAILLOL
MALLOY
MALONE
MARLEY
MASON
MAURIAC
McALLISTER
McCABE
McCAREY
McKENNA
McKENZIE
McLEOD
MERCER
MOLINA
MONTOYA
MORLEY
MORRISON
MUNDY
MURPHY

NASH
NAVARRO
NEWELL
NILSSON
NOLAN
NUNNALLY

O'BRIEN

ODELL

O'HARA

O'KEEFE

ONO

OROZCO

ORTEGA

ORTIZ

O'SHEA

PAXTON

PAYTON/PEYTON

PAZ

PHELAN

QUAID

QUINN

QUINTERO

RAFFERTY

RALEIGH

REDMOND

REED

REMINGTON

RILEY/REILLY

ROMERO

ROONEY

ROSS

ROWAN

RYDER

SAWYER

SHAW.

SHERIDAN

SINCLAIR

SLATER

SLOAN

SOTO

SPALDING

STONE

TAM

TANDY

TANNER

TATE

THAXTER

THOREAU

TIERNEY

TUCKER

TULLIVER

TULLY

TYSON

VEGA

VIGO

WADE

WESTON

WHELAN

WILEY

WILLOUGHBY

WILSON

ZAHN

ZECCA

ZIELLA

ZOLA

HERO SURNAME NAMES

We have long named our children after our heroes, with notables from presidents to soap opera stars inspiring legions of namesakes. But the newest twist on hero names is last names used as firsts. Coupled with the craze for surname names, this makes sense. The connection to the hero is more direct, and the name is more interesting to boot. Consider how much more powerful Mandela is than Nelson, Fitzgerald than Scott, Oakley than Annie. Appropriate hero surnames cover politics, sports, business, and the arts; work for both boys and girls (though some sound better for one sex than the other); and range far beyond the choices here. But these will give you a good start:

ALCOTT	GIACOMETTI
	GIBSON
BALZAC	GILLESPIE
BERGMAN	GORKY
BOGART	GUEVARA
CHANEL	HALE
CHAPLIN	HALSEY
CHURCHILL	HAMMETT
	HARPER
	HART
EARHART	HAZLITT
EMERSON	HENDRIX
	HERRERA
FITZGERALD	HUNTER
GANDHI	
GARCIA	JAGGER
GARVEY	
GATES	
GAUGUIN	KEATON
GEHRIG	KENNEDY
	KUROSAWA

LENNON	O'HARA
LINCOLN	OLIVIER
LODGE	ORWELL
LOEWY	
	PENN
	PICABIA
MacARTHUR	POE
MANDELA	POWELL
MARQUEZ	
McCARTNEY	
MISHIMA	RALEIGH
MONROE	RUNYON
MORRISON	
MOZART	TENNYSON
	THOREAU
	TWAIN
OAKLEY	
O'CASEY	WEBSTER
O'CONNOR	WHARTON

IMPORTS

Faster than you can say Leonardo DiCaprio, imported names have become the hottest of the hot. Given the naming interests and priorities of today's parents, these are the names that have everything. They have traditional connections, yet they're anything but boring and expected. They're unusual, some of them virtually unheard of on these shores. They carry personal meaning via their ethnic roots. They're decidedly masculine or feminine without being tied to conventional gender stereotypes. What more can you ask for in a name?

The pool of imported names is as wide as the world. For even more choices, check the extensive lists (p. 259) in the Tradition section. What follows are those exotic choices that we believe strike the perfect style note for these times.

GIRLS

ADRIANA
AIDA
ALESSANDRA
ALIZA
ALLEGRA
AMANDINE
ANABELLA
ANASTASIA
ANGELIQUE
ANOUK
ANYA
ARABELLA
ASIA
ASTRID
AURELIA
AZIZA

BASIA
BATHSHEBA
BIANCA
BRONWEN

CALISTA
CANDIDA
CARINA
CARLOTTA
CARMEN
CHANTAL
CHIARA
CLEA

CLEO
CONCHITA
CONSUELO
COSIMA

DAGNY
DANICA
DARIA
DEANDRA
DEIRDRE
DELILAH
DELTA
DEMETRIA
DESIRÉE
DIANTHA
DOMINIQUE

ELENA
ELODIE
ESMÉ
ESMERALDA
EUGENIE
EULALIA

FABIENNE
FERNANDA
FIONNULA
FLAVIA
FLEUR
FRANCESCA

GABRIELLA	MIGNON
GEMMA	MIRABELLE
GIOIA	
GIOVANNA	NADIA
GRANIA	NATALYA
GRAZIELLA	NATASHA
	NICOLETTE
ILIANA	NOELLE
INDIA	
INGRID	ODILE
ISABELLA	OONA
	ORIANA
JADE	OTTILIE
JASMINE	
JOCASTA	PALMA
JUNO	PALOMA
	PANDORA
KATYA	PAOLINA
	PHILLIPA
LILIANA	PIA
LINNEA	PILAR
LIV	PRIMA
LIVIA	
LOLA	RAFFAELA
LOLITA	RAINE
LOURDES	RAMONA
LUCIA	RAPHAELA
LUCIANA	RAQUEL
LUCIENNE	RENATA
	RHONWYN
MAEVE	ROMY
MARIELLA	
MARISOL	SABRINA
MERCEDES	SABRINE

SAFFRON	TALLULAH
SALOMÉ	TAMAR
SANNE	TAMARA
SASHA	TAMSIN
SASKIA	TATIANA
SERAPHINA	THALIA
SERENA	
SIDONIE	VALENTINA
SIGNE	VENETIA
SIMONE	VIOLETTA
SINEAD	VIVEKA
SOLANGE	VIVIANA
SORCHA	YASMIN

BOYS

ALDO	CARLO
ALEJANDRO	CLAUDIO
ALONZO	COSMO
AMADEO	
ANATOLE	DAAN
ANGUS	DANTE
ARAM	DIETER
ARLO	
ARNO	EMILIO
AUGUST	ENZO
AXEL	ETIENNE
BALTHAZAR	FABIAN
BARNABUS	FEDERICO
BENNO	FERGUS
BJORN	
BRAM	GUIDO
BRUNO	GUNTER

IVOR	OLAF
	ORLANDO
KNUT	OTTO
KRISTOF	
	PABLO
	PAOLO
LARS	PEDRO
LEONARDO	PHILIPPE
LORCAN	PIERS
LORENZO	
LUC	
LUCIEN	RAOUL
LUCIUS	ROCCO
	RUTGER
MARCO	SEAMUS
MARIUS	
	TANGUY
NIALL	TARQUIN
NICO	
NIGEL	WILLEM

THE BRITS & THE CELTS

A name from the British Isles may be exactly what you crave—a little bit exotic, but not overly so, a little bit familiar, but not run-of-the-mill either. These British imports, native to England, Scotland, Ireland, and Wales, have the perfect accent for today.

GIRLS

AILSA	BEATRIX
AMABEL	
ANWEN	CAMILLA

DAPHNE	JEMIMA
DEIRDRE	JESSAMINE
DELYTH	JESSAMY
DULCIE	
	KERENZA
ELSPETH	
	LETTICE
FELICITY	
FENELLA	MOIRA
FFION	MYFANWY
FINOLA	
FIONA	NICOLA
	PIPPA
GEORGINA	
GILLIAN	RHIANNON
GREER	ROSAMOND
GWENDOLYN	
	SIOBHAN
IMOGEN	
IONA	UNA

BOYS

ADRIAN	CALLUM
ALEC	CRISPIN
ALISTAIR	
AMBROSE	
ANGUS	DAMIAN
ARCHIE	DUNCAN
BASIL	EWAN

FELIX	MALCOLM
FERGUS	MUNGO
FRASER	
	NEVILLE
	NIGEL
GARETH	NOEL
GAVIN	
GRAHAM	
GUY	QUENTIN
	RALPH
HAMISH	REX
	ROLAND
	ROLF
INIGO	
	SEBASTIAN
LACHLAN	
LAIRD	TREVOR
LIONEL	TRISTAN

PLACE NAMES

In the mid-eighties we met a young girl named London. What an original name! we thought. How charming, how distinctive. Then we met a woman named Holland. Heard of a baby Indiana. Encountered a young Asia, a little Siena.

By the time Melanie Griffith and Melissa Gilbert gave birth, in the same year, to their baby Dakotas (one male, one female), what had seemed an offbeat style a short time before had mushroomed into a full-blown trend. Place names, drawn not from name books but from maps and often signi-

BUT NO IBERIA

A *Latin twist on the place name game:* Renan Almendarez Coello, host of Southern California's top-ranked Spanish-language morning radio show, and his wife named their three daughters Irlanda, Italia, and Francia.

fying a locale important to the child's parents, became one of the premier name fashions combining originality and personal meaning.

Today, Madison is among the Top Ten girls' names, and Austin is near the head of the boys' popularity lists. Savannah, Sierra, Cheyenne, and Chelsea make the girls' top one hundred, while Dakota, Dallas, and Devon rank among the most stylish boys' names. Those few Place Names that haven't been overtouristed are those far off the beaten name track: Ireland, chosen by Kim Basinger and Alec Baldwin for their daughter, was a delightful surprise; Lauryn Hill's Zion is an original choice combining place with the Bible; truly eccentric choices such as Sicily or Peru retain their vibrancy. A place with real significance to you or your family can always make an appropriate choice, whether it's an established option such as Georgia or one you've turned into a name—Wisconsin, say, or Reno or Thames.

One note: As with many names that start out unisex, Place Names are drifting further and further into all-girl territory. We don't even include a boys' list any longer, because many of the formerly male choices—Dakota, Devon—are now nearly as often used for girls. As with most unisex names, if you choose one for your son be aware that there's a strong possibility it will float further toward the female camp in years to come.

GIRLS

ABILENE	BOLIVIA
AFRICA	
ARABIA	CAIRO
ASIA	CALEDONIA
ASPEN	CALIFORNIA
ASSISI	CAROLINA
ATLANTA	CATALINA
AVALON	CHINA
	COLOMBIA

EDEN	MADISON
EGYPT	MAJORCA
ELBA	MALTA
	MIAMI
FLORENCE	MILAN
FLORIDA	
FRANCE	
	ODESSA
	OLYMPIA
GENEVA	
GENOA	
GEORGIA	PANAMA
GLASGOW	PERSIA
GUERNSEY	
	QUINTANA ROO
HAIFA	
HAVANA	
HIMALAYA	ROMA
HOLLAND	
	SAHARA
IBERIA	SAMARA
INDIA	SAMARIA
INDIANA	SAMOA
IRELAND	SAVANNAH
ITALIA	SICILY
ITHACA	SIENA
	SONOMA
JAMAICA	SONORA
JAVA	
JUNEAU	
	VALENCIA
KENYA	VENETIA
	VENICE
LOUISIANA	VERONA
LOURDES	VIENNA

UNISEX

ALBANY	LONDON
AMERICA	
AUSTIN	MACON
	MONTANA
BOSTON	MOROCCO
BRAZIL	
BROOKLYN	
	NAIROBI
	NEVADA
CHEYENNE	
CUBA	
	PACIFIC
DAKOTA	PARIS
DALLAS	PERU
DENVER	PHOENIX
DEVON	
DUBLIN	RIO
EVEREST	SCOTLAND
	SENEGAL
GALWAY	SIERRA
HARLEM	
HOUSTON	TANGIER
HUDSON	TROY
	TULSA
INDIO	
ISRAEL	YORK
JERSEY	ZAIRE

COMFY NAMES

You just can't help loving these friendly, unpretentious names: familiar as your favorite T-shirt, soft as Grandma's easy chair, warm as a hand-knit afghan. They don't aim to impress or intimidate or brazen their way through the world, but harken back to a sweeter, gentler time when extended families and helpful neighbors ruled the world.

Some of the Comfy Names—Annie, Becky, Jessie, Katie, Lizzie, Ben, Jack, Jake, Sam, and Max—have been stylish for so long now they can hardly be considered hot. But many others in this category—from Bea to Daisy, Gus to Ned—are far more adventurous while retaining the same down-to-earth quality. Choose the end of the style spectrum most comfortable to you.

GIRLS

ANNIE	FANNY
	FLORRIE
	FLOSSIE
BEA	
BECCA	
BECKY	GRACIE
BELLE	
BESS	HATTIE
BILLIE	
	JESSIE
CEIL	JOSIE
CORA	
	KATIE
DAISY	KITTY
DELLA	
DORA	
	LETTIE
	LIBBY
ELLIE	LIZZIE

LOTTIE	POLLY
LU	
	ROSIE
MAISIE	
MAMIE	SADIE
MILLIE	SALLY
MINNIE	SOPHIE
MITZI	
MOLLY	TESS
	TILLIE
NELLIE	WINNIE

BOYS

ABE	LEO
	LOU
BARNEY	
BEN	
	MACK
CAL	MAX
CHARLIE	MOE
CLEM	MORRIS
ELI	
	NAT
FRANK	NATE
FRED	NED
GUS	
	OSCAR
HARRY	
HENRY	
	SAM
	SOL
JACK	
JAKE	
JOE	WILLIE

GOOD GIRLS

There's a sense that after a generation of naming our daughters Dylan and Dakota and Dani, it might be okay to let girls be girls again. Feminism is firmly established, and little Felicity might just as well grow up to go to Harvard and become a nuclear physicist as if her name were Flannery.

These virtue names feel right for our times because they capture all those admirable qualities we could do with more of. The embodiment of Shaker simplicity and New England tradition, these names also manage to strike a modern note.

AMITY	HONOR
	HOPE
CHARITY	
CHASTITY	MERCY
	MODESTY
FAITH	PATIENCE
FELICITY	PLEASANT
	PRUDENCE
GRACE	VERITY

NAMES IN BLOOM

More hot good-girl names come from the garden, where botanical names, as sweet as Jasmine and Rose, as edgy as Ivy and Sage, grow rampant.

THE GENERICS

BLOSSOM	FLORA
FLEUR	POSEY

COMMON GARDEN VARIETY

ANGELICA	LAUREL
	LILY
CAMELLIA	
CLOVER	
	MARGUERITE
	MYRTLE
DAISY	
FERN	OLIVE
HAZEL	PANSY
HEATHER	POPPY
HOLLY	
IRIS	ROSE
IVY	ROSEMARY
JASMINE	VIOLET

WILDER FLOWERS

ACACIA	GARDENIA
AMARYLLIS	
AZALEA	HYACINTH
BRYONY	JONQUIL
	LIANA
DAHLIA	LILAC
FORSYTHIA	MAGNOLIA
FREESIA	MARIGOLD

PEONY	SEQUOIA
PETUNIA	SORREL
PRIMROSE	
	TANSY
RUE	VERBENA
	WILLOW
SAFFRON	
SAGE	ZINNIA

BIBLICAL BOYS

Biblical names, especially for boys, have been among the hottest of the hot for several decades now. And as one generation of names—Benjamin and Adam and Daniel, for instance—becomes widely used, parents turn to more unusual choices. Now, even the long-gray-beard names of the Old Testament prophets, Abraham and Moses, sound young and fresh again. Here, the latest group of biblical names heating up for boys.

AARON	EZEKIEL
ABEL	EZRA
ABRAHAM	
AMOS	GABRIEL
ASA	GIDEON
ASHER	
	HIRAM
CALEB	
	ISAAC
DARIUS	ISAIAH
ELIJAH	JARED
EMANUEL	JEREMIAH
EPHRAIM	JONAH

JOSIAH	PHINEAS
JUDAH	
	RAPHAEL
LEVI	REUBEN
MALACHI	SAMSON
MICAH	SAMUEL
MOSES	SIMEON
	SIMON
NATHANIEL	
NOAH	TOBIAS
OBADIAH	ZACHARIAS
OMAR	ZEBEDIAH

THE IRISH ROGUES

They're a bold lot, these Irish boys, elbowing their way into the center of the baby-naming arena. But how could we ignore them, with luminaries from Liam Neeson to Aidan Quinn, Conan O'Brien to Malachy McCourt claiming our attention? Whether they've captured our hearts by force of energy or charm we're not sure. Big brothers Brian and Ryan, Kevin and Sean may be fading away, but the new Irish Rogues are the bad-boy names everyone loves to love.

AIDAN	CONNOR/CONOR
	CORMAC
BARNABY	
BRADY	DECLAN
BRENDAN	DERMOT
BRENNAN	DESMOND
	DEVIN
	DONOVAN
CASEY	
COLIN	
CONAN	EAMON

FERGUS	McCAULEY
FINIAN	MILO
FINN	
FLYNN	NOLAN
GRADY	PADRAIG
GULLIVER	
	QUINN
KENNEDY	
KIERAN	
KILLIAN	REDMOND
	RILEY
	RORY
LIAM	
LORCAN	
	SEAMUS
MAGUIRE	
MALACHY	TULLY

RIDDLE OF THE MIDDLE

Middle names have suddenly become a new hot spot in the naming process, taking on a greater presence and significance than they've had since Peggy Sue got married. And why? Perhaps it's because so many more young women in the spotlight are using all three of their names—the Sarah Michelle Gellar/Sarah Jessica Parker/Jennifer Love Hewitt syndrome—or maybe it's because parents are realizing that this is an arena where they can be more creative than they can with their child's main name.

No longer do baby namers want to settle for ho-hum middle names that do nothing but euphonically bridge the all-important first and last names. Rather, middle names represent an opportunity to provide a spot for a favorite choice—say Felix or Frederica—that seems to cross the line into the overly eccentric when used as a first name. It can also be a safe slot for a name you really don't like that much but feel a certain obligation to include. This scenario doesn't arise as often these days as it once did, that of having to pay homage to Great Aunt Hortensia and thus pave a direct path to the family fortune. That kind of thinking, we hope, went out with screwball comedies and fifties sitcom plots, but there are still times when you do want to honor a beloved relative or friend whose name you like but don't love, and the middle position is the perfect place to put it.

Middle naming is also a good way to honor a special hero or heroine, someone you particularly admire in the arts, history, politics, or spiritual life, or whose values you would like your child to emulate. One musical couple we know gave their son the middle name of Amadeus, after Mozart, and of course the child grew up with a keen interest in the composer. Another gave their daughter the middle name Eleanor, honoring Mrs. Roosevelt, and a third used Ray, after jazzman Charles. And, because many parents feel that anything goes with a middle name, some choose a place name with significance for them—or even a word, such as Truth.

Last names are often first names these days, and they're even more often middle names. The long-held tradition of using the mother's maiden surname for a middle name is alive and thriving. Some parents are taking this practice a step further and considering other ancestral surnames as middle names, such as those of both maternal and pater-

---

MEANINGFUL MONOGRAMS

A *new study conducted by researchers from the University of California at San Diego says that people with initials such as ACE or GOD are likely to live longer than those whose initials spell out words like APE, DUD, RAT, or PIG. People with good monograms, such as JOY or WOW, lived 4.48 years longer than a control group of people with neutral or ambiguous monograms. Those with negative initials such as BUM or UGH, died an average of 2.8 years earlier.*

—*AUSTIN AMERICAN-STATESMAN*

nal grandmothers, that might otherwise be lost to history.

Another trendlet we've spotted is giving girls a boy's middle name, as in Jennifer Jason Leigh. Some possibilities noted: Duncan, Gary, Elliot, Michael. This is another way in which celebrities from the Spielbergs to the Beattys have been trendsetters, bestowing on their daughters such middle names as Max, Ray, Glenn, George, Allyn, Ira, Dean, and Lewis.

Finding an interesting middle name can also be a nice way of accommodating all members of the family. For one thing, it can give both parents a chance to have equal input on the issue of what to name their baby. One mother we know, for example, wanted to honor her Irish heritage by naming her son Liam, while her husband opted to give the child the middle name Henry (which she didn't particularly like), after his father. It can even be a way for older siblings to get in on the baby-naming act. Rosie O'Donnell gave her daughter Chelsea the middle name of Belle, her son's favorite Disney character, from *Beauty and the Beast*.

With middle names, just about anything goes. You may prefer traditional first names, for instance, yet honor your child's place of conception by using a place name in the middle. Or you can use one of the new word names as a middle name: One mom we know gave her son the middle name Red, for her favorite color. And multiple middle names, à la royalty, are fine too, to pay homage to both grandmothers, say, at once.

There are a couple of guidelines in this midname game. The first is to think of a balance of syllables. Kyle Jefferson Reed makes a stronger impression than Kyle Paul Reed, whereas Samantha Jane Kennedy is more rhythmic than, say, a mouthful such as Samantha Brittany Kennedy. The other is the old caveat about being careful what damage a certain middle initial can do to your child's monogram. So no Peter Ian Greenbergs, please, or Ashley Sarah Sloans— or your child will never forgive you.

The only other absolute rule is not to fall into using one of the last generation's Designated Middle Names—Ann or Marie, Lee or John—just because you can't think of anything better. If you still like the idea of a short, connective, one-syllable middle name, look for one that moves far away from the last generation's ubiquitous Sues and Lynns. Following is a list of ideas primarily for girls, though several can work for boys, too:

BAY	DELL
BECK	DOE
BELLE	DOONE
BESS	DREE
BLAINE	DREW
BLAIR	
BLAKE	EVE
BLANCHE	
BLYTHE	FAITH
BOYD	FAY
BREE/BRIE	FLANN
BRETT	FLEUR
BRITT	
BROOKE	GEORGE
BROWN	GLENN
BRYN	GRACE
	GRAY
	GREER
CASS	GWYNNE
CEIL	
CHAN	HART
CHASE	HOPE
CLAIR/CLAIRE/	
CLARE	JADE
CLAUDE	JAMES
COLE	JAY
CRAIG	JUAN
	JUDE
DALE	KAI
DEAN	KANE

KATE	RAE/RAY
KENT	RAINE
KERR	REECE/REESE
KYLE	ROONE
	ROSE
LAKE	ROY
LANE	RUE
LANG	RUTH
LARK	
LAURE	SAGE
LIV	SCOTT
LORNE	SEAN
LUZ	SETH
LYLE	SHAW
	SHAY/SHEA
MAE/MAY	SKYE
MAEVE	SLOAN/SLOANE
MAI	SPENCE
MAIRE	
MAUDE	TATE
MAX	TEAL
MERLE	TESS
MOSS	TROY
	TYNE
NEIL/NEAL	
NELL	WREN
	WYNNE
PAIGE	
PAUL	XAN/ZAN
PEARL	
PRU	YALE/YAEL
QUINN	ZANE

A GARDEN OF ROSES

Rose seems to be *the* middle name for girls these days, as evidenced by this rose garden of starbabies. (The Stallones liked it so much, they used it twice.)

Aidan **Rose**	*Faith Daniels*
Claudia **Rose**	*Michelle Pfeiffer*
Emerson **Rose**	*Teri Hatcher*
Hayley **Rose**	*Jeff Bridges*
Kelsey **Rose**	*Gabrielle Carteris*
Sarah **Rose**	*Marlee Matlin*
Sistine **Rose**	*Jennifer Flavin & Sylvester Stallone*
Sophia **Rose**	*Jennifer Flavin & Sylvester Stallone*
Stephanie **Rose**	*Jon Bon Jovi*

SO FAR OUT THEY'RE IN

How far out do you have to go to get to a truly cutting-edge name these days? Pretty far, with many categories, from old-fashioned names to place names, surname names to exotic names, making the leap to Hot and becoming fit for widespread consumption.

The newest names are those from little-explored frontiers. There are the ancient names revived for use after long periods of lying dormant, including mythological names from cultures around the world. There are boys' names for girls, not the androgynous names such as Taylor and Dylan that have become standard feminine fare but real masculine standards: James, Gregory, Zachary.

And then there are the farthest-out names of all, the word names that pick up where place names and virtue names leave off. Can you really name your baby Pike and Remember, Christmas and (perfect for a writer) Story? You can and, increasingly into the future, you will.

If hot choices like Gulliver and Hugo, Sawyer and Poppy are still not sizzling hot enough for you, you might dare to venture here.

WORD NAMES

With the explosion of unconventional names over the past few years, the parent in search of something really different may feel there is no ground left unexplored. That's not entirely true: The world of word names, names that for the most part have never been names at all, is set to open its boundaries.

At first glance, most of these names seem bizarre, too far out to be considered at all. And for many people, they will be. But bear in mind that this category does not come as completely out of the blue as it may initially seem. Think of it as a continuation of the place names, an adjunct to invented names and spellings, a step beyond names like Sunshine and Freedom first heard in the sixties.

Popular culture has been preparing us for the advent of word names. A few notable celebrities have chosen them for their children: Christie Brinkley's Sailor, Forest Whitaker's True, Sylvester Stallone's Sistine and Sage. In one memorable episode, *Seinfeld*'s George declared that if he had a child, boy or girl, he would name it Seven. And singer Erykah Badu *did* in fact name her son Seven. Then there are the celebrities who bear word names, from Tuesday Weld to the singer Seal. In traditional literature, we have Huckleberry Finn and Scarlett O'Hara. And soap opera characters, always on the cutting edge, have names like Star and Steel, Stone and Storm.

Perhaps best of all, the word names introduce hundreds of new name possibilities into the lexicon, opening up a universe of options to parents in search of a name that's highly unusual and yet embodies personal meaning. Not every word—not even very many words—qualify as name possibilities. We offer the following lists with a caveat, urging you to think long and hard of possible peer repercussions before you make your final choice.

NATURE NAMES

Nature names have been with us for several decades now, with a few—River, Willow, Stone, Star, Sky—becoming at least familiar to most people. And of course flower names such as Lily and Rose and gem names from Pearl to Ruby have been used for centuries. Yet nature offers an infinitely wider world of name possibilities for the adventurous parents. There are tree names, from Ash to Oak, and spice names: Cinnamon, Sage. There are names that refer to weather—Cloud and Storm—and those that are colors, from Azure to Indigo to Lilac. Nature names can connect to features of the earth—Quarry, Field—and to water—Ocean, Cascade—and those that relate to the sky and space—Meteor, Galaxy, Air. Animals and birds are represented here too—Finch, Fox, Pike—as are other things found in nature, from Forest to Fauna.

ACACIA
ACANTHUS
AIR
AMARYLLIS
AMBROSIA
ANEMONE
ANGORA
ARBOR
ARCADIA
ASH
AUBURN
AZALEA
AZURE

BAY
BEECH
BIRCH
BLAZE
BLUE
BRANCH
BROWN
BURR

CALICO
CALYX

CAMOMILE
CANYON
CARAWAY
CARNELIAN
CASCADE
CASHMERE
CASSIA
CATALPA
CAYENNE
CEDAR
CINNAMON
CITRON
CLOUD
COBALT
COLUMBINE
COMET
CORONA
CRIMSON

DIAMOND
DRAKE

ECHO
ELM

FAUNA	MICA
FENNEL	MIMOSA
FIELD	
FINCH	NORTH
FLAME	
FLINT	OAK
FLOWER	OCEAN
FOREST	
FORSYTHIA	PIKE
FOX	PINE
FREESIA	PRAIRIE
FROST	
	QUARRY
GALAXY	RAIN
GLADE	RED
GRANITE	RIVER
GRAVITY	RUSH
GREEN	
GROVE	SAGE
	SHADE
	SILVER
HARBOR	SKY
	SLATE
INDIGO	SNOW
	SPRUCE
JUNIPER	STAR
	STONE
LAKE	STORM
LARK	
LEAF	TAMARIND
LILAC	TARRAGON
	TEAL
MAHOGANY	THUNDER
MEADOW	TIMBER
MERCURY	
METEOR	WOLF

DAY NAMES

The first Africans in North America often bore day names—
names that signified the day of the week on which they
were born. Through the years, the African day-naming custom was Anglicized and expanded to include months, sea-
sons, holidays. While African-Americans, postslavery, left
their old day names behind, some of the names that connect
to times of the year have lived on. April, May, June, and
Dawn, of course, have long been well-used girls' names.
More recently, August, Summer, and Autumn have come
to the fore. Season Hubley and Spring Byington were actresses of some note. And who can forget Tuesday Weld
or Wednesday Addams? Day names worth considering now
include:

AFTERNOON	MARCH
ARIES	MONDAY
AUGUST	MORNING
AUTUMN	
	NOON
CALENDAR	NOVEMBER
CHRISTMAS	
DECEMBER	OCTOBER
EARLY	SCORPIO
EASTER	SEASON
	SEPTEMBER
GEMINI	SPRING
	SUMMER
JANUARY	SUNDAY
LIGHT	WINTER

POSTVIRTUE NAMES

The Puritans paved the way with virtue names, giving us
Hope and Charity, Faith and Honor, as well as several other
selections that have been all but lost to time: Justice, Rev-
erence, Purity. Now, it's time for a new complement of
virtue names, word names that set forth the values and ide-
als of our time. Some of these—Simplicity and Trust, for
example—relate directly to the classic Puritan virtue
names, while many others vary in syntax and viewpoint.
But they all evidence some ineffable human quality or feeling. At least two of the names here, Remember and Experience, were used by early New England settlers. As with
the virtue names, most of these are most appropriate for
girls, though some—such as True, the name of actor Forest
Whitaker's new son—can work as well for boys.

ADMIRE	ECCENTRICITY
AFFINITY	ELOQUENT
ALLIANCE	ENDEAVOR
AMIABLE	ENERGY
	ENTERPRISE
BENEVOLENT	ESSENTIAL
BLISS	ETERNAL
BLITHE	ETHEREAL
	ETHICAL
CHANCE	EXCELLENCE
CLARITY	EXPERIENCE
COMFORT	
DECLARE	FASCINATION
DEMOCRACY	FAVORITE (but be
DIPLOMACY	careful with this one)
DISCOVERY	FOREVER
DIVERSITY	FORTUNE
DIVINITY	FORWARD
DREAM	FREE

FREEDOM
FRIEND
FUTURE

GALLANT
GENEROUS
GENTLE
GLIMMER

HARMONY

ILLUMINATION
IMAGINE
INFINITY
INSPIRATION
INTEGRITY

JUSTICE

KISMET

LEGEND
LIBERTY
LIVELY

MEMORY
MIRACLE

MUSE
MYSTERY

PEACE
PHILOSOPHY
PLEASANT
POWER
PROMISE
PROSPER

REMEMBER
RHYTHM
RULE

SERENDIPITY
SERENITY
SIMPLICITY
SINCERITY
SOCIETY
SPIRIT
STRATEGY

TEMPERANCE
TENDER
TRUE
TRUST

PROFESSION NAMES

When Christie Brinkley named her third child Sailor, she set the course for a new brand of baby names, those that relate to an activity or profession. Scout, the name of Demi Moore and Bruce Willis's second daughter and the nickname of the young heroine of *To Kill a Mockingbird*, falls in this category, too. Other occupational names include:

> As for their baby's nautical name, [Christie] Brinkley explains: "Peter's family dates back to Captain Cook, who discovered the Big Island of Hawaii. It's also where we found out we were pregnant, so we called her Captain Cook during the pregnancy. That evolved into Sailor."
>
> —JIM JEROME, *LADIES' HOME JOURNAL*

ARCHER	JUDGE
BREWER	MASON
COOK	NAVIGATOR
DANCER	PAINTER
	PILOT
EXPLORER	RACER
	RANCHER
FARMER	RANGER
FIELDER	
	SAILOR
GARDENER	SCOUT
GLAZIER	
GUARDIAN	TEACHER
GUIDE	TRAVELER

WORD NAMES

The most adventurous of the adventurous word names are those that can't be fit into any familiar categories. These words become name-worthy by virtue of euphony or symbolism, or both. Words that make the grade have to do more than be easy on the ear. Atrocity and Captivity, for instance, Salary and Shallow, are attractive sounding words, but not fit for a child's name. Nor can the meaning be too simple: a name like Sweet, Pretty, or Sugar, for example, might belittle a child. And one like Splendid or Extraordinary could set too high a bar. A lot of words get eliminated by these rules. Those that remain are, admittedly, wild and woolly, but undeniably interesting.

ABACUS	CANTATA
ALCHEMY	CASTLE
ANALOGY	
ANCHOR	DANCE
ANSWER	
ANTIQUITY	
ARIA	ELEVEN
ARMOR	ENGLISH
ARROW	EVER
AVALANCHE	EVERY
AXIOM	
	FABLE
BLADE	
BOUNDARY	GAGE
BRIDGE	GENESIS
	GLASS
CADENCE	GRAVITY
CALLIOPE	
CAMEO	HALCYON
CAMERA	HEAVEN
CANOE	HISTORY

HOLIDAY	QUINTESSENCE
HORIZON	
	SAFARI
KISMET	SCIENCE
	SECRET
LYRIC	SEVEN
	SONNET
MUSIC	STEEL
	STERLING
OPERA	STORY
PACE	TAFFETA
PALACE	THEATER
PYRAMID	TRINITY

ENDANGERED SPECIES

In the ever-escalating search for distinctive names, forward to entirely new names and outward toward more exotic names aren't the only directions in which to go. You can also move backward, in search of those ancient names now teetering on the edge of oblivion.

There's an attic full of names waiting to be rediscovered. Some of the girls' names are long neglected variations on male names: Augusta and Cornelia, Henrietta and Josepha. Many of the boys names have biblical—Ezekiel, Phineas, Silas—or Greco-Roman—Thaddeus, Cyril—roots. And then there is an entire subcategory of long-dormant mythological names: Ulysses, for instance, or Minerva, the Roman goddess of wisdom and invention, the arts and martial strength. Less familiar names from myths of other cultures, from Irish to Hindu, also qualify for revival.

What all these names have in common is a quaint, quirky quality. Musty? Maybe. But if you gravitate toward names that combine the historic with the eccentric, these choices are perfect for you.

The parent who wants an unusual name can rest assured that these won't be heard in every playground and on every nursery school roll. Hardly any children in the United States are given these names anymore. In a recent complete list of names used for babies born in the state of Maine, for example, there was only one boy named Bartholomew and one girl called Evangeline.

GIRLS

ADA

AGATHA

AGNES

ALTHEA

ARAMINTA

AUGUSTA

CANDIDA

CHRISTABEL

CLAUDIA

CLEMENTINE

CORDELIA

CORNELIA

CRESSIDA

DESDEMONA

DRUSILLA

EDWINA

ELEONORA

ELVIRA

EMMELINE

ERNESTINE

ESMÉ

EUDORA

EULALIA

EVANGELINE

GENEVIEVE

GUINEVERE

HARRIET

HENRIETTA

ISIDORA

JACINDA

JOSEPHA

LUCRETIA

MYRTLE

OCTAVIA

PEARL

PHILOMENA

ROWENA

SIDONY

THALIA
THEODORA
THEODOSIA

URSULA

VIOLA

WILHELMINA

ZENOBIA
ZULEIKA

BOYS

ABSALOM
ARCHIBALD
ARTEMAS
AUBREY
AUGUSTINE

BALTHAZAR
BARNABAS
BARTHOLOMEW
BENEDICT

CASPAR
CECIL
CEDRIC
CLEMENT
CLIVE
CONRAD
CYRIL
CYRUS

DIGBY

EBENEZER
ELMO
ERASMUS

EUSTACE
EVANDER
EZEKIEL

FERDINAND

GILES
GUSTAV

HECTOR
HIRAM
HORATIO
HUMPHREY

ISHMAEL

JARVIS

LEANDER
LEMUEL
LEOPOLD
LINUS
LLEWELYN
LUCIUS

NICODEMUS	ROSCOE
	RUPERT
OBADIAH	
	SEPTIMUS
	SILAS
PERCIVAL	
PERCY	
PEREGRINE	THADDEUS
PHILO	TITUS
PHINEAS	
	ULYSSES
	URIAH
QUINCY	
	VIRGIL
RODERICK	
ROLLO	WALDO

MYTHOLOGICAL NAMES

GIRLS

ANANN	*IRISH*
ANCASTA	*BRITISH*
ANDROMEDA	*GREEK*
ANNIKI	*FINNISH*
ANNONA	*ROMAN*
APHRODITE	*GREEK*
ARANI	*INDIAN*
ARIADNE	*GREEK*
ARTEMIS	*GREEK*
ASTARTE	*PHOENICIAN*
ASTRA	*GREEK*
ATALANTA	*GREEK*
ATHENA	*GREEK*
AURORA	*GREEK*
BELINDA	*BABYLONIAN*
BRANWEN	*WELSH*

BRIGHID (*Breed*)	*IRISH*
CALLIOPE	*GREEK*
CALYPSO	*GREEK*
CASSANDRA	*GREEK*
CASSIOPEIA	*GREEK*
CERELIA	*ROMAN*
CERES	*GREEK*
CHANDA	*INDIAN*
CHLORIS	*GREEK*
CLIO	*GREEK*
CLIONA	*IRISH*
CYBELE	*GREEK*
CYNTHIA	*ROMAN*
DAMARA	*BRITISH*
DAMONA	*CELTIC*
DANA/DANU	*IRISH*
DAPHNE	*GREEK*
DEIRDRE	*CELTIC*
DELIA	*GREEK*
DEMETER	*GREEK*
DIANA	*ROMAN*
ECHO	*GREEK*
ELARA	*GREEK*
ELECTRA	*GREEK*
EURYDICE	*GREEK*
FAUNA	*ROMAN*
FLORA	*ROMAN*
FORTUNA	*ROMAN*
FREYA	*NORSE*
GAIA/GAEA	*GREEK*
GALATEA	*GREEK*
GODIVA	*BRITISH*
GWENDYDD	*WELSH*
(*GWED-eth*)	
HERMIONE	*GREEK*
HESTIA	*GREEK*
INGRID	*NORSE*
IRENE	*GREEK*
IRIS	*GREEK*
ISIS	*GREEK*

JANA	ROMAN
JOCASTA	GREEK
JUNO	ROMAN
KALI	HINDU
KALINDI	HINDU
KALMA	FINNISH
KARA	NORSE
LEDA	GREEK
LUNA	ROMAN
MAIA	GREEK
MINERVA	ROMAN
MORRIGAN	IRISH
NANNA	TEUTONIC
NIX/NIXIE	TEUTONIC
NORNA	NORSE
OLWYN	WELSH
PALLAS	GREEK
PANDORA	GREEK
PAX	ROMAN
PHAEDRA	GREEK
RANA/RANIA	NORSE
RHEA	GREEK
RHIANNON	WELSH
SELENE	GREEK
SULLA (Silla)	CELTIC
SURYA	INDIAN
TAMESIS	BRITISH
TAMRA	INDIAN
TARA	INDIAN
TERRA	ROMAN
THALIA	GREEK
VENUS	ROMAN

BOYS

ACHILLES	GREEK
ADONI	PHOENICIAN

ADONIS (though he'd better be *great* looking)	*GREEK*
AENGUS (*Angus*)	*IRISH*
AJAX	*GREEK*
ANGUS	*CELTIC*
ANTAEUS	*GREEK*
APOLLO	*GREEK*
ARAWN (*Roan*)	*WELSH*
ARES	*GREEK*
ARION	*GREEK*
ATLAS	*GREEK*
BALIN	*BRITISH*
BORVO	*CELTIC*
BRAN	*WELSH*
CADMUS	*GREEK*
DAEDALUS	*GREEK*
DAMON	*GREEK*
DIARMUID (*Dermud*)	*IRISH*
DONAR	*TEUTONIC*
DONN	*IRISH*
DYLAN	*WELSH*
ELIUN	*PHOENICIAN*
ENDYMION	*GREEK*
FERGUS	*IRISH*
FIONN	*IRISH*
GARETH	*BRITAIN*
GUNNAR	*NORSE*
HELIOS	*GREEK*
HERMES	*GREEK*
ICARUS	*GREEK*
JANUS	*ROMAN*
JUPITER	*ROMAN*
KRONOS	*GREEK*
LEANDER	*GREEK*
LOKI	*SCANDINAVIAN*
MARS	*ROMAN*
MERCURY	*ROMAN*
NAKKI	*FINNISH*

NEPTUNE	ROMAN
ODIN	NORSE
ORION	GREEK & ROMAN
ORPHEUS	GREEK
OSIRIS	EGYPTIAN
PARIS	GREEK
RA	EGYPTIAN
REMUS	ROMAN
SALEM	PHOENICIAN
SILVANUS	ROMAN
THOR	NORSE
ULYSSES	GREEK
VULCAN	ROMAN
ZEUS	GREEK

A GIRL NAMED BOY

With Taylor near the top of the girls' popularity lists, and such unisex choices as Madison, Morgan, Jordan, Bailey, and Mackenzie firmly amongthe most widely used names for girls, where's the next frontier for parents who would like masculine names for their daughters but want to move beyond the choices we've been hearing most often? Firmly in male territory, with Andrew and Graham, Jeremy and Thomas, names we've long thought of as exclusively male.

Hollywood has helped forge the path into this new area. There are the actresses with male names: Drew Barrymore, Glenn Close, Daryl Hannah, Sean Young. And then there is the increasing number of celebri-

WOMEN WILL BE MEN

Q: Why do so many of your female characters have men's names?
A: When I was growing up, my parents knew George Gershwin's sister. Her name was Frankie, which struck me as being extremely glamorous. Now, I just love men's names— they give characters a flip, jazz-age feeling.

—LOS ANGELES MAGAZINE, JUDITH KRANTZ

ties who've given their daughters boys' names, from Diane Keaton's Dexter Dean to Spike Lee's Satchel Lewis, from Steven Spielberg and Kate Capshaw's Destry Allyn to Sting's Eliot.

Giving boys' names to girls is less of an innovation than you might initially think. In Olde England, girls were commonly called Alexander, Aubrey, Basil, Douglas, Edmund, Eustace, Gilbert, Giles, James, Nicholas, Philip, Reynold, and Simon. And we've long been paving the modern-day road into this androgynous land, via such sixties boyish nickname names as Jody and Jamie and Ricki and later Victorian gentlemen's favorites such as Ashley and Lindsay and Courtney.

But these days, once a name crosses the line from masculine to feminine, it's unusual for it ever to travel back again. As more and more previously all-boy names are claimed by girls, we worry that boys will have fewer decidedly masculine choices left.

This may be bad news for boys, but it's good news for girls, giving them more and more interesting options. And many boys' names acquire new life when used for girls. Stalwarts like James and Neil, Gary and Seth seem melodic and jaunty and stylish again when applied to a female. Here are some of the best new choices for girls:

AARON	BECKETT
ABBOTT	BRADLEY
AIDAN	BRADY
ANDREW	BRENNAN
ARLO	BRONSON
AUBERON	BRUCE
AUGUST	
AUSTIN	
AVERY	CARMINE
	CARSON
	CARTER
BAILEY	CECIL
BARNABY	CHAZZ
BARRY	CHEVY

CLAUDE	EMERY
CLAY	EMMANUEL
CLOVIS	
CODY	FABIAN
COLE	FARRELL
COLIN	FINN
CONNOR	FLORIAN
CORNELL	FLYNN
CULLEN	
CURTIS	GARETH
	GARY
DALLAS	GEORGE
DAMIAN	GIDEON
DANE	GLENN
DARIUS	GRAHAM
DARREN	GREGORY
DARRYL	GRIFFITH
DEAN	
DEREK	HARLEY
DEWEY	HUNTER
DEXTER	
DOMINIC	IAN
DONOVAN	IRA
DUANE	IVO
DUNCAN	
DUSTIN	JAKE
DYLAN	JAMES
	JARED
EBEN	JASON
ELI	JAY
ELIAS	JEREMY
ELIOT	JONAH
ELISHA	JUBAL
ELLERY	JUDE
EMERSON	JULIAN

KEITH	QUENTIN
KENT	QUINCY
KENYON	
KIERAN	RAFAEL
KILLIAN	RALEIGH
KIMBALL	REED
KIRBY	REESE
KYLE	ROY
	RYAN
LAURENCE	SAWYER
LEANDER	SCOTT
LEO	SEAN
LEWIS	SETH
LIONEL	SEYMOUR
LOWELL	SIMON
LUCIAN	SPENCER
	STUART
MASON	
MAX	THEO
MICHAEL	THOMAS
MORLEY	TIERNEY
	TIMOTHY
	TOBIAS
NEIL	TRAVIS
NICHOLAS	TRISTAN
NOLAN	TROY
NORRIS	TYSON
ORLANDO	VAUGHN
	WENDELL
PATRICK	WYATT
PERRY	WYLIE
PETER	
PHILIP	ZACHARY

SO FAR IN THEY'RE OUT

With names moving in and out of fashion at an ever-accelerating rate of speed, the issue of trendiness becomes thornier and thornier. A name—say Madison or Montana—can sound interesting and new one month and terminally overused the next. No longer does a name date-stamp a child as belonging to a generation or even a decade as it did in the fairly recent past—now the optimum popularity of a name can be pinned down to a five-year period.

But so what? you may ask. Is there anything wrong with a child having a megapopular name? Well, no and yes. On the one hand, for the most part kids like having Top Ten names, being in with the in-name crowd. On the other hand, there is a certain surrendering of personal identity with and possession of a name when your Taylor is fated to spend her schooldays labeled Taylor B., because there are also Taylors C., D., and A. seated not far away.

Since so many first-time parents in particular are unaware of the names that are currently peaking, we present the following master list of So Far In They're Out Names, meaning that if you do decide to select one of them for your son or daughter, it will be with the knowledge that it carries with it all the plusses and minuses of a trendy name. So even if there aren't any Briannas or Baileys, Dakotas or Sierras on your block yet, that doesn't mean a thing—as fresh as some of them may sound to your ear, there's a good chance that a couple of other kids with the same name will be in your child's kindergarten class.

There are a few names here that can be considered classics: Hannah and Emma, for instance, or Matthew and Nicholas. These names definitely have more staying power than such trendy new names as Sierra and Tanner. But we include them here because of their recent explosion in popularity, and the likelihood of their being names your child will share with many of his or her contemporaries.

GIRLS

ALEXANDRA	KAYLA
ALEXIS	KAYLEE/CALLIE
ALYSSA	KELSEY
AMANDA	KIMBERLY
ASHLEY/ASHLYN	KYLIE
BAILEY	LAUREN
BRIANNA/BREANNA	LINDSEY/LINDSAY
BRITTANY	
BROOKE	MacKENZIE
	MADISON
CHELSEA	MEGAN
COURTNEY	MELISSA
	MICHAELA/
DAKOTA	MIKAYLA et al.
DANIELLE	MICHELLE
	MORGAN
EMMA	
	NICOLE
HALEY et al.	
HANNAH	RACHEL
JASMINE	SAMANTHA
JENNA	SAVANNAH
JENNIFER	SHELBY
JESSICA	SIERRA
JORDAN	STEPHANIE
KATELYN/KAITLYN	TAYLOR
et al.	TIFFANY

BOYS

ALEX	JONATHAN
ALEXANDER	JORDAN
AUSTIN	JOSHUA
	JUSTIN
BENJAMIN	
BRADLEY	KYLE
BRANDON	
	LOGAN
CAMERON	
CODY	MATTHEW
CONNOR	MAX
COOPER	
	NATHAN
DAKOTA	NICHOLAS
DUSTIN	
DYLAN	RYAN
ETHAN	SAMUEL/SAM
	SEAN
HUNTER	
	TANNER
IAN	TAYLOR
	TRAVIS
JACOB	TREVOR
JAKE	TYLER
JARED	
JEREMY	ZACHARY

BUT I'VE ALWAYS ADORED AMANDA

Oh, no! Ever since the days when you were playing house and cutting out paper dolls and listening to the song "Farewell, Amanda," that's been the name you've planned to give your first daughter. But now that the time has almost arrived, you find that thousands of other mothers got there first and Amanda is currently one of the most popular girl's names in the country. What to do?

Well, you've got two options. You can stick with your lifelong love and risk the perils of popularity described above. Or you can look for a worthy substitute, a name that relates to your first choice in either style or sound or ethnicity. To help you in the process, here is a list of possible substitutes, all at least a shade more creative and crisp than the original.

GIRLS

Instead of:

ALEXANDRA	ARABELLA, ALBANY, ANASTASIA
ALYSSA	ALEXA, ALICE
AMANDA	AMABEL, AMITY, MIRANDA
ASHLEY	AVERY, ASTRID
BAILEY	BELLAMY, BAY
BRIANNA	BREE, ARIANA, BRYONY, BIANCA
BRITTANY	BRONTË, PARIS, BRETT
CHELSEA	CELESTE, LONDON
COURTNEY	KENNEDY, CORDELIA
DANIELLE	LUCIENNE, DANICA
EMILY	EMMELINE, EMELIA, ELLERY
EMMA	GEMMA, ELIZA, JANE
HALEY	HELENA, HARLEY, HAZEL
HANNAH	DINAH, ANYA, LEAH
JASMINE	JADA, JAMAICA, YASMIN
JENNIFER	GENEVIEVE, GEMMA, JENICA

JESSICA . . . . .JESSA, JESSAMINE, JERSEY
JORDAN . . . . .GEORGIA, JUSTINE, GEORGE
KAITLYN . . . . .BRONWYN, KATYA
KAYLA . . . . .LAYLA, KAY, KAIA
KELSEY . . . . .GELSEY, ELLA
KIMBERLY . . . . .KIRBY, KIMBALL
KRISTIN . . . . .INGRID, BRITTA, CHRISTIANE
LAUREN . . . . .LAUREL, LAURENCE, NORA
MADISON . . . . .MAISIE, INDIANA, MADALENA
MEGAN . . . . .REGAN, MARGARET, MARINE
MELISSA . . . . .LARISSA, MELANTHA, MELISANDE
NICOLE . . . . .NICO, NICOLA
RACHEL . . . . .TAMAR, RAQUEL, RUTH
SAMANTHA . . . . .SUSANNAH, SAMARA, SAWYER
SARAH . . . . .SAHAR, SERENA, SALLY
SHELBY . . . . .TRILBY, SICILY
TAYLOR . . . . .THALIA, THEA, TALIA

BOYS

AARON . . . . .ABEL, ABNER, ASA
ALEX . . . . .ALEC, LEX
ALEXANDER . . . . .CONSTANTINE, ALASDAIR
AUSTIN . . . . .DALLAS, AUGUST
BRANDON . . . . .BRAM, BRANIGAN
CAMERON . . . . .ANGUS, MALCOLM, CAMPBELL
CHRISTOPHER . . . . .CRISPIN, CHRISTO, COSMO
CODY . . . . .RIDER, CROSBY, CASSIDY
CONNOR . . . . .QUINN, GRADY
COOPER . . . . .KENYON, SLATER
DUSTIN . . . . .DUNCAN, DUFF
DYLAN . . . . .FINN, KILLIAN, DEXTER
JACOB . . . . .JAMES, JETHRO, JONAH
JAKE . . . . .JOE, MOE
JORDAN . . . . .GEORGE, OWEN, GORDON

JOSHUA	JOSIAH, ISAIAH
JUSTIN	JULIAN, JASPER
KYLE	KAI, KANE
LOGAN	HOGAN, LORCAN
MATTHEW	MATTHIAS, MARCUS
MAX	MAC, GUS
RYAN	CORMAC, RILEY
SEAN	SEAMUS, SHAW
TREVOR	GRAHAM, ADRIAN, COLIN
TYLER	TOBIAS, CYRUS
ZACHARY	ZEBEDY, ZANE, BARNABY

WE DIDN'T SAY IT . . .

UNCOOL NAMES

DYLAN	DAKOTA
TAYLOR	CHELSEA
CONAN	SHANE

—L.A.'s *Buzz* MAGAZINE

FASHION LIMBO

There is a whole generation of names that are decidedly not in, but may not be out forever. Rarely chosen by contemporary name-givers, they are suspended in a state of stylistic limbo, a great proportion of them consigned there because they were overused for and by our own parents. Chances are, in fact, that you'll find your own name on this list as well as those of your mom and dad.

Some of them, in the cyclic pattern of these things, will inevitably be rediscovered by our own children when it comes time to name their babies. And, no doubt, we will be more than a little disconcerted by the idea of having grandchildren named Phyllis or Donald or Arlene or Gary, just as our parents are dismayed at this generation's little Sams, Maxes, and Rosies.

But others of these names will not fare so well (or so badly, depending on your point of view), and will eventually pass onto a future edition of the So Far Out They'll Probably Always Be Out list.

GIRLS

ADELE	DOREEN
ANITA	DOROTHY
ANNETTE	
ARLENE	EILEEN
AUDREY	ELAINE
	ESTELLE
BARBARA	
BERNICE	FRANCINE
BETSY	
BETTY	GAIL
BEVERLY	GLORIA
BONNIE	
BRENDA	HEIDI
	HELENE
CANDY	
CAROL	IRENE
CARRIE	IRIS
CHARLENE	
CHERYL/SHERYL	JANET
CINDY	JANICE
	JEAN
DARLENE	JEANETTE
DENISE	JOAN
DIANE	JOANNE
DOLORES	JODY
DONNA	JOY

JOYCE
JUNE

KAREN
KIM

LARAINE/LORRAINE
LAVERNE
LEONA
LINDA
LISA
LORETTA
LUCILLE
LYNN

MARCIA/MARSHA
MARCY
MARGERY/
    MARJORIE
MARIAN
MARIANNE
MARILYN
MARLENE
MARYLOU
MAUREEN
MAXINE
MINDY
MONA
MYRA

NADINE
NANCY
NANETTE
NOREEN
NORMA

PAM
PATTY
PAULA
PEGGY
PENNY
PHYLLIS

RENEE
RHODA
RHONDA
RITA
ROBERTA
ROCHELLE
RONA
ROSALIE
ROSEANNE

SANDRA/SONDRA
SHARI
SHARON
SHEILA
SHELLEY
SUZANNE
SYLVIA

TERESA
TRACEY
TRUDY

VIVIAN

WENDY

YVONNE

ZELDA

BOYS

ALAN	HAROLD
ARTHUR	HARRIS
	HOWARD
BARRY	
BRUCE	IRA
	IRWIN
	IVAN
CARL	
CARY	
CLARK	JAY
CLIFFORD	JEROME
	JOEL
DARREN	KENNETH
DARRYL	
DEAN	
DENNIS	LANCE
DONALD	LARRY
DUANE/DWAYNE	LEE
DWIGHT	LEONARD
	LUTHER
ERNEST	MARSHALL
EUGENE	
	NEIL
GARTH	NORMAN
GARY	
GERALD	RALPH
GERARD	RANDOLPH
GILBERT	RAYMOND
GLENN	ROGER
GRANT	ROLAND

RONALD	VICTOR
ROY	VINCENT
SIDNEY	
STUART/STEWART	WALLACE
	WALTER
TERRY	WARREN
TODD	WAYNE

SO FAR OUT THEY'LL PROBABLY ALWAYS BE OUT

When you talk about baby names, there are two words that are very risky to use: always and never. After all, in the first edition of this book, we stated firmly that two names that would never come back were Raymond and Murray. Well, since then, two hip media stars—Jack Nicholson and Lisa Kudrow—have used them for their sons, and others have resurrected such long-slumbering selections as Clara and Ella and Lorraine and Renee and Zelda and Wolfgang, just as Elijah and Isaiah and Abigail are making their way up the popularity charts, and we have a nonmouse movie star named Minnie. Nevertheless, although it is with some trepidation, we submit the following list of names we're pretty sure are so far out they'll never come back as baby names. Just don't remind us of what we said when Hester and Herman make it to the top of the list in the year 2020.

THE EUGENE SYNDROME

I call it the Eugene Syndrome," [Jim] Carrey says, "because my middle name is Eugene: I always figured my parents named me that to keep me humble. You can never get too cool with a name like Eugene."

—LOS ANGELES TIMES

GIRLS

BERTHA	IRMA
BEULAH	
	MILDRED
DORIS	MYRNA
	SELMA
ETHEL	SHIRLEY
EUNICE	
	THELMA
GERTRUDE	
GLADYS	VELMA
	VERDA
HESTER	
HORTENSE	WANDA

BOYS

ADOLPH	HERBERT
ALVIN	HERMAN
ARNOLD	HUBERT
	HYMAN
BERNARD	
BERTRAM	IRVING
BURTON	
	JULIUS
EARL	
EDGAR	LEON
EDWIN	LESTER
ELMER	
	MARVIN
FRANKLIN	MAURICE

LVIN   RUDOLPH
ERVYN
MILTON   SEYMOUR
MORTIMER   SHELDON
MYRON   SHERMAN
                        STANLEY

OSBERT   WILBUR
OSWALD   WILFRED

POPULARITY

Style may in many ways be personal, but it's never isolated: A name's fashion status can only be determined in relation to what everybody else is doing. Here, we look at what the rest of the country—and the rest of the world—is doing about names. You'll find lists of the most popular names in the United States and in several other countries as well. You'll see what the rich and famous, who often influence our own tastes and ideas, are naming their children. And you'll get an insight into how famous names, real and fictional, current and historic, are influencing naming trends.

THE 100 MOST POPULAR
NAMES FOR 1998

For the first time this year, thanks to Michael Shackleford of the Social Security Administration, there exists an accurate record of the names given to more than three million babies born in the U.S. in 1998. This represents over ten times as many current names as have been available in the past, more evenly distributed across the country, including the full complement of variations and spellings.

And a very full complement it is! The most striking aspect of the Social Security list is the wide range of spellings that serve to make some names much more widespread than they appear on any one state's top ten or twenty. The perfect case in point is the new number-one name for girls, Kaitlyn. And Katelyn and Caitlin. And of course Caitlyn, Kaitlin, Katelynn, Katlyn, Kaitlynn, Katelin, Caitlynn, Katlin, Katlynn, and Kaytlyn. The most popular spelling of the name, Kaitlyn, barely edges into our consciousness at number thirty-six. But taken together, the variations topple last year's number one, Emily, still the most popular name (by far) with one main form. Beyond the enormous variety of forms of the most popular names, the sheer volume of names is staggering. Creativity abounds, and names that are wildly adventurous are still far from unique. A boy named Kade? Last year, there were 320 of them! Heath? 228! There were 177 girls born named Armani, almost a thousand Deja's, over two thousand Maya's.

On the girls' list, spelling variations significantly reshuffle the deck. For purposes of clarity, we include on the list here only those spellings that account for more than one thousand babies, and cite them in order of frequency, but often counted many more variations in the final tally. (For a list of the full range of spelling variations of the most popular names, see page 76.) Girls' names that moved up the ladder when different spellings were counted are, most significantly, Haley, thirty-seven under that spelling but number twelve when you tote up all spellings, and Makayla, seventy-two in the top one hundred for girls under that spelling alone, but seventeen when you consider all spellings. Brianna, Jasmine, Gabrielle/Gabriella, and Madeline are other names that are dramatically more popular when all spellings are counted. Michael still hangs on, by a few hundred votes, to the top spot on the boys' list. Jacob, which has risen to number one in several states, comes close to unseating the longtime king of boys' names, but can't quite manage it unless you count the three thousand boys who last year were called simply Jake—which we don't. Elsewhere, spelling and variations do less to rig the positions of the names on the boys' list than they do on the girls'. Only a few names—notably Nicholas, Zachary, Jonathan, Eric, and Connor—get a big boost from counting different spellings. But the boys' Top Ten includes exactly the same names, in slightly reshuffled order, as it did last year. Christian, Dylan, and especially Noah are heading up on the larger list. Stalwarts such as John, Robert, and Thomas are slipping down, evidence of a swing back in tastes toward more adventurous boys' names, with conventional choices once again going out of favor.

Continuing last year's trends, girls' names on the way up include Abigail, Sydney, Emma, Destiny, Jordan, Savannah, Julia, Olivia, Natalie, and Bailey. Boys' names Cameron and Hunter are moving up along with Logan, Bailey, Cooper, Connor, Dalton, Cole, and Tanner. Christian seems to be picking up some of the wind Christopher is losing. And for both sexes, every name containing the two magic syllables "Alex" seems to be gaining steam—in particular Alexis, Alexander, Alexandra, Alexandria, and of course just plain Alex.

On individual state lists, Michael took the top spot in the majority available (the latest available state name figures are for 1997), with Jacob number one in at least twelve states. Front-running boys in at least one other state included William (in South Carolina), Austin, Christopher, José (in Texas and California), Nicholas, and Joshua. On the girls' side, Emily was most often the number one name. Hannah led in at least seven states, while Sarah, Ashley,

Taylor, and Alexis (tops in Louisiana for the second year in a row) were in first place in others.

In some interesting data released by the state of West Virginia's Department of Vital Records a year ago, it was found that mothers in different age groups favor different names. For example, for mothers under twenty, the most popular names were the trendy Tyler and Brittany, for those twenty to twenty-four it was Tyler and Kayla, twenty-five to twenty-nine, Jacob and Emily, thirty to thirty-four, Zachary and Emily, and the top choices for mothers over thirty-five were old classics Matthew and Sarah. Here, the top one hundred names for girls and the top one hundred for boys in 1998.

THE TOP 100 GIRLS' NAMES, 1998

1. KAITLYN/KATELYN/CAITLIN/CAITLYN/KAITLIN/KATELYNN
2. EMILY
3. SARAH/SARA
4. HANNAH/HANNA
5. ASHLEY
6. ALEXIS/ALEXUS
7. BRIANNA/BREANNA/BRIANA
8. SAMANTHA
9. MADISON
10. TAYLOR
11. JESSICA
12. HALEY/HAILEY/HAYLEY
13. MEGAN/MEGHAN
14. ELIZABETH
15. KATHERINE/KATHRYN/CATHERINE
16. ALYSSA/ALISSA/ALLYSSA
17. MAKAYLA/MIKAYLA/MICHAELA
18. JASMINE/JASMIN/JAZMIN/JAZMINE

19. KAYLA
20. RACHEL/RACHAEL
21. LAUREN
22. BRITTANY/BRITTNEY
23. GABRIELLE/GABRIELA/GABRIELLA
24. VICTORIA
25. ABIGAIL
26. ALLISON/ALISON/ALLYSON
27. AMANDA
28. JENNIFER
29. REBECCA/REBEKAH
30. MADELINE/MADELYN/MADELEINE
31. ANNA/ANA
32. SYDNEY
33. EMMA
34. OLIVIA
35. MORGAN
36. NICOLE
37. DESTINY
38. DANIELLE/DANIELA
39. STEPHANIE
40. ALEXANDRA
41. JORDAN/JORDYN
42. COURTNEY
43. JULIA
44. MACKENZIE/McKENZIE
45. NATALIE
46. ISABELLA/ISABEL/ISABELLE
47. SIERRA/CIERRA
48. KAYLEE
49. AMBER
50. KELSEY
51. ERICA/ERIKA
52. SAVANNAH
53. CHRISTINA/KRISTINA

54. MARIA
55. BAILEY
56. BROOKE
57. CARLY
58. MARY
59. MARISSA/MARISA
60. MARIAH
61. CHEYENNE
62. SHELBY
63. MICHELLE
64. KIMBERLY
65. LINDSEY/LINDSAY
66. VANESSA
67. SOPHIA/SOFIA
68. CASSANDRA/KASSANDRA
69. JADE/JADA
70. ANDREA
71. KYLIE /KYLEE
72. PAIGE
73. KRISTEN/KRISTIN
74. JENNA
75. MIRANDA
76. CHELSEA
77. SABRINA
78. TIFFANY
79. KELLY
80. CRYSTAL
81. LAURA
82. ALEXANDRIA
83. ADRIANA/ADRIANNA
84. CAROLINE
85. ARIANA/ARIANNA
86. LESLIE
87. CLAIRE
88. KATIE

89. AUTUMN
90. DIANA
91. CASSIDY
92. CHLOE
93. CASEY
94. ALEXA
95. AMY
96. MONICA
97. JACQUELINE
98. ALICIA
99. HEATHER
100. ANGELA

THE TOP 100 BOYS' NAMES, 1998

1. MICHAEL
2. JACOB/JAKOB
3. MATTHEW/MATHEW
4. NICHOLAS/NICOLAS
5. JOSHUA
6. CHRISTOPHER
7. BRANDON
8. ZACHARY/ZACKARY/ZACHERY
9. AUSTIN
10. TYLER
11. ANDREW
12. DANIEL
13. JOSEPH
14. JONATHAN/JOHNATHAN/JONATHON
15. WILLIAM
16. JOHN
17. DAVID
18. RYAN

19. ANTHONY
20. JAMES
21. JUSTIN
22. ALEXANDER
23. DYLAN/DILLON
24. CHRISTIAN/CRISTIAN
25. KYLE
26. ROBERT
27. BRIAN /BRYAN
28. JORDAN
29. ERIC/ERIK/ERICK
30. SAMUEL
31. JOSÉ
32. STEVEN/STEPHEN
33. KEVIN
34. NOAH
35. BENJAMIN
36. THOMAS
37. CAMERON
38. NATHAN
39. HUNTER
40. CALEB/KALEB
41. CONNOR/CONNER
42. AARON
43. ETHAN
44. CODY
45. JASON
46. LOGAN
47. LUIS
48. ADAM
49. TIMOTHY
50. CHARLES
51. SEAN
52. JUAN

53. JARED
54. GABRIEL
55. ALEX
56. MARK/MARC
57. RICHARD
58. PATRICK
59. TREVOR
60. NATHANIEL
61. ISAIAH
62. JACK
63. CARLOS
64. DEVIN
65. COLIN/COLLIN
66. EVAN
67. ISAAC
68. JEREMY
69. CHASE
70. ANGEL
71. ELIJAH
72. IAN
73. ADRIAN
74. JESSE
75. DAKOTA
76. LUKE
77. JESUS
78. JEFFREY/JEFFERY
79. COLE
80. ANTONIO
81. MAXWELL/MAX
82. GARRETT
83. TANNER
84. BLAKE
85. KENNETH
86. SPENCER

87. MASON
88. MIGUEL
89. DALTON
90. SETH
91. COLTON
92. PAUL
93. VICTOR
94. TRISTAN
95. ALEJANDRO
96. BRYCE
97. LUCAS
98. BRENDAN
99. TRAVIS
100. MARCUS

POP SPELLINGS

Many of the top one hundred girls' names sport several new and invented spelling variations. Our Most Popular list includes those spellings that account for more than one thousand babies. Here, following the most widely used spelling of each name, are other variations culled from the Social Security Administration list. But lest you believe that these spellings are used by just a handful of parents, all the spellings here were used more than a hundred times last year, and many—Kailey and Ashleigh, Bryanna and Baylee, Makenzie and Katlynn, to mention a few—approach the thousand mark.

ABBY	Abbey/Abbie
ABIGAIL	Abbigail/Abigayle
ASHLEY	Ashlee/Ashleigh/Ashly/Ashlie
BAILEY	Baylee/Bailee/Bayleigh/Baileigh
BRIANNA	Breana/Bryana/Breeanna
CAMERON	Camryn/Kamryn/Kameron

CARLY	Carley/Carlie/Karli/Karlie/Karlee/Carlee/Karly/Carli/ Karley
CASEY	Kasey/Kaci/Kaycee
CHELSEA	Chelsey/Chelsie
CHEYENNE	Cheyanne/Shyanne/Shyann/Chyanne
COURTNEY	Kourtney/Cortney/Kortney
DESTINY	Destinee/Destiney/Destini/Destany/Destinie
ERICA	Ericka/Erykah
HALEY	Hallie/Hailee/Haleigh/Haylee/Halle/Halie/Haylie
JASMINE	Jazmyn/Jasmyn/Jazmine/Jasmyne
KAITLYN	Katlyn/Kaitlynn/Katelin/Caitlynn/Katlin/Katlynn/ Kaytlyn
KAYLA	Kaila/Cayla/Kaylah
KAYLEE	Kayleigh/Kaylie/Kaleigh/Kailee/Kaylee/Kalie/Caleigh/ Cailey
KELSEY	Kelsie/Kelsi/Kelsea/Kelcie
KYLIE	Kiley/Kyleigh
KYRA	Kira
LAUREN	Lauryn/Loren
MADELINE	Madalyn/Madelynn/Madilyn
MADISON	Maddison/Madisyn/Madyson/Madisen
MAKAYLA	Mikaela/Mckayla/Michaela/Mikala/Makala/Micayla/ Mykayla/Makaela
MARIAH	Mireya/Moriah
MEGAN	Meagan/Meaghan
MIRANDA	Maranda/Myranda
RILEY	Rylee/Reilly/Rylie
SAVANNAH	Savanah/Savana
SYDNEY	Sidney/Sydnee/Cydney/Sydni

MAKE WAY FOR JOSÉ

Move over, John. Make way for José, which in 1998 became the most popular baby boy's name in California and Texas. For much of the last two centuries, experts say, immigrants chose so-called "American" names as a way of assimilating into their new lives. Not so long ago, José would probably have been Joseph . . . but no longer. "This gives us a window on society of how much things have changed," said Edward Callary, professor of English at Northern Illinois University and editor of the American Name Society's Journal. "Thirty years ago, most people would not have given their child an ethnic name. A lot of folks tried to blend in and fold into American society as quickly as they could."

But even in the choice of José, some Latino parents say they are bowing to American sensibilities. It is widely recognized and easy to pronounce. "Imagine the problems I would have to pass my name on to my son," said Gildardo Vasquez.

—MEGAN GARVEY AND PATRICK J. McDONNELL,
LOS ANGELES TIMES

MEGANAME

Is it Hayley? Bailey? Kayla or Kaylie? No, it's Meganame!

When you tally the most popular names, there are some related names with dozens of spelling variations that tend to get lost in the count so that the true scope of their popularity is disguised. That's what's happened with the Hayley, Bailey, et al family.

These names are linked by sound and structure. Instead of thinking of them as a single girls' name, think of them asTaylor-Hayley-Bailey-Kaylie-Kayla-Mikayla-Mackenzie-McKenna. You might theoretically also throw Kaitlyn, Kelsey, Kylie, and Madison into the stew. And add a dizzying number of spelling variations, from Baylee to Hallie, Michaela to Caitlin.

The result: an axis of names that is given, in some states, to more than four times as many girl babies as receive the number-one name. And in many cases, because of all their variations, these names don't even show up on local popularity lists, so all the parents who choose Bailey and Hayley, Mikayla and McKenna are unaware of how spectacularly popular these names are.

REGIONAL FLAVOR

Over the years, certain names have taken on regional accents, often as much from literature and movies as from real life. What, for example, could Scarlett be but a southern belle, and Rhett but her male counterpart? Prudence and Priscilla have a distinctly New England aura, and it's hard not to picture Dallas riding the range. So although this may smack of stereotyping and, in an era when national media influences have blurred geographical differences, little Scarlett Prudence may at this moment be playing in her Boise backyard, we still offer these lists for parents seeking a name with a zonal feel.

SOUTHERN BELLES & BEAUS

GIRLS

ABRA	BETHIA
ACACIA	BEULAH
ALTHEA	BLOSSOM
ARABELLA	
ATLANTA	CALISTA
AURELIA	CALLA
AURORA	CAMELIA
	CAMILLA
BELLE	CATALINA
BETHANY	CHLOE

CLARISSA	LACEY
CLEMENTINE	LAVINIA
CORDELIA	LETITIA
CORINNE	LOUELLA
	LUCINDA
DAISY	
DELIA	
DELILAH	MAGNOLIA
DELTA	MARIAH
DESIRÉE	MELANTHA
DIANTHA	MELISANDE
DINAH	MIRABELLE
DIXIE	MIRANDA
DULCY	
	ODELIA
EMMALINE	
ESMÉ	
EUDORA	PEYTON
EVANGELINE	
	RUBY
FALLON	
FLORIDA	
	SABRINA
GEORGIA	SAVANNAH
	SCARLETT
HALLIE	SELENA
HARPER	SUSANNAH
HYACINTH	
	TALLULAH
IVY	TANSY
JASMINE	
JEMIMA	VIOLET
JEZEBEL	VIRGINIA

BOYS

ABBOTT	JARED
ABSALOM	JASPER
ALONZO	JEFFERSON
ASA	JETHRO
ASHLEY	JUDAH
BARNABY	KENYON
BENEDICT	KIMBALL
BLAKE	LOGAN
BRETT	
BURL	MACON
	MOSES
CAMERON	MOSS
CHAUNCEY	
CLAY	QUENTIN
DARCY	REED
DAVIS	RHETT
DEVEREUX	RUFUS
DEX	
DORIAN	SAWYER
	SCHUYLER
GARETH	
GUY	TANNER
	THADDEUS
HARPER	TRAVIS
HYATT	
	VIRGIL
JABEZ	
JACKSON	YANCY

WESTERN COWBOYS

AUSTIN	JACK
	JAKE
BEAU	JEB
BEN	JED
BRADY	JESSE
BUCK	
	LUKE
CASSIDY	
CHEYENNE	MATT
CLINT	
CLYDE	
CODY	SAM
	SIERRA
DALLAS	
DALTON	WYATT
GANDY	ZEB

NEW ENGLAND NAMES

GIRLS

ABIGAIL	FAITH
AGATHA	
AMITY	
	GRACE
CLARA	
	HONOR
	HOPE
EDWINA	
ELIZA	
EMILY	KETURAH

MARTHA	UNITY
MATILDA	
MAUDE	
	VERITY
PATIENCE	
PRISCILLA	WINIFRED
PRUDENCE	
PRUNELLA	ZENOBIA

BOYS

AMBROSE	HIRAM
ARCHIBALD	HOMER
AUGUSTUS	HUGH
BARTHOLOMEW	ICHABOD
	ISAIAH
CALEB	ISHMAEL
CALVIN	
CHESTER	JEREMIAH
CLIFFORD	JONAH
CORNELIUS	JOSIAH
DEXTER	LELAND
DUDLEY	LEMUEL
	LOWELL
EBENEZER	
ELIHU	NATHANIEL
EMORY	NOAH
EVERETT	
EZRA	OGDEN
FRANCIS	PRESCOTT

QUINCY	WINSLOW
	WINSTON
SPENCER	
	ZACHARIAS
TITUS	
TOBIAS	

WHAT THE REST OF THE WORLD IS DOING

Several other countries have released their own most popular lists, which are interesting in that they demonstrate both how similar and dissimilar baby names are around the world. From our continent, we have some statistics from Canada. In primarily French-speaking Quebec, the top names for 1997 were:

BOYS   GIRLS

1. SAMUEL	CAMILLE
2. GABRIEL	AUDREY
3. ALEXANDRE	SABRINA
4. WILLIAM	ALEXANDRA
5. MAXIME	GABRIELLE
6. OLIVIER	CATHERINE
7. NICOLAS	SARAH
8. MATHIEU	LAURENCE
9. VINCENT	AMELIE
10. DAVID	JESSICA

ENGLAND & WALES

The most up-to-date list for British babies born in 1997 has the following as the top five:

BOYS   GIRLS

| 1. JACK | CHLOE |
| 2. JAMES | EMILY |

3. THOMAS	SOPHIE
4. DANIEL	JESSICA
5. JOSHUA	MEGAN

Britain being far from a classless society, however, we find quite a different 1998 list compiled from the births registered in the upscale *London Times*. As you will see, these names (particularly the boys') stick more with royal and classic choices and eschew the purely trendy:

BOYS

1. THOMAS
2. WILLIAM
3. JAMES
4. HARRY
5. CHARLES
6. OLIVER
7. ALEXANDER
8. GEORGE
9. EDWARD
10. BENJAMIN

GIRLS

OLIVIA
LUCY
ISABEL
CHARLOTTE
EMILY
ALICE
ALEXANDRA
SOPHIE
ISABELLA
IMOGEN

SCOTLAND

In neighboring Scotland, these names took the Top Ten places:

BOYS

1. RYAN
2. ANDREW
3. LIAM
4. JACK
5. CONNOR
6. SCOTT

GIRLS

EMMA
AMY
LAUREN
SHANNON
REBECCA
CHLOE

7. JAMES	MEGAN
8. DANIEL	SARAH
9. ROSS	HANNAH
10. JORDAN	RACHEL

NORWAY

Norway, which has strict laws governing first names—only established personal names on an official list can be used, released the following Top Ten:

BOYS	GIRLS
1. ANDREAS	INGRID
2. MARKUS	IDA
3. KRISTIAN	MARTE
4. MARTIN	KAROLINE
5. KRISTOFFER	SILJE
6. THOMAS	JULIE
7. JONAS	CAMILLA
8. FREDRIK	KRISTINE
9. DANIEL	MARIA
10. DARIUS	VILDE

THE NETHERLANDS

In the Netherlands, the most popular names are short and straightforward. "American names" such as Demi are widely popular—but are shunned by the upper classes. Many Dutch parents favor names from other European countries, particularly French names such as Juliette or Fleur or Italian ones like Guido.

BOYS	GIRLS
1. THOMAS	SANNE
2. TIM	ANNE
3. KEVIN	LAURA

4. RICK	LISA
5. DAAN	KIM
6. TOM	ANOUK
7. NICK	IRIS
8. NIELS	DEMI
9. MAX	AMBER
10. LARS	LOTTE

GERMANY

BOYS   GIRLS

1. ALEXANDER	MARIA
2. MAXIMILIAN	SOPHIA
3. LUCAS	JULIA
4. PHILIPP	LAURA
5. DANIEL	ANNA
6. JAN	SARA(H)
7. FLORIAN	LISA
8. NIKLAS	KATHARINA
9. FELIX	VANESSA
10. DOMINIK	MICHELLE

FRANCE

And from the Nantaise region of France, we have a Top Ten list for mid-1998, with some surprising standings. Quentin? Killian? Hallo?

BOYS   GIRLS

1. QUENTIN	CHARLOTTE
2. CORENTIN	MATHILDE
3. KILLIAN	CLOE/CHLOE
4. NICOLAS	MARINE
5. MATHIEU	CLARA

6. ADRIEN	LEA
7. PIERRE	LUCIE
8. TANGUY	CAMILLE
9. BASTIEN/	MANON
SEBASTIEN	
10. CLEMENT	ROMANE

GOOD-BYE, DICK; GOOD-BYE, JANE

First-time parents, unaware of today's wild baby-naming trends, often ask, "Where do you guys get this stuff?" No, we don't make it up. We track class lists and birth announcements, on the statistically grounded theory that more adventurous names favored by fashion-forward big-city parents tend to make their way over the years to the population at large. Here, a list of the names of children at two hip nursery schools, one in New York City and one in Berkeley, California, that evidence many of the naming trends detailed in our What's Hot and So Far Out They're In sections. And there's nary a Dick or Jane in sight.

GIRLS

ALEXANDRA	IVY
AMELIE	
AUDREY	
AVA MARIE	KATIE
	KYLE ROSE
CHARLOTTE	
CLARA	LEAH
ELANA	MIA
ELIZABETH	MICHELA
EMILY	MOLLY
FIFER	NAAMA

ROSE	TALYA
RUBY	TATANKA
	TESS
	THEODORA
SAMANTHA	
SIRI	
SOFIA	WILLA
SONYA	
STEPHANIE	
SYDNEY	ZOE

BOYS

ALEJANDRO	MATTHEW
ALEXANDER	MILO
ASSAF	
	OCTAVIO
CHARLES	OSCAR
	OWEN
EMIL	
EVAN	
	RYDER
GAUDENZ	
GUS	SPENCER
HAROLD/HAL	
	TIMOTHY
JOSEPH	TRYSTAN
JOSHUA	TYLER
JULIAN	
	WILL
KIRK	WILLEM

STARBABIES

William and Harry rocketed in popularity among Times readers naming their babies immediately after the death of Diana, Princess of Wales. At the same time, Charles dipped dramatically. As the nation mourned the Princess, new parents appear to have paid their own tribute by naming their children after her sons. The name William appeared twice as often in the September birth columns as it did in any other month; Harry's appearances were up a third that month, while Charles went into temporary decline. . . . Diana's Christian name is, however, nowhere near as popular as the Princess was herself and the name appeared only once in the birth columns—back in the spring.

—HELEN RUMBELOW,
BRITAIN

Whether we care to admit it or not, we're all influenced to some degree by what celebrities do and say, how they wear their hair, and choose their clothes, and decorate their homes. We're also extremely interested in what they name their babies, partly because they've set so many trends in this area, but also because with names, the playing field is leveled—we don't need money or talent or beauty or fame to choose star-quality names for our own children—just star-quality taste and cool.

Stars have been blazing fresh trails for several years now, beginning when, almost simultaneously, Melanie Griffith and Don Johnson had a daughter they named Dakota and Melissa Gilbert had a son she also named Dakota. The confluence of these choices started two important naming trends, opening up a whole new territory of unisex names, and putting Western place names on the map. Other high-profile ce-

---

ROYAL UPDATE

*Charles and Camilla are slowly winning public accep-
tance, at least among those discerning classes who announce the birth of their children in* The Times. *William
is holding his own, and Harry is moving up fast on the
inside track. Of the 3,421 children whose arrival has
been posted in these columns during 1998, the popularity of Charles as a first name has moved up one place
to fifth. Among girls, Camilla is a new entry, creeping
in at number 20. . . . Thomas has replaced James as the
top male name, one boy in every 15 being named after
the doubting apostle. The girls, for the second year running, are headed by Olivia, a name virtually unknown
to British babies until the Eighties.*

—ALAN HAMILTON & SENAY BOZTAS,
THE TIMES, LONDON

---

lebrities followed suit, calling their kids Montana, Sierra,
and Cheyenne, and before long some of these newly coined
names were among the most popular in America.

Stretching the limits even further were the names of the
three Demi Moore–Bruce Willis girls. First came Rumer
Glenn, inspired by the Anglo-Indian novelist Rumer God-
den. She was followed by Scout LaRue, whose first name
harks back to the nickname of the tomboy character in *To
Kill a Mockingbird.* And finally, they were joined by the
saucy Tallulah Belle.

But surely the most publicized and eagerly awaited celebrity baby name decision was that buzzing around Madonna's little girl. For months, there were discussions in
newspaper and magazine columns, on television and radio
shows, until finally the pundits declared that a name had
been chosen. And the name was—Lola. It seemed like a
perfect choice, a name that oozes sex and determination,
one that suited Madonna herself. Whatever Lola wants,

Lola gets. But then, at the last minute, it was announced that Mama Madonna didn't want the name Lola for her child at all, choosing instead a dark horse of a name that was less flashy, more unusual, but in the end even more appropriate for her offspring. Madonna's little girl would be called Lourdes, the name of the French town where the original Madonna is said to have appeared to Saint Bernadette. And her nickname is—Lola.

But even though we're not all rushing to name our own babies Lourdes or Scout or Rebop (as Todd Rundgren did), the trend among celebrities toward ever-more-outrageous baby names reflects and influences our own increasing penchant for distinctive names and also inspires us mere mortals to stretch the baby-naming boundaries further and further beyond Madison and Montana. They've pointed the way toward a new world of place name (Kim Basinger and Alec Baldwin's Ireland, for example), characters from literature (Gary Oldman's Gulliver), boys' names for girls (Diane Keaton's Dexter Dean), word names (Christie Brinkley's daughter Sailor), formerly fusty names (Jack Nicholson's Raymond), and in many other novel directions as well.

To help make sense of how starbaby names dovetail with the major naming trends today, we divide this list into categories you'll recognize from the Style section. We've restricted our list to relatively recently born children of well-known celebrities. Middle names appear when they were accessible. And again we admit that we do realize that none of these children arrived without two parents, and offer our apologies to those lesser-known parents who might not have received billing here.

BOYS' NAMES FOR GIRLS

Aidan Rose	*Faith Daniels*
Alix Ray	*Faith Daniels*
August Anna	*Garth Brooks*
Bailey Jean	*Melissa Etheridge*
Destry Allyn	*Kate Capshaw & Steven Spielberg*
Dexter Dean	*Diane Keaton*

Dominik ....*Andy Garcia*
Dylan Frances....................*Sean & Robin Wright Penn*
Eliot Pauline......................*Sting*
Emerson Rose....................*Teri Hatcher*
Jordan Alexandra ....*Leeza Gibbons*
Langley Fox ....*Mariel Hemingway*
Morgan...........................*Clint Eastwood*
Reilly Marie ....*Roma Downey*
Remington Elizabeth...........*Tracy Nelson & Billy Moses*
Riley Paige ....*Howie Mandel*
Ryan Elizabeth ....*Holly Robinson & Rodney*
                               Peete
Satchel Lewis ....*Spike Lee*
Schuyler Frances...............*Tracy Pollan & Michael J.*
                               Fox
Skylar ....*Sheena Easton*
Spencer ....*Debbe Dunning*
Taylor Mayne Pearl ....*Garth Brooks*
Tyson..............................*Nenah Cherry*
Wylie Quinn Annarose.......*Richard Dean Anderson*

COMFY NAMES
Annie......................*Jamie Lee Curtis*
Annie Maude ....*Glenn Close*
Billie Catharine ....*Carrie Fisher*
Daisy ....*Markie Post*
Daisy ....*Lucy Lawless*
Harry Spencer ....*Richard Dreyfuss*
Henry.......................*Dennis Hopper*
Henry.......................*Julia Louis Dreyfuss & Brad Hall*
Henry Pays ....*Amanda Pays & Corbin Bernsen*
Jack..........................*Luke Perry*
Jack..........................*Ozzie Osbourne*
Jack..........................*Joanne Whalley & Val Kilmer*
Jack..........................*Meg Ryan & Dennis Quaid*
Jack Antonio.............*Antonio Sabato, Jr.*
Jack Daniel................*Ellen Barkin & Gabriel Byrne*
Jack Henry.................*Susan Sarandon & Tim Robbins*
Jack Paris ....*Cheryl Tiegs*
Jake (twin)................*Niki Taylor*

Jesse James Louis ....*Jon Bon Jovi*
Joe ....*Christine Lahti*
Luke William ....*Rick Schroder*
Maggie Marie.............*Pat Sajak*
Millie......................*Amy Grant*
Molly Evangeline........*John Goodman*
Rainie ....*Andie MacDowell*
Ruby.......................*Matthew Modine*
Sadie ....*Michael Ontkean*
Sadie Leigh...............*Elvira (Cassandra Peterson)*
Sam Michael.............*Tracy Pollan & Michael J.Fox*

IMPORTS
Alaia ....*Stephen Baldwin*
Alessandra.....................*Andy Garcia*
Alvaro ....*Lorenzo Lamas*
Amandine ....*John Malkovich*
Amedeo ....*John Turturro*
Anneliese ....*Kelly LeBrock & Steven Seagal*
Arpad Flynn ....*Elle Macpherson*
Bianca............................*Jean-Claude Van Damme*
Brigidine..........................*Sinead O'Connor*
Colette............................*Dylan McDermott*
Dante Lorenzo ....*Chazz Palminteri*
Enzo ....*Patricia Arquette*
Etienne ....*Sheryl Lee Ralph*
Fifi Trixiebelle ....*Paula Yates & Bob Geldof*
Francesca Ruth ....*Frances Fisher & Clint Eastwood*
Giacomo Luke Summer........*Sting*
Giovanna ....*Vanna White*
Greta...............................*David Caruso*
Greta Simone.....................*Phoebe Cates & Kevin Kline*
Izabella............................*Hunter Tylo*
Juliette Loraine ....*Janine Turner*
Katia ....*Denzel Washington*
Katya ....*Hunter Tylo*
Lourdes Maria Ciccone ....*Madonna*

Luca Bela ....*Jennie Garth*
Malu Valentine ....*David Byrne*
Mercedes ....*Joanne Whalley & Val*
                        Kilmer
Najee (boy) ....*LL Cool J*
Nala...............................*Keenan Ivory Wayans*
Nayib (boy).......................*Gloria Estefan*
Paloma ....*Emilio Estevez*
Pedro.............................*Frances McDormand &*
                        Joel Coen
Prima Sellechia ....*Connie Selleca & John Tesh*
Raphael ....*Juliette Binoche*
Romy Marion ....*Ellen Barkin & Gabriel*
                        Byrne
Saoirse Roisin....................*Courtney Kennedy & Paul*
                        Hill
Sasha (girl).......................*Kate Capshaw & Steven*
                        Spielberg
Sindri (boy)......................*Bjork*
Sofia ....*Lionel Richie*
Sofia Luisa........................*Mikhail Baryshnikov*
Tatiana Cecilia...................*Caroline Kennedy & Ed*
                        Schlossberg
Willem Wolf ....*Billy Idol*
Wolfgang..........................*Valerie Bertinelli & Eddie*
                        Van Halen

PLACE NAMES

Austin..............................*Sela Ward*
Austin..............................*Tommy Lee Jones*
Austin Bryce.....................*Paula Zahn*
Brooklyn Joseph.................*"Posh Spice" Victoria*
                        Adams & David Beckham
Cairo ....*Beverly Peele*
Caledonia Jean-Marie ....*Shawn Colvin*
Chelsea Belle.....................*Rosie O'Donnell*
Dakota (girl).....................*Melanie Griffith & Don*
                        Johnson
Dakota Mayi (boy) ....*Melissa Gilbert*
Deni Montana ....*Woody Harrelson*

Georgia May.......................*Jerry Hall & Mick Jagger*
Georgia Tatom....................*Harry Connick, Jr.*
India Emmeline...................*Marianne Williamson*
Indio.................................*Deborah Falconer & Robert Downey, Jr.*
Ireland Eliesse....................*Kim Basinger & Alec Baldwin*
Italia.................................*LL Cool J*
Kenya Julia Miami ....*Nastassja Kinski & Quincy Jones*
Lourdes Maria.....................*Madonna*
Madison (girl)....................*Sissy Spacek*
Montana Eve ....*Judd Hirsch*
Montana James ....*Richard Thomas*
Paris (boy).........................*Blair Underwood*
Paris Michael Katherine.......*Michael Jackson*
Phoenix Chi........................*"Scary Spice" Melanie Brown*
Rio....................................*Sean Young*
Savannah Jane.....................*Jimmy Buffett*
Sierra Alexis.......................*James Worthy*
Sonora Ashley.....................*Kelly McGillis*
Zion ....*Lauryn Hill & Rohan Marley*

CENTURY NAMES
August.......................*Lena Olin*
Beatrice ....*Emma Samms*
Belle Kingston.............*Donna Dixon & Dan Ackroyd*
Charlotte.....................*Sigourney Weaver*
Chester ....*Rita Wilson & Tom Hanks*
Cicely Yasin...............*Sandra Bernhard*
Clara Mathilde............*Ewan McGregor*
Eleanor......................*Diane Lane & Christopher Lambert*
Elinor........................*Katie Couric*
Ella...........................*Gary Sinise*
Eulalia Grace..............*Marcia Gay Hardin*
Homer Banks...............*Bill Murray*
Isabel Ira Ashley.........*Annette Bening & Warren Beatty*

Isabella......................*Andrew Lloyd-Weber*
Isabella Jane................*Nicole Kidman & Tom Cruise*
Isabelle Holmes............*C. C. Dyer & Geraldo Rivera*
Jasper Armstrong..........*Wynton Marsalis*
Josephine ....*Linda Hamilton & James Cameron*
Louis..........................*Bill Pullman*
Louisa Jacobson ....*Meryl Streep*
Mable.........................*Tracey Ullman*
Madeline.....................*Lea Thompson*
Mariah........................*Kerry Kennedy & Andrew Cuomo*
Matilda ....*Elizabeth Perkins*
May ....*Madeleine Stowe & Brian Benben*
Miles..........................*Lionel Richie*
Miles Guthrie ....*Susan Sarandon & Tim Robbins*
Miles William..............*Elisabeth Shue*
Oliver..........................*Martin Short*
Olivia ....*Denzel Washington*
Victoria ....*Tommy Lee Jones*

BIBLICAL NAMES
Aaron..............................*Robert De Niro*
Benjamin ....*Annette Bening & Warren Beatty*
Delilah Belle ....*Lisa Rinna & Harry Hamlin*
Elijah ....*Tiffany*
Elijah ....*James Spader*
Elijah Judd...........................*Wynnona Judd*
Eve......................................*Bono*
Ezra Samuel.........................*Paul Reiser*
Ezekiel ....*Beau Bridges*
Gabriel ....*Jason Alexander*
Gabriel Luke Beauregard.......*Jerry Hall & Mick Jagger*
Gabriel Kane.......................*Isabel Adjani & Daniel Day-Lewis*
Hannah................................*Kristin Scott Thomas*
Hannah Margaret ....*Jilly Mack & Tom Selleck*

Hannah Jo...........................Elizabeth Perkins
Hannah Nika.......................Helen Slater
Isaac Harris.........................Annie Potts
Jacob Eli.............................Albert Brooks
Jacob Nicholas....................James Caan
Jared Brandon.....................Paula Zahn
Jonathan.............................Paulina Porizkova & Rik
          Ocasek
Lydia.................................Bill Paxton
Noah..................................Jason Alexander
Noah Alexis........................Kim Alexis
Samuel...............................Sally Field
Sarah Jude..........................Kiefer Sutherland
Sarah Margaret....................Andie MacDowell
Sarah Rose..........................Marlee Matlin
Selah..................................Lauryn Hill & Rohan
          Marley
Simeon...............................Wynton Marsalis
Zachary..............................Cheryl Tiegs & Tony Peck

LAST NAMES FIRST
Bailey...........................Anthony Edwards
Beckett..........................Melissa Etheridge & Jvlie
          Cipher
Cameron........................Emma Samms
Cameron Marley..............Jimmy Buffett
Carter............................Alan Thicke
Cassidy Erin...................Kathie Lee & Frank Gifford
Cooper..........................Tim Matheson
Decker Nilsson................Nikki Sixx
Emerson Rose.................Teri Hatcher
Grady Thomas.................Harry Smith
Gulliver Flynn.................Gary Oldman
Holden...........................Dennis Miller
Holden Richard................Rick Schroder
Hopper Jack....................Robin Wright & Sean Penn
Hunter (twin, boy)...........Niki Taylor
Jackson Frederick............Patti Smith
Jackson James.................Katey Sagal
Jackson Lewis.................Spike Lee

Jefferson.........................Tony Randall
Kelsey..........................Kelly McGillis
Kelsey Rose....................Gabrielle Carteris
Kendall Nicole.................Bruce Jenner
Langley Fox....................Mariel Hemingway
Mallory Loving (girl)........Rick Derringer
Marston...........................Hugh Hefner
Mason.............................Cuba Gooding, Jr.
Mason............................Laura San Giacomo
Matalin Mary ....Mary Matalin & James
                              Carville
McCanna.......................Gary Sinise
McKenna Lane................Mary Lou Retton
Parker Jaren ....Rosie O'Donnell
Presley Tanita..................Tanya Tucker
Quinn............................Sean Young
Reilly............................Roma Downey
Remington ....Tracy Nelson & Billy Moses
Sawyer...........................Kate Capshaw & Steven
                              Spielberg
Truman Theodore.............Rita Wilson & Tom Hanks
Tully..............................Deirdre Hall
Walker Steven ....Adrienne Barbeau
Weston...........................Nicolas Cage

NATURE NAMES
Ivy-Victoria..........Sheryl Lee Ralph
Jasmine ....Michael Jordan
Jasmine Page........Martin Lawrence
Lily Dolores.........Amy Madigan & Ed Harris
Lily Marie ....Kathy Ireland
Lily Max ....Meredith Viera
Peaches ....Paula Yates & Bob Geldof
Rose ....Rene Russo
Sage (boy)..........Tracey Gold
Storm (girl).........Nikki Sixx
Summer...............Dr. Dre
Willow...............Gabrielle Anwar
Zephyr ....Karla De Vito & Robby Benson

CLASSICS

Alexandra Lyn	*Lorenzo Lamas*
Caroline	*Katie Couric*
Catherine Clare	*Crystal Gayle*
Charles	*Julia Louis Dreyfuss & Brad Hall*
Charles	*Jodie Foster*
Christina Maria Aurelia	*Maria Shriver & Arnold Schwarzenegger*
Christopher Casey	*Sean "Puffy" Combs*
Christopher Sargent Shriver	*Maria Shriver & Arnold Schwarzenegger*
Daniel Jack	*Natasha Richardson & Liam Neeson*
Emily Grace	*Alex Trebeck*
Emily Marie	*Gloria Estefan*
Emma	*Eric Roberts*
Emma	*Christine Lahti*
Eve	*Bono*
Grace	*Wynnona Judd*
James Powell	*Annie Potts*
John Albert Victor	*Tracey Ullman*
John Bouvier Kennedy	*Caroline Kennedy & Ed Schlossberg*
John David	*Denzel Washington*
John Henry	*Michelle Pfeiffer*
John Owen	*Rob Lowe*
John Stacy	*Jane Seymour*
Joseph	*Kristin Scott-Thomas*
Julia Jones	*Shaun Cassidy*
Julia Laurette	*Tony Randall*
Julian	*Robert De Niro*
Julian Murray	*Lisa Kudrow*
Katharine Eunice	*Maria Shriver & Arnold Schwarzenegger*
Lucy	*Mimi Rogers*
Matthew Edward	*Rob Lowe*
Matthew Jay	*Connie Chung & Maury Povich*

Matthew Julian	*Eddie Money*
Michael Richard Antonio	*Natasha Richardson & Liam Neeson*
Nicholas	*Vanna White*
Nicholas Morgan	*Marilu Henner*
Thomas	*Dana Carvey*
William Dalton	*Adrienne Barbeau*

EXOTIC, UNUSUAL, UNIQUE

Angus Moore	*Amanda Pays & Corbin Bernsen*
Aquinnah Kathleen	*Tracy Pollan & Michael J. Fox*
Arie	*Jody Whatley*
Arissa	*Kelly LeBrock & Steven Seagal*
Atticus	*Isabella Hoffman*
Braison Chance	*Billy Ray Cyrus*
Brawley King	*Nick Nolte*
Bria Lianna	*Eddie Murphy*
Buck	*Roseanne*
Chelsy	*Scott Bakula*
Chorde	*Snoop Doggy Dog (Calvin Broadas)*
Coco	*Sting*
Dashiell	*Harry Anderson*
Declyn Wallace	*Cyndi Lauper*
Dex	*Dana Carvey*
Dree Louise	*Mariel Hemingway*
Esmé	*Anthony Edwards*
Heavenly Hirani Tiger Lily	*Paula Yates*
Hud	*John Mellencamp*
Jelani (boy)	*Wesley Snipes*
Jett (boy)	*Kelly Preston & John Travolta*
Kathlyn Bening	*Annette Bening & Warren Beatty*
Lara	*Bob Saget*
Letesha	*Ice T*
Liberty Irene	*Jean & Casey Kasem*

Loewy.....................................*John Malkovich*
Lola.....................................*Annie Lennox*
Lolita...................................*Brian De Palma*
Lulu.....................................*Edie Brickell & Paul Simon*
Maesa ....*Bill Pullman*
Pixie ....*Paula Yates*
Rebop ....*Todd Rundgren*
Rumer Glenn.............................*Demi Moore & Bruce Willis*
Sailor Lee ....*Christie Brinkley*
Samaria ....*LL Cool J*
Scout LaRue (girl)......................*Demi Moore & Bruce Willis*
Scout Gabriel (boy) ....*Tai Babilonia*
Seven ....*Erykah Badu*
Shayla Rae..............................*Mary Lou Retton*
Shayne Audra...........................*Eddie Murphy*
Sistine Rose ....*Jennifer Flavin & Sylvester Stallone*
Slade Lucas Moby....................*David Brenner*
Sonnet Noel ....*Forest Whitaker*
Sosie Ruth ....*Kyra Sedgwick & Kevin Bacon*
Speck Wildhorse......................*John Mellencamp*
Tali......................................*Annie Lennox*
Tallulah Belle.........................*Demi Moore & Bruce Willis*
Trixie...................................*Damon Wayans*
Zoey ....*Lea Thompson*

AND THE OTHERS ...

Adrian Edward ....*Edie Brickell & Paul Simon*
Alastair ....*Andrew Lloyd-Weber*
Ali (girl).........................*Ruth Pointer*
Allie Colleen....................*Garth Brooks*
Allison Grady...................*Heather Menzies & Robert Urich*
Ashley Jade ....*Howard Stern*
Ava ....*Aidan Quinn*

Ava Elizabeth................*Heather Locklear & Richie Santora*

Beau Grayson................*Tanya Tucker*

Bobbi Kristina................*Whitney Houston & Bobby Brown*

Brandon ....*Pamela Anderson & Tommy Lee*

Brandon Scott ....*Tracy Austin*

Claudia Rose..................*Michelle Pfeiffer*

Cody Alan ....*Robin Williams*

Cody Newton ....*Kathie Lee & Frank Gifford*

Connor..........................*Ruth Pointer*

Connor Antony...............*Nicole Kidman & Tom Cruise*

Devin Christian ....*Vanessa Williams*

Dylan............................*Pierce Brosnan*

Dylan Jagger..................*Pamela Anderson & Tommy Lee*

Dylan John ....*Joan Cusack*

Elliot.............................*Robert De Niro*

Garrett ....*Bo Jackson*

Hayley Rose ....*Beau Bridges*

Jennifer Katharine ....*Bill Gates*

Jillian...........................*Vanessa Williams*

Justin ....*Andie MacDowell*

Kristopher Steven............*Jane Seymour*

Leila Ruth ....*Deborah Roberts & Al Roker*

Leila George ....*Greta Scacci & Vincent D'Onofrio*

Liam McAllister ....*Rachel Hunter & Rod Stewart*

Lorraine Broussard..........*Rebecca Broussard & Jack Nicholson*

Lucas Autry ....*Willie Nelson*

Lucian...........................*Steve Buscemi*

Malcolm........................*Denzel Washington*

Marlon ....*Dennis Miller*

Maxwell ....*Andrew Dice Clay*

Maya Grace ....*Garrison Keillor*

Michaela Andrea.............*Kerry Kennedy & Andrew Cuomo*

Mikaela.........................*Deborah Norville*

Mikaela George	*Kate Capshaw & Steven Spielberg*
Milo Sebastian	*Ricki Lake*
Myles Maximillian	*Sherilyn Fenn & Toulouse Hardy*
Myles Mitchell	*Eddie Murphy*
Owen	*Christopher Reeve*
Owen Joseph	*Phoebe Cates & Kevin Kline*
Sebastian	*James Spader*
Shelby Steph (boy)	*Reba McEntire*
Sophia	*Rebecca DeMornay & Patrick O'Neal*
Sophia Rose	*Jennifer Flavin & Sylvester Stallone*
Spencer	*Cuba Gooding, Jr.*
Spencer Michael	*Gena Lee Nolin*
Stanley Kirk, Jr	*M. C. Hammer*
Stella del Carmen	*Melanie Griffiths & Antonio Banderas*
Stella Irene Augustus	*Donna Dixon & Dan Ackroyd*
Stephanie Rose	*John Bon Jovi*
Theo	*Kate Capshaw & Steven Spielberg*
Travis Sedg	*Kyra Sedgwick & Kevin Bacon*
Tristan River	*Natasha Henstridge*
Ty Christian	*Pam Dawber & Mark Harmon*
Vincent	*Sophie Marceau*
Zelda	*Robin Williams*
Zoe	*Rosanna Arquette*
Zoe	*Woody Harrelson*

TV RECEPTION

If a new name crops up, seemingly out of nowhere, all across the country, chances are it can be found in the pages of *TV Guide* or—even more likely—*Soap Opera Digest*. Sometimes there's a bit of a gap, the time it takes for impressionable young viewers to reach childbearing age, but surprisingly often, the impact is almost spontaneous.

This is a pattern that dates back to the very beginnings of television. It first became noticeable when the phenomenally popular westerns of the 1950s and 1960s reintroduced a genre of names that hadn't been heard in this country for almost a century—grizzled old great-grandpa names like Joshua, Jason, Jeremy, and Jesse. Practically before you could say Ponderosa, those very names had taken on enough muscle and magic to start replacing old stalwarts like Robert and Richard on baby name popularity lists.

That was also the era of cute-kid TV names, often in the form of unisex nicknames. There were boy Kellys and girl Kellys, boy Jodys and girl Jodies, reflecting and affecting the newborns in real life. A more glamorous element entered in the *Charlie's Angels* seventies, an age of Sabrinas and Kimberlys and Tiffanys and other dainty three-syllable names. When *Dynasty* exploded onto the small screen in 1981, it created a mini-baby-naming boom all its own. Blakes of both sexes appeared in ever-increasing numbers on birth announcements and, in its various spellings, Krystle/Krystal/Crystal vaulted onto popularity charts. As for Alexis Carrington, she was at least partly responsible for a still rampant epidemic of Alexi—not only Alexises and Alexes but Alexas, Alexanders, Alexandras, Alexandrias, and Lexies. *Dynasty*'s creators also played with the idea of surname and male names for girls—Fallon, Kirby, and others—which would explode in the nineties.

But for decades it has been the daytime dramas that have been most in the vanguard of baby-naming trends. The classic case is the name Kayla. When the character of Kayla Brady was introduced on *Days of Our Lives* in 1982, the name was barely mentioned in any of the standard baby-naming manuals. But within a few years, Kayla began an unprecedented leap up the lists, still registering in the top fifteen a decade and a half later. Soaps also anticipated the trend of using place names for people—there were Egypts and Indias, Sierras and Friscos back when the current parents of little Dakotas and Dallases were still in junior high.

This timeline displays the key TV character names, and

the shows they appeared in, over the past four decades, with the most trendsetting set in boldface.

1955	*Cheyenne*	CHEYENNE
	Gunsmoke	**MATT**
1956	*Maverick*	BART
		BRET
		BEAU
1957	*Bachelor Father*	KELLY (f)
	The Real McCoys	LUKE
1958	*Wanted Dead or Alive*	JOSH
1959	*Bonanza*	**ADAM**
1963	*Wagon Train*	COOPER
1964	*Bewitched*	**SAMANTHA**
	Peyton Place	**ALLISON**
1965	*I Spy*	KELLY (m)
1966	*Family Affair*	JODY (m)
	As the World Turns	AMANDA
	The Secret Storm	BROOKE (still a soap favorite)
1968	*Here Come the Brides*	**JASON**
		JEREMY
		JOSHUA
1970	*The Secret Storm*	INDIA
1972	*Bob Newhart*	EMILY
	The Waltons	OLIVIA
1974	*Good Times*	FLORIDA (an early place name)
	General Hospital	CAMERON
	Ryan's Hope	MAEVE (an early ethnic Irish name)
1975	*General Hospital*	KYLE
1976	*Bionic Woman*	JAIME
	Charlie's Angels	SABRINA
1977	*Eight Is Enough*	**NICHOLAS**
	The Edge of Night	LOGAN
		RAVEN
	Search for Tomorrow	KYLIE
1978	*The Avengers*	EMMA
	Diff'rent Strokes	**KIMBERLY**

	WKRP in Cincinnati	BAILEY (f)
	Dallas	JENNA
1979	*Charlie's Angels*	**TIFFANY**
	Facts of Life	BLAIR
	Hart to Hart	JONATHAN
		JENNIFER
	The Edge of Night	PAIGE
1980	*Another World*	MIRANDA
		TAYLOR (m)
	The Guiding Light	MORGAN (f)
	As the World Turns	HALEY
1981	*Dynasty*	BLAKE (m)
		KRYSTLE
		FALLON (f)
		ALEXIS
	Falcon Crest	COLE
1982	*As The World Turns*	ARIEL
	Days of Our Lives	**KAYLA**
	Family Ties	**ALEX**
		MALLORY
	Dynasty	KIRBY (f)
	Santa Barbara	SYDNEY (f)
	Young and the Restless	**ASHLEY** (appeared earlier on *The Doctors*)
	Newhart	STEPHANIE
1983	*One Life to Live*	COURTNEY
	Search for Tomorrow	HOGAN
	Dallas	JENNA
	Scarecrow & Mrs King	AMANDA (hits prime time)
1984	*Kate & Allie*	EMMA
	Cosby Show	THEO
		VANESSA
	Days of Our Lives	**JASMINE**
	Dynasty	BRAD
	Another World	HUNTER
1985	*Another World*	**BRITTANY**
	As the World Turns	HOLDEN
		SIERRA (m)

	Days of Our Lives	**SAVANNAH**
	Falcon Crest	CASSANDRA
		JORDAN (f)
	The Colbys	MILES
	General Hospital	**JADE**
1986	*Matlock*	**TYLER** (m)
	As the World Turns	**DUNCAN**
	L.A. Law	**KELSEY** (attorney ANN KELSEY'S surname)*
		GRACE
1987	*Cheers*	**SAM**
		REBECCA
	A Different World	JALEESA
	thirtysomething	HOPE
		MELISSA
		BRITTANY (child)
	Miami Vice	CAITLIN
	As the World Turns	**TAYLOR** (f)
	My Two Dads	NICOLE
1988	*Murphy Brown*	MURPHY
	As the World Turns	CALEB
	Days of Our Lives	LEXIE
	General Hospital	COLTON
1989	*Anything but Love*	HANNAH
	Days of Our Lives	COLIN
	Baywatch	TREVOR
	The Cosby Show	OLIVIA (child)
1990	*Beverly Hills 90210*	**BRANDON**
		DYLAN
	thirtysomething	LEO (baby)
	All My Children	**CEARA** (an anything-goes spelling)
	As the World Turns	**CONNOR** (f)
	Days of Our Lives	TANNER

*She bestowed it on the adopted baby daughter she was forced to return to the birth mother in a heartrending episode that not only launched the name Kelsey but also spawned an important trend toward using mothers' maiden names as first names.

1991	*Blossom*	SIX
	Another World	SPENCER
1992	*Mad About You*	JAMIE (interesting because her nickname is the male JAMES)
	Murphy Brown	AVERY (the show's baby was male, but most of its namesakes were girls)
	Another World	KELSEY
	Days of Our Lives	**AUSTIN** (appeared earlier on *Edge of Night* and *One Life to Live*)
	Loving	**COOPER**
1993	*All My Children*	KENDALL (f)
	As the World Turns	DAMIAN
	Blossom	KENNEDY (little girl)
	Dr. Quinn, Medicine Woman	**MICHAELA** (also called Mike)
	Hangin' with Mr. Cooper	GENEVA
	Late Night with Conan O'Brien	CONAN
	Melrose Place	SYDNEY (f)
	The X-Files	FOX
1994	*Ellen*	PAIGE
	Friends	CHANDLER
		ROSS
	Party of Five	JULIA
		BAILEY (m)
		GRIFFIN
		OWEN (child)
	Sister, Sister	TIA
	As the World Turns	BETHANY
	Young and the Restless	**KEESHA**
1995	*Baywatch Nights*	**DESTINY**

	Guiding Light	ABIGAIL
	Loving	**BRIANNA**
1997	*Mad About You*	MABEL (baby)
	Buffy the Vampire Slayer	XANDER
	Just Shoot Me	MAYA
		HANNAH (child)
1998	*Days of Our Lives*	ELVIS (baby)
	Boy Meets World	TOPANGA
	Felicity	FELICITY

MULTIPLE PERSONALITIES

Some soap names work overtime, pedaling between several different shows. The following are some of the names that have appeared on at least two daytime dramas—some of them as many as five (Olivia, Julia):

MALE	FEMALE
AUSTIN	ALEXANDRA
	AMANDA
BO	ANGELA
BRANDON	APRIL
COLE	BROOKE
DAMIAN	CARLY
DEREK	
DYLAN	DINAH
EVAN	EMMA
	EVE
GRANT	
	FELICIA
HART	

	GILLIAN
IAN	GRACE
LEO	HANNAH
LUCAS	HOPE
MARCUS	ISABELLA
MILES	
	JADE
NED	JULIA
PIERCE	KEESHA
	KELSEY
RYAN	
	LEXIE
SHANE	LILA
	LILY
TYRONE	LYDIA
ZACK	MARGO
	MIRANDA
	MOLLY
	NATALIE
	OLIVIA
	RUBY
	SAMANTHA
	TAYLOR
	TESS
	TIFFANY
	VANESSA

THEY CAME FROM OUTER SPACE

Recent space operas and mythic dramas have added their own eccentric entries (with an emphasis on the letters 'z' and 'x') into the name game. Among them are Ezri, Jadzi, Xena, and Yara (female) and Callisto, Dax, Fox, Joxer, and Neelix (male).

IT TAKES ONE TO PLAY ONE

Not only do some soap opera characters have some wildly inventive names, but often so do the actors who portray them. A few examples:

FEMALE	MALE
ALLA	CRUISE
CADY	DAX
ESTA	INGO
JENSEN	KALE
KAM	KIN
KIMBERLIN	ROARK
SABRYN	SHEMAR
SCHAE	
VANITA	

AND TIDE WAS THE SURFER DUDE WHO HAD AN AFFAIR WITH DAWN

We *even named characters after Procter & Gamble products. Dawn was named after the dishwashing soap and Cal's horse Comet, after the cleanser."*

—JOHN KUNTZ, SCRIPTWRITER FOR *AS THE WORLD TURNS*, IN *SOAP OPERA MAGAZINE*

DISNEY WORLD

When Rosie O'Donnell was naming her daughter Chelsea, her older son, Parker, pushed for the name of his favorite movie character, Belle in *Beauty and the Beast*, and the compromise was made for the little girl to be called Chelsea Belle. Over the years, Disney characters have provided naming inspiration for generations of parents. Before the movie of the same name, for example, Bambi was rarely if ever used as a girl's name, but after the movie's release, and despite the fact that the deer in question was male, there soon were thousands of little girl Bambis across the land. More recently, another name that was influential was that of Ariel, the title character of *The Little Mermaid*.

Here is a list of Disney names that might be considered by prospective parents and that could give their bearers a special connection to the leading purveyor of children's popular culture in America. Be warned, however, that some of these are names of bad guys, and others play pretty minor parts.

A SCHOOL OF MERMAIDS

As any parent with school-age children knows, names are subject to fashion, and the source for trendy names is often the movies: there may be five Ariels in your daughter's fourth-grade class, because a character by that name was the heroine of Disney's The Little Mermaid, in 1989, but just try finding an Ariel in the play group where you deposit your preschooler. (Mulan, anyone?)

—BRENDAN LEMON, THE NEW YORKER

GIRLS

ABIGAIL	The Fox and the Hound and The Aristocats
ADELAIDE	The Aristocats
ALICE	Alice in Wonderland
AMELIA	The Aristocats
ANASTASIA	Cinderella
ANITA	One Hundred and One Dalmatians
ARIEL	The Little Mermaid
AURORA	Sleeping Beauty
BAMBI	Bambi (male character)
BELLE	Beauty and the Beast
BIANCA	The Rescuers and The Rescuers Down Under
CALLA	The Gummi Bears (TV)
CALLIOPE	Hercules
CARLOTTA	The Little Mermaid
CLEO	Pinocchio
CLIO	Hercules
DAISY	cartoons
DINAH	Alice in Wonderland

ENA	*Bambi*
ESMERALDA	*The Hunchback of Notre Dame*
FELICIA	*The Great Mouse Detective*
FIFI	cartoon shorts
FLORA	*Sleeping Beauty*
HYACINTH	*Fantasia*
JENNY	*Oliver and Company*
KATRINA	*The Adventures of Ichabod and Mr. Toad*
LUCY	*One Hundred and One Dalmatians*
MARIAN	*Robin Hood*
MIM	*The Sword in the Stone*
MINNIE	cartoon shorts
MOLLY	*TailSpin* (TV)
NALA	*The Lion King*
OLIVIA	*The Great Mouse Detective*
PERDITA	*One Hundred and One Dalmatians*
POLLY	*The Rescuers Down Under*
SARABI	*The Lion King*
SARAH	*Lady and the Tramp*
THALIA	*Hercules*
URSULA	*The Little Mermaid*
VANESSA	*The Little Mermaid*
WENDY	*Peter Pan*
WINIFRED	*The Jungle Book*

BOYS

ABU	*Aladdin*
AKELA	*The Jungle Book*
AMOS	*The Fox and the Hound*
ANGUS	*Ichabod and Mr. Toad*
BARTHOLOMEW	*The Great Mouse Detective*
BASIL	*The Great Mouse Detective*
BORIS	*Lady and the Tramp*

BROM	*The Adventures of Ichabod and Mr. Toad*
BRUNO	*Cinderella*
CASEY	*Dumbo*
CHRISTOPHER	*Winnie the Pooh*
CLAUDE	*The Hunchback of Notre Dame*
CODY	*The Rescuers Down Under*
DEMETRIUS	*Hercules*
DEWEY	cartoons
ERIC	*The Little Mermaid*
GASTON	*Beauty and the Beast*
GIDEON	*Pinocchio*
GUS	*Cinderella*
HUGO	*The Hunchback of Notre Dame*
IAGO	*Aladdin*
JAFAR	*Aladdin*
JAKE	*The Rescuers Down Under*
LUKE	*The Rescuers*
MAX	*The Little Mermaid*
MEEKO	*Pocahontas*
OLIVER	*Oliver and Company*
ORVILLE	*The Rescuers*
OTTO	*Robin Hood*
PEDRO	*Lady and the Tramp*
PERCY	*Pocahontas*
PETER	*Peter Pan*
PHILLIP	*Sleeping Beauty*
PHOEBUS	*The Hunchback of Notre Dame*
RAFIKI	*The Lion King*
RAMA	*The Jungle Book*
ROBIN	*Robin Hood*
ROSCOE	*Oliver and Company*
RUFUS	*The Rescuers*
SEBASTIAN	*The Little Mermaid*
SIMBA	*The Lion King*
STEFAN	*Sleeping Beauty*
THADDEUS	*Toad of Toad Hall*
THOMAS	*The Aristocats*
TIMON	*The Lion King*
TIMOTHY	*Dumbo*

TOBY	*Robin Hood* and *The Great Mouse Detective*
TOD	*The Fox and the Hound*
WALDO	*The Aristocats*
WINSTON	*Oliver and Company*
ZAZU	*The Lion King*

THERE'S ONLY ONE UMA

If you have one of these names, what it means is that when you make a phone call, you'll never be asked "Ving who?" On the other hand, nothing necessarily lasts forever, including uniqueness. There are a lot more Elvises around than there used to be, including a soap opera baby, but there's still only one Elvis. In terms of one-person names, these seem to be permanently assigned to their current owners:

ALANIS Morrisette
ALFRE Woodard
ARETHA Franklin
ARSENIO Hall

BJORK
BONO

CALISTA Flockhart
CHARLIZE Theron
CUBA Gooding, Jr.

DELROY Lindo
DEMI (b. Demetria) Moore
DENZEL Washington
DJIMON Hoursou
DWEEZIL Zappa

EMO Phillips
ENYA (c. Eithne)
ERYKAH (b. Erica) Badu

FAMKE Jannssen

IMAN

JADA Pinkett
JUDGE (b. Edward) Reinhold

KEANU Reeves (it means "cool breeze over the mountain" in Hawaiian)
KIEFER Sutherland

MADONNA
MAYIM Bialik
MONTEL Williams

NENAH Cherry
NEVE Campbell

OPRAH Winfrey

PARK Overall
PICABO Street

STONE Phillips
SWOOSIE Kurtz

RIDDICK Bowe
ROMA Downey
RUSH Limbaugh

TIPPER (b. Mary Elizabeth) Gore
TREAT Williams

UMA Thurman (a Tibetan name chosen by her Buddhist scholar father)

SADE (b. Helen)
SALMA Hayek
SELA Ward
SHADOE (b. Terry) Stevens
SHANIA Twain
SHAQUILLE O'Neal
SIGOURNEY (b. Susan) Weaver
SINBAD
SKEET (b. Brian) Ulrich

VIGGO Mortensen
VING (b. Irving) Rhames

WHOOPI (b. Caryn) Goldberg
WINGS Hauser
WINONA Ryder

THE GODDESS UMA

Uma Thurman has three brothers: Dechen, Ganden, and Mipam. The four siblings all have Tibetan names because their father, Robert A. F. Thurman, the Jey Tsong Khapa Professor of Indo-Tibetan Buddhist Studies at Columbia University, was the first American to be ordained as a Tibetan Buddhist monk by the Dalai Lama, in 1965. Uma means "the Middle Way" in Tibetan and is the name of the mother goddess in Indian mythology.

MUCH ADO ABOUT NAMING

With names like Olivia and Julia, Duncan, Sebastian, and other favorites of the Bard of Avon experiencing a revival, you might want to consider a more expansive playbill of Shakespearean choices:

GIRLS

ADRIANA	*The Comedy of Errors*
ALICE	*The Merry Wives of Windsor*
AUDREY	*As You Like It*
BEATRICE	*Much Ado About Nothing*
BIANCA	*The Taming of the Shrew, Othello*
CASSANDRA	*Troilus and Cressida*
CELIA	*As You Like It*
CHARMIAN	*Antony and Cleopatra*
CLEOPATRA	*Antony and Cleopatra*
CORDELIA	*King Lear*
CRESSIDA	*Troilus and Cressida*
DESDEMONA	*Othello*
DIANA	*All's Well That Ends Well*
DORCAS	*The Winter's Tale*
EMILIA	*Othello, The Winter's Tale*
FRANCISCA	*Measure for Measure*
HELENA	*A Midsummer Night's Dream, All's Well That Ends Well*
HERMIONE	*The Winter's Tale*
IMOGEN	*Cymbeline*
ISABEL	*Henry V*
ISABELLA	*Measure for Measure*
JACQUENETTA	*Love's Labour Lost*
JESSICA	*The Merchant of Venice*
JULIA	*Two Gentlemen of Verona*
JULIET	*Romeo and Juliet*
JUNO	*The Tempest*
KATHARINA (KATE)	*The Taming of the Shrew*
LAVINIA	*Titus Andronicus*
LUCIANA	*The Comedy of Errors*
MARGARET	*Much Ado About Nothing*
MARINA	*Pericles*
MIRANDA	*The Tempest*
NELL	*The Comedy of Errors*

NERISSA	*The Merchant of Venice*
OCTAVIA	*Antony and Cleopatra*
OLIVIA	*Twelfth Night*
OPHELIA	*Hamlet*
PAULINA	*The Winter's Tale*
PERDITA	*The Winter's Tale*
PHEBE	*As You Like It*
PORTIA	*The Merchant of Venice, Julius Caesar*
REGAN	*King Lear*
ROSALIND	*As You Like It*
ROSALINE	*Love's Labour Lost*
TAMORA	*Titus Andronicus*
TITANIA	*A Midsummer Night's Dream*
URSULA	*Much Ado About Nothing*
VIOLA	*Twelfth Night*
VIRGILIA	*Coriolanus*

BOYS

ABRAHAM	*Romeo & Juliet*
ADRIAN	*The Tempest*
ADRIANO	*Love's Labour Lost*
ALONSO	*The Tempest*
ANGELO	*Measure for Measure*
ANGUS	*Macbeth*
ANTONIO	*The Tempest, Two Gentlemen of Verona, The Merchant of Venice, Much Ado About Nothing*
ANTONY	*Antony and Cleopatra*
ARIEL	*The Tempest*
BALTHASAR	*Romeo and Juliet, The Merchant of Venice, Much Ado About Nothing*
BALTHAZAR	*A Comedy of Errors*
BENEDICK	*Much Ado About Nothing*
BENVOLIO	*Romeo and Juliet*

CALIBAN	*The Tempest*
CAMILLO	*The Winter's Tale*
CLAUDIO	*Measure for Measure, Much Ado About Nothing*
CLEON	*Pericles*
CORIN	*As You Like It*
CORNELIUS	*Hamlet*
DEMETRIUS	*A Midsummer Night's Dream*
DION	*The Winter's Tale*
DUNCAN	*Macbeth*
EDMUND	*King Lear*
FABIAN	*Twelfth Night*
FERDINAND	*The Tempest*
FRANCISCO	*Hamlet*
GREGORY	*Romeo and Juliet*
HENRY	Several plays
HORATIO	*Hamlet*
HUMPHREY	*Henry VI, Part II*
KENT	*King Lear*
LENNOX	*Macbeth*
LEONARDO	*The Merchant of Venice*
LORENZO	*The Merchant of Venice*
LUCIUS	*Timon of Athens, Titus Andronicus, Julius Caesar*
LYSANDER	*A Midsummer Night's Dream*
MALCOLM	*Macbeth*
NATHANIEL	*Love's Labour Lost*
OBERON	*A Midsummer Night's Dream*
OLIVER	*As You Like It*
ORLANDO	*As You Like It*
ORSINO	*Twelfth Night*
OWEN	*Henry IV, Part I*
PHILO	*Antony and Cleopatra*
PROSPERO	*The Tempest*
ROSS	*Macbeth*
SAMPSON	*Romeo and Juliet*
SEBASTIAN	*Twelfth Night, The Tempest*
STEPHANO	*The Merchant of Venice, The Tempest*

TIMON	Timon of Athens, Measure for Measure
TOBY	Twelfth Night
VALENTINE	Two Gentlemen of Verona, Twelfth Night

GULLIVER versus ROMEO

When asked about his son Gulliver's unusual name, Gary Oldman explained to People magazine, "I was inspired by the character from Gulliver's Travels. My wife [photographer Donya Fiorentino] was a great sport about it." Maybe it was a happy compromise. "I also wanted to name him Romeo," said Oldman, "which would have been doing the boy a favor. Any boy named Romeo is going to get the chicks."

BRIT LIT

The annals of British literature, from the pastoral poets of the seventeenth century, through Jane Austen and Dickens, and up to more modern times, are a rich source of imaginative names:

GIRLS

ADELINE	Lord Byron
AGATHA	Evelyn Waugh
ALETHEA	Samuel Butler
ALTHEA	Richard Lovelace
AMANDA	Noel Coward
AMELIA	Henry Fielding, W. M. Thackeray
ANASTASIA	Charles Dickens
ANTHEA	Robert Herrick, Barbara Pym

ARABELLA	*Charles Dickens*
BATHSHEBA	*Thomas Hardy*
BELINDA	*Alexander Pope*
CANDIDA	*George Bernard Shaw*
CECILIA	*Charles Dickens*
CHARLOTTE	*Jane Austen, Charles Dickens*
CHASTITY	*Evelyn Waugh*
CHRISTABEL	*Barbara Pym, Samuel Coleridge*
CLARICE	*P. G. Wodehouse*
CLARISSA	*Samuel Richardson, Charles Dickens, Virginia Woolf*
CORDELIA	*Evelyn Waugh*
CORINNA	*Robert Herrick*
CRESSIDA	*Barbara Pym*
DAHLIA	*George Meredith, P. G. Wodehouse*
DINAH	*Lawrence Sterne*
DOMENICA	*Evelyn Waugh*
ELECTRA	*Robert Herrick*
ELIZA	*Jane Austen, George Bernard Shaw*
EMMA	*Jane Austen*
ESTELLA	*Charles Dickens*
EUSTACIA	*Thomas Hardy*
EVANGELINE	*P. G. Wodehouse*
FLEUR	*John Galsworthy*
FLORA	*Charles Dickens, Sir Walter Scott*
FORTITUDE	*Evelyn Waugh*
GEORGIANA	*Jane Austen, Charles Dickens*
GUINEVERE	*Arthurian Legends*
HONORIA	*Charles Dickens*
JEMIMA	*Jane Austen, Beatrix Potter*
JULIANA	*Andrew Marvell*
JUSTICE	*Evelyn Waugh*
JUSTINE	*Lawrence Durrell*
LAVINIA	*Charles Dickens*
LEILA	*Lord Byron*
LETITIA	*Jane Austen*

LILIA	*E. M. Forster*
LUCASTA	*Richard Lovelace*
LUCRETIA	*Charles Dickens*
LYDIA	*Jane Austen*
MALTA	*Charles Dickens*
MARIGOLD	*Barbara Pym*
MATILDA	*Charles Dickens*
MAUD	*Alfred, Lord Tennyson*
MERCY	*Charles Dickens, Evelyn Waugh*
MORGAN	*Arthurian Legends*
NELL	*Charles Dickens*
PERDITA	*Evelyn Waugh*
PIPPA	*Robert Browning*
PLEASANT	*Charles Dickens*
PRIMROSE	*Barbara Pym*
ROMOLA	*George Eliot*
ROWENA	*Sir Walter Scott*
SELINA	*Jane Austen*
TAMSIN	*Barbara Pym*
TESS	*Thomas Hardy*
THOMASIN	*Thomas Hardy*
VELVET	*Enid Bagnold*
ZULEIKA	*Sir Max Beerbohm*

BOYS

ALARIC	*Barbara Pym*
AMBROSE	*P. G. Wodehouse, Evelyn Waugh*
AUGUSTINE	*P. G. Wodehouse*
AUGUSTUS	*Charles Dickens*
BARNABY	*Charles Dickens*
BARNEY	*Charles Dickens*
BARTHOLOMEW	*Charles Dickens*
CHEVY	*Charles Dickens*
CRISPIN	*Barbara Pym*
DARCY (surname)	*Jane Austen*
DIGBY	*Barbara Pym*
DORIAN	*Oscar Wilde*

DUNCAN	*Evelyn Waugh*
EBENEZER	*Charles Dickens*
ELIJAH	*Charles Dickens*
EPHRAIM	*Charles Dickens, Barbara Pym*
EUSTACE	*P. G. Wodehouse*
FELIX	*Evelyn Waugh, Barbara Pym*
FERDINAND	*Charles Dickens*
FITZWILLIAM	*Jane Austen*
GARETH	*Arthurian Legends*
GILES	*Barbara Pym*
GRAY	*W. Somerset Maugham*
GULLY	*Joyce Cary*
HIRAM	*Charles Dickens*
HORATIO	*Charles Dickens*
HUMPHREY	*Tobias Smollett, Evelyn Waugh*
IVOR	*P. G. Wodehouse, Evelyn Waugh*
JASPER	*P. G. Wodehouse*
JEREMIAH	*Charles Dickens*
JOSIAH	*Charles Dickens*
JUDE	*Thomas Hardy*
LEMUEL	*Jonathan Swift*
NICODEMUS	*Charles Dickens*
NICOL	*Sir Walter Scott*
OBADIAH	*Anthony Trollope*
OLIVER	*Charles Dickens*
ORLANDO	*Virginia Woolf, P. G. Wodehouse*
PEREGRINE	*Tobias Smollett, Evelyn Waugh*
QUEBEC	*Charles Dickens*
QUENTIN	*Sir Walter Scott*
REX	*Evelyn Waugh*
RODERICK	*Tobias Smollett*
ROLLO	*Barbara Pym*
RUPERT	*P. G. Wodehouse*
SEBASTIAN	*Evelyn Waugh*
SEPTIMUS	*Charles Dickens, Virginia Woolf*
SILAS	*George Eliot*
TOBY	*Charles Dickens*
TRISTRAM	*Arthurian Legends, Lawrence Sterne*

IMAGE

What's really in a name?

In this section, we examine that Shakespearean puzzle to determine what kind of images are embodied in a name, and how much information those images convey.

Some names have a Traditional image while others feel Creative—that's the easy part. Here we tell you everything you ever wanted to know about the sixty most classic names, and also offer a long list of names with a creative flavor.

In these days of highly inventive baby-naming, we analyze the issue of Unusual Names: How unusual is too unusual for your child? And if you're tired of both usual and creative names, which names have a more straightforward, down-to-earth image?

We explore the implications of nicknames here, too. And if you want a name that will help your child fit in with the crowd as well as stand out, this is where you'll find it.

And we wrestle with that most taboo of American subjects as it relates to names: class. Are there really names that sound classy, and those that don't? We tell all.

WHAT'S REALLY IN A NAME?
POWER, IMAGE, AND NAMES

*A*ll names carry an image. That much is indisputable. We perceive some names as sounding stronger, more serious than others, some names as being attractive and intelligent and others not.

But how important, how influential is that image? By your choice of a name, do you really set your child up for being thought of as smart or energetic, sexy or unreliable for the rest of his or her life? Or can a name shape your child's destiny in an even more elemental, insidious way, by conveying power through its very sounds and rhythms?

Through the years and over the ages, from ancient times to the present, there are those who have believed—and who would have you believe—that names are everything, that the image of a name is all-important in determining your child's future.

Primitive people believed that the name was the vessel for the person's soul or spirit. There are many superstitions relating to names and their power to influence someone's life for good or evil, to bless them with riches and a long future, or to drain their very lifeblood from them, hastening their death and even the deaths of those in their families.

It may be easy to dismiss these sorts of traditional beliefs as nonsense, yet as recently as 1937 name expert W. E. Walton wrote: "A person's first name may be a determining factor in his development of personality, acquisition of friends, and in all probability in his success or failure in life."

At the time of this writing we went on the Internet, that thoroughly modern vehicle for the dissemination of information, and checked in at the name site of the Kabalarian Society, which analyzes what it considers the power inherent in over 150,000 names, from P-Nut to Padmavathamma, based on its own Mathematical Principles.

Here is the Kabalarian's reading of Pamela:

The first name of Pamela creates a rather dual nature. You can appear to be two entirely different people, depending upon what environment you are in. . . . You are inclined to be termperamental and impulsive, overemotional and generous. The beauties of nature, fine music, art and literature you find very inspiring. . . . You must guard against indulgence in any form, particularly in the emotions, and also in the desire for sugars and starchy foods.

Seems wacky? Consider that in Italy, standard baby-naming books carry similar predictions about a child's personality and destiny based on his or her name. A boy named Enrico, for instance, will be calm and reflective and, when he's in love, will be faithful and devoted. His lucky number is one; his best day, Sunday; and his lucky precious metal, gold.

And much closer to home and mainstream social science, UCLA professor Albert Mehrabian has undertaken extensive surveys in which people rate names on six qualities: success, morality, health, warmth, cheerfulness, and masculinity-femininity. His book, *The Name Game*, lists every name with its number rating on each of these characteristics, noting which names are perceived as being highest and lowest in each category.

While this is an interesting exercise, perceptions of names change over time, sometimes quite rapidly. A name that sounds successful, say, or masculine one year might seem anything but a few years later. And our ideas about many of these names vary radically from what Mehrabian's panel decided. Brad, for instance, gets one of the highest ratings, a 90, in success. At what? Surfing? Bruce is seen as one of the most masculine names, yet its widespread image is as anything but.

We can see why Moses and Solomon, Lincoln and Ernest got high marks for morality, but why Herman? Why Filbert and Myrtle? Just because they sound too old to do anything nasty? Charlie indeed sounds cheerful, yet Abigail, which means happiness, gets one of the lowest ratings for cheer. Maggie hasn't got much chance of success,

Eleanor's not very healthy, Jessica's not really feminine—gee, this doesn't sound entirely accurate to us.

In surveying the research on the power of names, there is a lot of back and forth: studies that show one thing about image, and then further studies that show the complete opposite.

One well-publicized study from a few decades ago seemed to demonstrate that having a well-liked name could lead to academic success. Teachers graded the essays of children with popular names such as Lisa and Michael higher than those by children named Elmer and Bertha.

Yet other, much larger studies disproved the link between names and grades. One analysis of the grades of nearly 24,000 second-to-eleventh graders in a Midwestern public school system found no correlation between name popularity or desirability and academic achievement. Another study of 724 high schoolers in the Midwest found no correlation between names and grade-point average, achievement tests, and social competence and empathy tests. Researcher Martin Ford at Stanford reasoned that in some cases having an unusual or undesirable name might have a negative effect on a child's achievement, but it was just as likely that it would build character.

Another highly publicized study from Tulane University showed that hypothetical beauty pageant contestants with attractive names such as Jennifer and Christine won out over contestants with less desirable names such as Ethel and Harriet.

Still another study, which assigned two names found to have a high variation in attractiveness, Christy and Gertrude, to the same actress found that the names had no effect on how appealing people judged her looks and behavior to be.

Names, some more than others, carry stereotypes that can lead people to make judgments. A 1992 investigation of names in television at SUNY-Stonybrook found that people judged a hypothetical woman named Andrea Wolcot to be highly educated, they saw Kathy and Elisa as waitresses, Ruby was seen as a black jazz singer. Kimberly Channing was seen as a spoiled preppy girl and Marina a gypsy con woman. Avery and Bret get rich, Stanley Nmitski and Clyde Regan are criminals.

But our real-life experiences tend to overshadow whatever judgments we make about names on a theoretical basis. Kenneth Steele and Laura Smithwick, psychologists at Mars Hill College in North Carolina, found that people judge certain names as good (David, Jon, Joshua, and Gregory) or bad (Oswald, Myron, Reginald) and tend to assign positive and negative characteristics to people based on those names if, that is, they haven't met or seen the specific individual, and have no other information but the name. Once the subjects in the experiment were shown photos of the theoretical Joshuas and Reginalds, judgments based solely on the names were erased.

Interestingly, a name's most potent influence may be on the person who bears it. A British book called *The Cognitive Psychology of Proper Names* says that the intimate relationship between one's given name and one's sense of identity accounts for the frequency with which psychotics, particularly schizophrenics, forget their names, refuse to tell them, or adopt new ones.

Children tend to be extremely interested in their own names, which springs from their developing sense of selfhood. Educators have

> ## FREUDIAN ANALYSIS
>
> A *human being's name is a principal component in his person, perhaps a piece of his soul.*
>
> —SIGMUND FREUD

found that the name is an ideal vehicle with which to engage children in learning. The first thing most kids can write is their names, and once they learn the letters in their own names they use those as a jumping-off point to other words. Children are attracted to lists containing their own names and interested in differences between their names and their friends' names, which can be a way for them to start learning to read and write.

It's easy to get caught up in the mania over the image and power embodied in a name during the months you're

ON BEING A STANLEY

Stanley is your brother-in-law, your C.P.A., your cousin in drapes. He collects stamps, washes his car, belongs to Triple A, and keeps a weather eye on the gas mileage. He is, that is, as all of us are, the fiction of his sound, all his recombinant glottals, labials, fricatives, and plosives . . . He is, I mean, the vibrations of his name.

—FROM A LECTURE BY STANLEY ELKIN

on the hunt for the perfect choice. At the time, it can feel like your child's name is one of the few things you really have control over, and it's essential as one of your first important parenting acts that you make the perfect choice. It can seem as if the name you pick will make all the difference in whether your child will be seen as an intelligent, attractive, creative, interesting person or not.

And yet in your heart, you know that's not true. What's really in a name? A lot, we believe, but not everything. Choosing a great name for your child may be important, but it's nowhere near as important as making him or her feel secure, overseeing his education, and being a loving parent.

THE CLASSICS: SIXTY TRADITIONAL NAMES THAT TRANSCEND TIME

What's the definition of a classic name? One that's not only rooted in history, but that's been consistently well-used throughout the ages, finding fans in the twentieth century as it did in the twelfth. Classic names transcend class and religion and nationality to appeal to a wide range of parents, from royals on down to the hoi polloi. A great traditional name is hard to find, not least because there simply aren't that many of them around. Here are our picks for the top sixty Traditionals, thirty for girls and thirty for boys, that work as beautifully today as they have over the centuries.

GIRLS

ALICE. Forever associated with Lewis Carroll's heroine in *Alice's Adventures in Wonderland* and *Through the Looking Glass and What Alice Found There,* Alice still retains an aura of long, streaming hair and pastel-hued ribbon hairbands, which was reinforced by such sentimental songs as *Sweet Little Alice Blue Gown.* Stemming from an ancient German word meaning "nobility," it moved from Alalheidis to the French shortening Adaliz, which arrived in England as Aliz. The name enjoyed enormous popularity following the publication of *Alice in Wonderland* in 1865, remaining in the top twenty-five names in this country until 1925, but it then gradually began to fade as a baby name, especially after it took on a blue-collar tinge with the characters Alice Kramden on *The Honeymooners* and Linda Lavin's TV waitress, to be replaced by such variations as **Allison** and **Alyssa.** In England the name has survived as an aristocratic and even royal name and was number six on the most recent *Times of London* most popular names list, which reflects the current taste of the British upper class. Literary-minded parents might favor the name because of the unusual raft of excellent contemporary writers called Alice: the Alices Munro, Walker, Hoffman, Adams, McDermott, and Elliott Dark.

ANN, ANNE. Ann is the English form of the Hebrew name Hannah (which means "God has favored me"); in the Old Testament, Hannah was the mother of Samuel. Traditionally, Anne is also believed to have been the name of the mother of the Virgin Mary, which led to its great popularity in the Christian world. The Ann spelling was much more common in the nineteenth century, then was surpassed by the longer (French) version, especially with the birth of England's Princess Anne in 1950. In this country, Ann was in the Top Ten in 1925, but now **Annie,** a short form that was near the top of the Most Popular List around the turn of the twentieth century; **Anna,** the Greek form of the name; and especially the original **Hannah** are much more popular choices.

CAROLINE.   This name comes from **Carolina,** the Italian female form of Charles, and was introduced to the English-speaking world by Caroline of Ansbach, the German wife of George II, who became Queen in 1727. It was a favorite eighteenth-century name and has moved in and out of favor ever since, to be replaced in the 1930s and forties by **Carol,** then was given a high-profile gloss when it was picked by America's royal family, the Kennedys, and by Grace Kelly for her daughter, the Princess of Monaco. **Carolyn,** the form used by John F. Kennedy, Jr.'s wife, is a twentieth-century variation. The quintessential yuppie name of the eighties, Caroline retains its classy image, but has slipped a few rungs on the fashion ladder.

CHARLOTTE.   Charlotte is another Italian female offshoot of Charles, this time via Carlo and **Carlotta.** Before the late eighteenth century it was considered a French name and rarely used in England or America, until Britain's King George III married a German princess named Charlotte-Sophia. Charlotte has had a long reign as a popular literary name, used for the heroines of novels ranging from Goethe's *The Sorrows of Young Werther* to the endearing spider in E. B. White's *Charlotte's Web.* In the early 1990s, it was the number-one girl baby's name in England, and is beginning to be reappreciated in this country as well.

CHRISTINE, CHRISTINA.   All the names with this first syllable are derived from the Greek *chrio,* meaning "I anoint." The initial record of these two short forms of **Christiana** dates from the third century, via St. Christina, a martyred Roman noblewoman. It reached the British Isles late in the eleventh century, a time when the name **Christian** was used for both sexes. Christina became a royal name in both Spain and Sweden (Greta Garbo played Queen Christina in one of her best-known films). Christine (the French form) was at the height of its popularity in this country in the 1970s, when it reached number ten on the Hit Parade; these days Christina is the preferred choice.

CLAIRE, CLARE.   Claire, not surprisingly, comes from the Latin word meaning "clear, bright." Its first association was with St. Clare of Assisi, a follower of St. Francis and the founder, in 1212, of a benevolent order called the Poor Clares. Because she reportedly "witnessed" a mass being celebrated a great distance away, Clare was proclaimed, believe it or not, the patron saint of television in 1958 by Pope Pius XII. The name has been quite quietly used in this country, never ascending to the great heights of popularity it has in England, although the Claire spelling seems to be picking up some steam at present, as are its derivatives, **Clarissa** and **Clara. Clair** is another accepted spelling.

DEBORAH.   Deborah is the Hebrew word for "bee" and later, perhaps because of that insect's musical humming, also came to mean "eloquence." The first mention of this ancient name is in the Book of Genesis, where Deborah was Rebecca's faithful nurse. The later biblical bearer of the name was a formidable judge, poet, and prophetess who predicted the fall of the Canaanites and sang a famously expressive song of triumph when the Israelites were victorious. This name was very popular among the Puritans of the late seventeenth century, partially because the bee was a symbol of industriousness, an admired virtue. Deborah was then revived in the twentieth century, peaking around 1960, when it was second only to Mary, and it seemed that every other kid on the block was a **Debbie. Debra** is a twentieth-century variation.

DIANA.   One of the most enduring of the ancient goddess names, Diana, which means "divine" in Latin, was the Roman goddess of the moon and of the hunt, represented in myth as both beautiful and chaste. It was not used as an English Christian name until well into the sixteenth century, coming into general use only around 1750, partly because until then some ecclesiastics were hesitant to baptize girls with a pagan name. In America, Diana took even longer to take hold, infrequently used until the middle of the twentieth century, and even then it was the French form **Diane** that was more commonly heard. In contemporary times, it is certain to be associated with Diana, Princess of Wales, for a long while. Despite the Princess's popularity, however, the name's popularity has not been revived, here or in England.

ELEANOR. This name derives from the French Provencal form of Helen, Alienor, which came to England when Eleanor of Aquitaine married King Henry II in the twelfth century, and was popularized when Edward I erected many memorial "Eleanor" crosses to his wife, "Good Queen Eleanor," in the next century. Jane Austen's character **Elinor** Dashwood, the embodiment of sense in *Sense and Sensibility,* publicized that spelling of the name, and Eleanor Roosevelt was its most famous twentieth-century bearer. It was one of the first somewhat staid classic names to be revived by today's stylish parents. Short form **Ellie** has recently hit Britain's Most Popular list.

ELIZABETH. In Hebrew, this name means "God has sworn," and in the New Testament it was borne by the mother of John the Baptist. Her significance as the first person to recognize the impact of Mary's child would inspire Christians to honor the name Elizabeth. It became even more widely used via the royal families of England from the fifteenth century on, in particular with Elizabeth Tudor, who ruled the country for half a century, giving her name to the Elizabethan Age—during her reign 25 percent of girls born were named in her honor. The name was transported to this country by the colonists, three Elizabeths arriving on the *Mayflower,* and has had a remarkably consistent popularity: It was number three in 1875 and is still in the Top Ten in many states today. Elizabeth may also have spawned more offshoots and pet names than any other appellation, from **Betty** to **Betsy** to **Beth** to **Libby** to **Lisa** to **Liz.**

EMILY. Emily, which in 1997 was the most popular baby girl's name in America, derives from the Roman family name, Aemilius. It was Geoffrey Chaucer who introduced the name as Emily in "The Knight's Tale" section of *The Canterbury Tales*. It did not come into common use until after 1800, then, stimulated by two renowned writers, Emily Brontë and Emily Dickinson, it became among the most well-used names in both Britain and the United States by 1870. Emily had been climbing steadily toward the top since the early 1980s, its combination of strength and femininity appealing to a wide range of parents.

EMMA. Although Emma has sometimes been used as a short form of Emily, they have completely different origins. Emma comes from the Old German word meaning "universal" or "whole," and, along with many other names, was brought to the English-speaking world by the Normans when Queen Emma, "Fair Maid of Normandy," married the English King Ethelred the Unready in 1002. The literary heroines of Jane Austen's *Emma* and Flaubert's *Madame Bovary* cast further light onto the name. By the end of the nineteenth century, it was in the British Top Ten, then faded until the character of Emma Peel in the massive TV hit, *The Avengers,* brought it back. Always more popular in England than in the United States, it has finally come into its own here as a somewhat fresher alternative to Emily.

EVE. The meaning usually attributed to this name is "life-giving," or "breath of life," quite fitting for the first woman, created from one of Adam's ribs. In Genesis, Adam gave names to all the animals, and then to his wife, who was the "mother of all living." However, since, according to the Old Testament, Eve was believed to have brought sin into the world, her name has not been overly popular. And the serpentlike character in the 1950 film *All About Eve* didn't help much either. There is, however, an old tradition that children named Eve are always long-lived, which may account for the fact that the name was used even when Old Testament names were uncommon. At one time it was not unusual to name one twin Eve and her brother Adam. Eve was not used at all in the Puritan colonies, and has never appeared on the top fifty lists since then.

FRANCES. Frances, which means "free woman," is the feminine form of Francis—although, until the seventeenth century, the two spellings were used interchangeably for both sexes. In England the name did not appear until it was given to Henry VII's granddaughter. Frances became a favorite name among the Tudor aristocracy, then began being used, in the eighteenth century, more democratically. St. Frances (Mother) Cabrini, the first American citizen to be canonized, founded the Missionary Sisters of the Sacred Heart and helped Italian immigrants in America. The name saw its greatest popularity in this country around 1900, when it reached the Top Ten (and when its short form, **Fanny,** was popular in its own right), and now it is being used by some of the hippest Hollywood parents, such as Courtney Love and Robin Wright and Sean Penn.

GRACE. A Puritan-attribute name like Hope, Faith, and Charity, this name's original meaning referred to a person attaining a state of grace in the theological sense rather than a physical characteristic. In Greek mythology, the Three Graces were nature goddesses who spread joy throughout the world. The name was used in the Colonies, particularly the Puritan ones, and reached its high point in the last quarter of the nineteenth century—it was number eleven in 1875, and Grace Kelly came to be seen as the embodiment of its image. Modern parents are beginning to favor this pure and elegant appellation, often using it as a middle name.

HELEN. The most illustrious of all female Greek names, Helen means "the bright one," and it very early on became associated with beauty thanks to Helen of Troy, the daughter of Leda and Zeus, whose exquisite face was said by Christopher Marlowe to have "launched a thousand ships," and whose seizure by the Trojan prince Paris ignited the ten-year Trojan War. In England, the popularity of this name was due originally to St. Helena, the mother of Constantine the Great and daughter of the Old King Cole of nursery rhyme fame. Heard first as **Elena,** the *H* wasn't used until the Renaissance, when the study of classical literature revived Homer's epics and the story of the beautiful Greek queen. Not being the name of a biblical saint, however, Helen disappeared for centuries, suddenly making a comeback in the mid-nineteenth. Since then Helen and the colloquial form **Ellen** have alternated in popularity—Helen reached number three in 1900—although there aren't many babies named either Helen or Ellen these days. But who knows? Perhaps the likability of Helen Hunt and the aristocratic elegance of **Helena** Bonham Carter will give the name a boost.

JANE.   Jane is the most common female form of John, developing from the Old French and replacing the earlier Joan. At one time in this country, the use of the name was so widespread that *jane* became a slang term for *girl*. Still a popular name in England, it reached its highest point of U.S. popularity in 1925, but has not been on the American top fifty since then. For a time it was most often seen as half of such double names as Mary Jane and Betty Jane, and then became virtually replaced by such more modern-sounding variants as **Janet, Janice,** and **Jeanette.** But of all such similar names as **Jane, Joan, Jean, Janet,** and **June,** Jane stands the greatest chance of being revived.

JEAN.   Jean is, like Jane and Joan, a medieval variant of the Old French Jehann, and at one time its use was almost totally restricted to Scotland, still retaining a Scottish accent today. Its use peaked in this country in the 1920s and 1930s (it reached number nine in 1925), but has been declining ever since, despite the lingering popularity of the song *I Dream of Jeannie with the Light Brown Hair* and the recycled TV standard, *I Dream of Jeanie.*

JULIA. Julia is the feminine form of the old Roman family name, Julius, and was a common Christian name among early Romans. Borne by several early saints, it was used by Shakespeare in *Two Gentlemen of Verona* and was popular with the classical and romantic poets, only to be replaced for much of this century by the less euphonic, more straightforward **Julie.** Julia is now, thanks to such attractive influences as the Julias Roberts, Ormond, and Louis-Dreyfuss, making a strong return with sophisticated baby-namers, along with its male cognate, **Julian. Juliet** and **Juliana** are other chic variations.

KATHERINE. This name goes back to a Greek form, Aikaterine, the meaning of which is unknown. Its popularity in the Western world is due to the story and cult of the martyred fourth-century St. Katharine of Alexandria, who, according to legend, was such a brilliant Egyptian princess that she refuted the arguments of all the wisest men of her country with her defense of Christianity. After being killed with a spiked wheel, her body was carried by angels to Mount Sinai. The **Katharine** spelling is related to the Greek adjective *katharos,* meaning "pure." It is a royal name in England, belonging to the wives of Henry V, Henry VIII (including the formidable Katherine of Aragon), and Charles II, as well as the French Catherine de Medici. The **Catherine** spelling predominates in England and France; **Kathryn**, a twentieth-century form, is still the number two spelling here; the shortened form **Kate**—a favorite of William Shakespeare's—became one of the standard English names as well early on. Other related names, including **Karen, Kay, Kathleen, Kitty,** and **Kathy,** have had periods of popularity of their own, but today it is Katherine that is being chosen by conservative parents, with the name in all its variations at number fifteen.

LAURA. Laura is a feminine version of **Laurence,** both of which relate to the bay laurel, the leaves of which have long been an emblem of victory. Laura was first popularized in modern English via the love sonnets of the Italian poet Petrarch, which were largely addressed to a woman with that name. It was imported into England and America in the nineteenth century, and was given a thrust into the spotlight by the movie and song *Laura* in the 1940s, remaining in the top twenty-five in 1960. It was largely replaced by **Laurie, Lori, Lauren,** and to a lesser degree, **Laurel,** in recent years, though Laura seems now to be making a comeback in its own right and in its original form is the most stylish version of the name.

LOUISE. Louise is the French feminine form of Louis, **Louisa** being the Latin version. They both came into widespread English usage during the seventeenth century, when all things French were exerting a potent influence. Louise had its greatest period of popularity in this country from the end of the nineteenth century until about 1930, and has made a definite return in England in recent years, with some signs of new life stirring on this side of the Atlantic as well.

LUCY. Lucy is related to the Greco-Roman word *lux,* via the Latin Lucia, which means "light." In Roman times, the name was often given to a child born around daybreak. St. Lucy was a fourth-century Sicilian martyr whose cult became very popular in England in the Middle Ages, after which the name moved in and out of favor, increasing greatly in the eighteenth century, and returning again in the counterculture 1960s. On a recent London *Times* list, it was still the second most popular name.

MARGARET. Margaret comes from the Greek word meaning "pearl," which carries with it the ancient Persian meaning, "child of light." The popularity of the name derives from the third-century St. Margaret of Antioch, one of the four great virgin martyrs and patroness of women in childbirth, who was said to have been, like St. George, a slayer of dragons—the legend goes that she was swallowed alive by Satan in the form of a dragon, but on making the sign of the cross, burst out of the monster and killed it. Margaret was among the most common names in medieval England, along with Elizabeth, Joan, Agnes, Maud, and Alice. Margaret is another name that was especially popular in Scotland, sometimes considered the national Scottish female name, and was a royal name in both Scotland and England, as well as in Scandinavia and Austria. It did not come into full bloom in this country until the turn of this century, when, despite competition from some of its own variations and nicknames, such as **Margery, Peggy, May,** and **Daisy,** it remained in the top twenty for fifty years.

MARY. The New Testament form of **Miriam** (via the Greek **Mariam**), Mary was the mother of Christ as well as the name of numerous saints and Queens of England and Europe. Considered in the Middle Ages to be connected with the sea, it was not in general use before 1200, being considered too sacred for ordinary mortals. But by the time of the English colonization of America, it was the most common name for girls and remained so until it was replaced by Linda in 1948. Mary has been in decline in this country ever since. Until very recently, a quarter of all Irish girls were still baptized Mary. Historically, there were so many Marys that many pet names were invented to distinguish them from one another, some of which—**Marian, Molly, Polly, Minnie, Mamie, Mae**—became distinctive names on their own. **Maria** is a widespread variant throughout the Western world, while **Marie,** the French form, was popular here in the middle of the twentieth century. These days, Mary is a rarer choice for a baby girl than Madison or Morgan.

RACHEL. In Hebrew, Rachel means "little lamb," a symbol of gentleness and innocence, and the character in the Old Testament, the wife of Jacob and mother of Joseph and Benjamin, is described in the Bible as "beautiful and well-favored." Like Rebecca, Rachel has always been common as a Jewish name and began to be used by others at the time of the Reformation. In this country it began to be revived in the 1970s and now stands at number twenty on the girls' Most Popular list, having reached the Top Ten for the first time in 1995. **Rachael** is an accepted spelling variation.

REBECCA. In the Old Testament, Rebecca (spelled there **Rebekah**) was the beautiful wife of Isaac and the mother of Jacob and Esau, and was one of the few biblical characters to show compassion for animals. The name, which means "knotted chord," symbolizing a faithful wife, was brought to the New World by the earliest settlers, and was especially well used in New England, where it was often the fifth or sixth most popular name. It was the name adopted by Pocahontas at her baptism, and is also identified with the lovely heroine of Sir Walter Scott's *Ivanhoe*, as well as the eponymous character in the novel and classic film, *Rebecca*. In recent history, Rebecca made a strong comeback, along with other Old Testament stalwarts such as Rachel, Sarah, Samuel, and Benjamin, in the late 1960s and early 1970s, and has been in the top thirty for the past several years.

SARAH. Sarah has been the leading biblical girls' name for two decades now, ranking currently at number three. According to Genesis, it was God who said to Abraham, when his wife was ninety years old, "As for **Sàrai** thy wife, thou shalt not call her Sarai, but Sarah shall her name be," and thus the name Sarah (which means "princess") was born. The name came into English popularity after the Reformation, and by the seventeenth century it was often the third most popular name for girls, following Mary and Elizabeth. By the late nineteenth century, it was beginning to sound somewhat dowdy, and was often replaced by its nickname, **Sally.** The **Sara** spelling, by the way, was originally the Greek adaptation.

SUSAN, SUSANNAH. These names are derived from the Hebrew Shoshana, which means "lily." In the biblical story of Susannah and the Elders, the beautiful and pure Susannah was saved by the clever stratagems of Daniel, who proved that she had been falsely accused. It was a common name, often spelled **Susanna,** in early America, reaching its greatest popularity in the eighteenth century. The simplified Susan gradually began to take over, zooming way ahead in the 1940s, still holding the number four spot in 1950 and 1960, but is rarely used today. Susannah, however, has definite style power.

VIRGINIA.   The first English child to be born in America was christened Virginia, a feminine form of the Roman family name Virginus. Sir Walter Raleigh had called his newly founded colony in the New World Virginia, in honor of Elizabeth I, the "Virgin Queen," and little Ms. Dare was given the name for the same reason. This was an early example of a name becoming used first in America and then spreading to other parts of the world. The name had been borne previously by a young Roman woman who was, according to legend, killed by her own father to spare her from the amorous clutches of a despised political official. Virginia enjoyed a sudden burst of popularity around 1870, which lasted through the 1950s, peaking in the 1920s. With comparable names such as Elizabeth and Katherine becoming overused classics, Virginia may be getting ready to step up to the plate.

BOYS

ALEXANDER.   A Greek name that means "defender of men," Alexander has been popular for 3,000 years. In Homer's *Iliad* it was said to have been given as a nickname to Paris of Troy for saving his father's herdsmen from cattle rustlers. The name was borne by several characters in the New Testament and some early Christian saints. It was a Macedonian royal name, gaining worldwide fame in the fourth century B.C. via Alexander the Great, who conquered most of Asia Minor, Egypt, and Babylon while still in his twenties and who, after his death, became the hero of a cycle of popular "Alexander romances" similar to those about King Arthur. Alexander became a royal name in Scotland in the twelfth century and has always been a particular favorite in that country, as well as in Russia, and today it is the twenty-second most popular name for boys in America—though combined with its short form, **Alex,** it edges into the Top Ten.

ANDREW. Andrew is a Greek name (from Andreas) that means "manly." It is found in the New Testament— borne by the Galilean fisherman who was the first to be called by Christ to become one of the twelve Apostles— and St. Andrew is the patron saint of Scotland, Greece, and Russia. The name was quite consistently common from the Middle Ages on, brought to the New World by Scottish immigrants, and was borne by two U.S. Presidents—Jackson and Johnson. Andrew is now one of the most popular boy's names in the English-speaking world, boosted by the royal naming of England's Prince Andrew in 1960, and in one Harvard study it was cited as the boys' name most favored by highly educated mothers. It is now number eleven on the most popular list.

BENJAMIN. The biblical name Benjamin was borne by one of the founders of the twelve tribes of Israel, the youngest of the twelve sons of Jacob, who was the favorite of his fathers and brothers. As a result, at times the name has been used to signify a favored child and also for the son of older parents. It means "son of the right hand," representing strength and good fortune. The name was brought to the Puritan colonies by early settlers and proceeded to become more popular in New England than it was in Britain, especially with the celebrity of Benjamin Franklin. After centuries of waning use, Benjamin made a comeback in the 1960s, not only because biblical names were back, but because of the influence of the leading character in *The Graduate*, and is still popular today, especially in the era of Ben Affleck and Ben Stiller.

CHARLES. Charles, a Germanic name that stems from a word (*carl*) meaning "man," was made famous via Charles the Great, better known as Charlemagne, who founded the Holy Roman Empire in the early ninth century. A royal favorite in England and France, the name was so widely used in the Middle Ages that many early historical bearers are identified by such nicknames as Charles the Bald and Charles the Fat. Although it took a while to take off in this country, it reached third place in 1875 and remained in the U.S. Top Ten until 1950, when it started to slip, and is now at number fifty. **Charlie** and **Charley** are the more stylish nicknames, with **Chuck** no longer on anyone's agenda. Jodie Foster chose this elegant classic for her son.

CHRISTOPHER.   Deriving from the Greek word meaning "bearing Christ," Christopher's use as a first name developed in honor of the giant-sized third-century martyr, originally called Offeros, who was believed to have carried the infant Jesus, heavy with the sins of the world, on his shoulders across a river to safety—which explains why Christopher is the patron saint of travelers. There was also a medieval belief that if you looked at a picture of St. Christopher you would be protected all day. The name was very popular among early Christians, as it made them feel that they were symbolically bearing Christ in their hearts. In English-speaking countries Christopher moved in and out of favor for centuries, hitting a high in the 1940s (probably due to the beloved, gentle image of Christopher Robin), and is currently the sixth most popular boy's name in America.

DANIEL.   Daniel is a biblical name meaning "God is My Judge." The Old Testament Prophet Daniel was an Israelite slave who curried great favor through his skill at interpreting dreams, and whose faith protected him when he was condemned to die in a den of lions. The name was popular among Jews, early Christians, and, because of its resemblance to some Celtic names, has been a favorite Irish name as well. It is currently the twelfth most popular boys' name in America.

DAVID.   David, which means "beloved" in Hebrew, is another Old Testament perennial. In the Bible, David was the second King of Israel, who as a boy killed the giant Philistine Goliath with a slingshot. Considered by some the greatest King of Israel, he was also renowned as a poet, with many of the Psalms attributed to him. The Star of David is the symbol of Judaism and the national emblem of the State of Israel. This name is also very popular in

Scotland, where it is a royal name, and in Wales, of which David (also called Dewi) is the patron saint. In this country, it reached as high as number two on the 1960 popularity list, was still number three in 1970, and on most recent lists stood in seventeenth place.

EDWARD. Edward, which means "happy protector," is one of the most abiding of all Old English names, having survived from before the Norman Conquest to the present. It was the name of several Saxon kings and eight English kings, and is now the name of the youngest son of the current Queen. The name was an early arrival in the New World—there were several in the Jamestown Colony and six Edwards sailed on the *Mayflower*. The Puritans, however, were less enthusiastic about the name, as it was attached to a nonbiblical saint. In more recent times, Edward was in the top twenty-five until around 1960, when it started to slip, but now appears to be making a nickname-less (no **Eddie**, no **Ed**) comeback—think Edward Norton, Edward Furlong, and Edward Burns—though **Ned** may be acceptable to some parents.

FRANCIS. This name has an interesting history in that it stems from a nickname. The young Giovanni Bernadone, later to become famous as the nature-loving St. Francis of Assisi, was nicknamed **Francesco**, or little Frenchman, because his wealthy merchant father traded extensively with France, and because the then-worldly youth spoke French. In 1210, he founded the Order of the Friars Minor, later called Franciscans or Greyfriars because of the color of their habits—twelve traveling preachers who emphasized poverty, humility, and love for all living creatures, and whose ideas spread throughout Europe. St. Francis of Assisi became the patron saint of ecology, and another Francis, St. Francis de Sales, is the patron saint of writers and editors. The name was first used in England in the early sixteenth century and was popular in this country among the early colonists. It peaked in the middle of the nineteenth century, after which it was superseded by its short form, **Frank**, and also began to be used (spelled Frances) as a girl's name, which made it less desirable for boys. In recent years, its masculine use has been pretty much confined to Irish and Italian Roman Catholics.

FREDERICK. Frederick is a name that translates from the Old High German as "peaceful ruler." One not-so-peaceful ruler was Frederick the Great, eighteenth-century King of Prussia, an enlightened despot who was a brilliant soldier and laid the foundations of the powerful Prussian military state. The modern use of the name in English-speaking countries was influenced by the Victorian vogue for Germanic names. In America, it came over with the German immigrants in the 1850s and remained popular until the 1930s, after which it faded. There is now a Society of Freds, trying to restore and defend the dignity of the name.

GEORGE. George comes from a Greek word meaning "farmer," and is linked with the patron saint of England, the legendary dragon-slaying Roman martyr, St. George. In the Middle Ages St. George was closely associated with knighthood and chivalry. From 1714 on, four kings named George ruled England successively for more than a century, and a George was, of course, the father of our own country. It was among the five most common names in America from 1830 to 1900, remaining in the Top Ten until 1950, but although it is still way up there in England, it is rarely used for American babies today.

HENRY. Henry is a Germanic name, with the fairly irrelevant meaning, "home rule." It was a favorite among the Norman conquerors who brought it to England in the French form, Henri, which was more or less transliterated into Harry, the normal English usage until the seventeenth century. A British royal name from the eleventh to the seventeenth century, Henry was borne by eight English kings (all nicknamed Harry, just as the present young Prince is), and was pretty much restricted to the aristocracy until the widespread popularity of Henry V, the spirited Prince Hal of Shakespeare's *Henry IV*. The name was revived at the end of the nineteenth century when biblical names started to fade. In this country, Harry and Henry were both in the top fifteen at the turn of the century, but neither was even in the top fifty much after 1950. Still, although Henry has been off the popularity charts for decades, it has recently been picked up by several trendsetting celebs (see Comfy Names, under Starbabies, p. 93) and is favored by upwardly mobile parents.

JACOB. A name of uncertain origin, Jacob was featured in the Bible as belonging to one of the most important patriarchs in the Book of Genesis, father of twelve sons who each gave his name to a tribe of Israel. Jacob's Ladder refers to a vision seen by the patriarch of a stairway reaching from earth to heaven, a name also given to a ladder-looking plant. In this country, from early Colonial times, the name was associated with both the Jewish and German communities—it was the third most popular name among German immigrants. Anti-German feeling during the two World Wars almost wiped out the use of the name in that period, but it came back strong with the Jakes of the Age of Aquarius, and is currently climbing to the very top of the list, at a very strong number two.

JAMES. James, the Latinized form of Jacob, was the name of two of the twelve Apostles and three other figures in the New Testament, and James also has the distinction of being the name of more U.S. Presidents than any other. The name was particularly prevalent in Scotland, where it was attached to royalty for over a century. In the seventeenth century, the name, as in James I, for example, was pronounced Jeames (*Jeems*). Still near the top of the list in England—James has now dropped to number twenty in America and is more often than not used in full, modern parents eschewing its former nicknames of **Jim** and **Jimmy**, with **Jamie** the only possibly acceptable variation.

JOHN. This name, which is of Hebrew origin, has been throughout history (and until relatively recently in America) the most popular name for boys in English-speaking countries, and its many foreign cognates (such as **Ian, Evan, Sean, Ivan, Hans, Juan,** and **Giovanni**) have rated equally high in the rest of the Western world. It has been so common, in fact that it's been used to represent Everyman—from John Bull to John Doe to John Q. Public. John stems from the Hebrew word meaning "God is gracious," and became a well-used name around 1200, largely because of the two prominent saints, John the Baptist and the Evangelist. In total, however, there are eighty-two canonized St. Johns. In the early years of American history, about a fifth of all men answered to this name, and at the same time in England it was more like one quarter. The pet form **Jack** has been used independently for centuries and is a current favorite among celebrity baby-namers (see Starbabies, Comfy Names, p. 93) as well as fashion-conscious parents.

JOSEPH. Joseph is an important name in the Judeo-Christian tradition, both as Old Testament favorite son of the patriarch, Jacob, who gave him the coat of many colors, and whose brothers sold him into slavery, and also as the righteous carpenter husband of the Virgin Mary; while St. Joseph is the protector of working men. The widespread use of the name dates from the seventeenth century, when foreign forms such as José and Giuseppe also proliferated. After 1900, Joseph was a particular favorite with Catholics, especially those with an Italian heritage; and in this century it has always been among the fifteen most popular names, currently listed at number thirteen.

MATTHEW. Matthew, which is Hebrew for "gift of the Lord," was one of the four Evangelists, author of the first Gospel in the New Testament, who had been known by the name of Levi before he embraced Christianity. The name was well used from the Middle Ages until the beginning of the nineteenth century, when it began to wane. It came back strongly, partly as the result of such western TV heroes as Marshall Matt Dillon in the sixties, and is still in third place today, close behind Michael and Jacob. **Mathew** is a spelling variation.

MICHAEL. A name that crosses religious and ethnic lines perhaps more than any other in its unparalleled modern popularity, Michael's literal meaning is "Who is like the Lord?" In the Bible Michael is one of the seven archangels (one of only two recognized by Jews, Christians, and Muslims alike), and their leader in battle. Also a conqueror of Satan and the weigher of good deeds and bad at the Last Judgment, Michael became the patron saint of soldiers, as well as of bankers, policemen, and radiologists. His popularity assured the early spread of the name throughout Europe, and it became royal as well via nine Byzantine emperors, five Romanian kings, and a tsar of Russia. Always a favorite in Ireland, where it is often spelled **Micheal** (the nickname **Mick** is sometimes used as a generic, if un-PC, term for an Irishman), its entrance into this country paralleled the heavy Irish immigration of the mid–nineteenth century. Michael knocked Robert out of first place in 1950, and has remained there ever since.

NICHOLAS. Nicholas is a name of Greek origin that means "victory of the people." St. Nicholas is a saint with many charges: Not only is he the patron saint of Greece and Russia and of Christmas, but he is also responsible for the welfare of children, sailors, scholars, brides, bakers, thieves, merchants, and pawnbrokers. There are countless legends concerning his miracles and acts of bravery, such as calming storms and restoring dead boys to life. Santa Claus is the Dutch version of St. Nicholas. Nicholas was the name of five Popes, a Danish king, and two emperors of Russia. In early American history, Nicholas was used most frequently by Dutch colonists, and later by German and Greek immigrants as well. Nicholas now stands at its highest point ever in the history of American baby-naming, most recently rated at number four.

PATRICK. A Latin name meaning "of noble birth," Patrick is associated with the saint who was originally named Sucat. Born in England and educated in France, Patrick was sold as a slave in Ireland, eventually becoming the patron saint and apostle of that country, devoting his life to converting the Irish to Christianity. Not surprisingly, then, the name Patrick has been especially linked with Irish immigrants in America, although for a long period of time the Irish reverentially avoided the use of the name. Patrick has been swept along with the present wave of popularity of Irish names, currently climbing back onto the charts.

PAUL. Paul was the name taken by Saul of Tarsus, formerly a vehement persecutor of Christians, at the time of his conversion after seeing a vision of Christ telling him to preach. There have been five Pope Pauls, and as Pablo and Paolo, the name has been a classic of Latin culture. Paul was hardly used in England until the seventeenth century, the time when it was brought to the colonies, where it remained steadily, but not flashily, bestowed on babies for three hundred years. From 1900 to 1960, Paul ranked a consistent sixteenth to eighteenth place, but it is scarcely heard from today. It has been much more successful in England where, in the 1980s, it reached second place, probably influenced by mothers who had been adoring adolescent McCartney fans.

PETER. Peter, which means "rock" in Greek, has special significance because it is the only New Testament name to be credited to Christ Himself, who changed the name of Simon to Peter (in the form of Cephos), because he felt he would be the "rock" of the new religion ("Thou art Peter and upon this rock I will build my Church."). And St. Peter is, of course, keeper of the Gates of Heaven. It was a common name in the Middle Ages, then suffered a setback, as did many New Testament names, with the Protestant Reformation. In Britain its use was spurred by the fondness for the character, Peter Pan, and in Russia, Peter the Great developed his country into a modern nation. Peter's high point of popularity here was from roughly 1930 to 1960—though it never climbed very high on any popularity lists—and today it stands just outside the top hundred.

PHILIP. Philip, which means "lover of horses" in Greek, was very popular in the classical period, being the name of the father of Alexander the Great. It was borne by one of Christ's Apostles, but is not thought of as a biblical name. Philip's royal associations include six French and five Spanish rulers, and the present husband of England's Queen Elizabeth. Often spelled with two *l*'s, Philip was most commonly used in modern America pre-1960, and like Peter and Paul, is currently on hiatus.

RICHARD. Richard is a Germanic name meaning "strong ruler." It belonged to three English kings, one of whom, Richard I ("The Lion-hearted"), was influential in establishing the popularity of the name. In Elizabethan England, Richard usually stood in fourth place among boys' names, and continued to be in roughly the same position in the New World, common enough to become one of the "Tom, Dick, and Harry" trio. After some ups and downs, it reached as high as fifth place in 1950, but is rarely used for the babies of today, showing no signs of the kind of revival seen with James, John, Thomas, and William. Whether this name's decline has been related to the decline of Richard Nixon (who was actually named after Richard the Lion-hearted), we can only surmise.

ROBERT. Robert is an Anglo-Saxon name, deriving from the far more cumbersome Hreodbeorht, and meaning "bright fame." It was borne by three Scottish kings, most notably Robert the Bruce, who freed Scotland from British domination. The name became so popular in England after 1066 that it developed no less than six major short forms, including **Robin** and **Bob.** Robert was the top name in America for twenty-five years, from 1925 to 1950, and even now stands toward the bottom of the top twenty-six.

SAMUEL. This Old Testament name has the Hebrew meaning of "heard by God," referring to the fact that Samuel's mother, Hannah, had vowed that if God would give her a male child, she would dedicate him to God, and when she did have a son, it was evidence that her voice had been heard. Samuel was a Hebrew judge and prophet of great historical importance, and the significance of his naming was particularly appealing to women who were under social pressure to populate a new land. By the time of the settling of the New World, Samuel was already quite common in England, and became even more so in the colonies, particularly among the Puritans, at times achieving second place, just behind John, a pervasiveness reflected in the symbol of the United States being called Uncle Sam. It began to decline around 1800, when Old Testament names were beginning to sound fusty, but came back in the sixties and is now in the top thirty, a favorite, along with its short form **Sam**, among fashionable parents.

STEPHEN.   Stephen derives from the Greek word meaning "crown," referring to the wreath of leaves awarded to athletic champions in ancient times, and was the name of the first Christian martyr, stoned to death as a blasphemer. His name reflects his martyr's crown, as martyrdom was regarded then as a kind of victory. The feast of St. Stephen is celebrated the day after Christmas. The *ph* spelling preserves the Greek tradition, but the later, streamlined, version, **Steven** has become the more common choice by far in this country (Stephen still reigns in England)—it was in seventh place here from 1960 to 1970, having dropped in recent years out of the top twenty-five.

THOMAS.   Thomas, which means "twin," in Aramaic, was first given by Jesus to an apostle named Judas to distinguish him from Judas Iscariot. One of the Twelve Apostles, he was referred to as the Doubting Thomas because initially he refused to believe in Christ's resurrection. And the fact that this made him seem more human and fallible contributed to the spread of his name. In England Thomas was originally used only as a priest's name, but the martyrdom of St. Thomas à Becket in 1170 established the name as one of the most popular in England, usually the third highest, following John and William, and reached top place there in the early 1990s. On this side of the Atlantic, Thomas was the second most common name in the Jamestown colony, and has been consistently used ever since.

TIMOTHY. A Greek name meaning "Honoring God," Timothy was the companion of St. Paul, to whom he addressed two epistles. The name had been in use among the Greeks at least since the time of Alexander the Great, but was not prevalent in Europe until the sixteenth century when the revival of classical studies led to the use of the names of antiquity. It reached its high point in the 1960s, when there were lots of little Timmys on TV, and is still well used by modern parents.

WILLIAM. A Germanic name, William has, over the years, been second only to John (which took over in the thirteenth century) as the most widely used British and American boy's name. In the Elizabethan Age, 22.5 percent of all males were named William. It first came into vogue via William the Conqueror in 1066, and has never really been out of fashion since. It was number one in this country at the end of the nineteenth century and remained in the Top Ten through 1960, currently ranking number fifteen. Now with the British Princes Harry and William—the latter called **Wills** by his late mother—more and more in the spotlight, both their names have taken on an attractive and youthful aura. All the boys named **Bill** in the last generation have been replaced by those called **Will** or **Willie.**

UNUSUAL NAMES

*M*ore and more parents today are interested in giving their children unusual names. The pool of names from which parents are choosing is growing ever wider and deeper, as parents grow more adventurous and individual in their tastes. But even the most open-minded of parents has to ask the question: At what point is a name *too* unusual?

The only possible answer: It depends.

Certainly, the line separating unusual names from "normal" ones is constantly being redrawn these days. With choices such as Taylor, Kayla, Sydney, Sierra, Savannah, Destiny, Autumn, and Cheyenne among the top names for girls, and Brandon, Tyler, Justin, Dylan, Jordan, Cody, Kyle, and Logan edging out the Roberts and Thomases on the formerly staid Most Popular List for boys, there is virtually no distinction between names that are unconventional and those that are widely used.

Today, fewer children receive one of the Top Ten names—and more are given unusual or unique names—than in years past. According to one expert, only a quarter of the babies born in the late eighties received one of the Top Ten names, versus a full *half* of the children born in 1900. Now, just ten years later, an even smaller proportion of the babies born are given Top Ten names, while more and more children get unusual or unique names.

Why does this matter? Because a child's name is only unusual, or not, in the context of the names of other children in his or her community. When a large proportion of the kids have unusual names—as they do in Manhattan, or Hollywood, or in an African-American neighborhood in New Orleans, say—then having an unusual name will make your child feel like one of the crowd. But the same unusual name might make a child stand out, perhaps uncomfortably so, in a conservative small town in New England or the Midwest.

And then there's the question of what kind of unusual the name is. Some name scholars have attempted to differentiate between unusual names that are invented along the lines of current tastes and fashions and those that are outmoded—those that are perceived as attractive, in other words, and those that are not. The not-so-surprising findings: Attractive names, unusual or common, are better.

Of course, who your child is can be central to how he fares with an unusual name. The trouble with that is, your baby's personality can be kind of hard to predict when he or she's only a few hours old. Looks might be one indicator. A child whose looks are likely to make him stand out in a crowd—one with bright red hair, for instance—might do better with a regular-guy name, while a more ordinary-looking kid might welcome the distinction of being called Inigo or Jasper.

But how do all the little Vivianas and Frazers feel about their names? If you name your son Malachy, will he hate you forever? Are you setting up Kendra and Isolde for a lifetime of shame?

Not really, according to psychologists. People with unusual names do not like their names any less than people with ordinary names do, found one study, which said that 18 percent of men and 25 percent of women considered their names unusual. There is some evidence that girls tend to feel better about having uncommon names than boys do. Girls are more likely to have unusual names—there's simply a larger pool of girls' names than boys' names, and girls are given names from the top twenty less often than boys. Since girls with distinctive names are apt to find that other people like their names, they are more likely to accept the names themselves.

One study found that 40 percent of men and 46 percent of women did not like their names—but half of those women didn't like them because they were too common! An early name study found no difference between neurotic tendencies in girls with unusual names such as Janapea, Vondelier, and Honthalena and those named Dorothy, Helen, and Mildred—although these days, Dorothy, Helen, and Mildred would tend to be the odd ducks.

In dealing with an unusual name, confidence seems to count for a lot. An-

NEWT'S NAME

Newt Gingrich spent his last day in Congress on the "Tonight" show. "I'm grateful to the country that a guy like me, with a weird name . . . would be allowed to lead the country like that," the outgoing Speaker told host Jay Leno.

—*PEOPLE ONLINE DAILY*

DON'T TRY THIS AT HOME

Here are some names gleaned from actual records of actual names given to actual babies in the past year.

GIRLS	BOYS
ABRAXIS	BLEYD
ALLURA	
AMAZEN	CROCKETT
CADENCE	GADGE
CHAMPAGNELLE	GJERGJ
CHANCELLOR	KUGAR
CHHAYHOUTH	KWIK
JEALOUSA	MAVERICK
JOURNEY	
	SIR
KRIMSAN	SWADE
LEXUS	ZENITH
	ZOKIAK
MAGENTA	
MYSTYCAL	
PAISLEY	
SUGAR	
TRWISTA	

other study found that women with masculine-sounding names—Dean, Earl, Randy, Zeke, the kind of boyish fare that is becoming standard for girls today—who liked or accepted their names enough to use them were less anxious, less neurotic, and had more leadership potential than women who substituted more feminine nicknames.

Who chooses unusual names? Mothers with less education, according to research by Harvard sociology professor Stanley Lieberson, are more likely to select unusual names for their children, especially for their daughters, than mothers who've graduated from college. He also found that African-American mothers of all classes and educational levels are more likely to choose unusual or unique names than white mothers.

But today, as personal meaning becomes more important in the choice of a name, as parents look to celebrate ethnic identity and increasingly prize individuality in their children, unusual names are becoming more, well, common.

The upshot: Having an unusual name is likely to become less of a burden, and more of a mark of distinction, over time.

WHY BRIYANA SPELLS TROUBLE

The impulse may be benevolent enough. Why not, many parents wonder, find a name that has it all? A name that's familiar, fashionable, attractive, easy to like, and that's also original and creative and—hey, why not go all the way!—completely unique.

And so Abigail, thousands of years after King David's wife, hundreds of years after John Quincy Adams's mother, becomes Abbigayle. Anna morphs into Anah. Hayley (the way child star Mills spelled it) might be Haley, Halley (like the comet), Hailey, or Haylee. Rylee? Kearston? Konnor? Kaine? *Basta!*

Parents today are wild about invented spellings, that much is clear from the rosters of baby names across the country. Variations such as Kaitlyn and Katelynn have become much more prevalent than the original Caitlin, and Ashleigh and Brittney are now accepted names in their own right. But unpopular as it's certain to make us, we have to stand up and say it's time to stop the spelling insanity.

Today's epidemic of inventive spellings has its roots in

TOBY IN A TOMMY WORLD

Like being 6-foot-10 and having to duck through doorways, the curse of dysappellatia colors one's whole existence. It is the sore thumb that never heals. Perennial Top Five targets of schoolyard bullies, the ill-named live in dread of introductions, with the inevitable looks of confusion and the pity they elicit from every Tom, Dick and Holly we meet. . . . So—Dave, Nancy, Mike—spare me your patronizing comments about how "neat" it would be to have a "distinctive" name. Maybe now, in the afterglow of our current baby-naming Golden Age— where diversity is celebrated and every playground teems with Baileys and Logans and Skylars—maybe now it's OK. But for those of us arriving in the Eisenhower years, uncommon meant un-American . . . I was a Toby in a Tommy world.

—TOBY MULLER, "GROWING UP TOBY," *LOS
ANGELES TIMES MAGAZINE*

the 1960s and early 1970s, when so many Pattys and Terrys and Sherrys became Pattis and Terris and Sherris. Even the President's daughter jumped on the bandwagon, shedding Lucy for Luci Baines Johnson. Barbra Streisand nudged the trend along when she dropped an *a*, though stars have long favored the dramatic spelling, from Carole Lombard to Jayne Mansfield, Diahann Carroll to Dyan Cannon.

But the trend really caught fire in 1981, when along came the sweet and gentle character Krystle Carrington on the hugely successful show, *Dynasty*. Krystle spawned not only her own perfume, but a rash of characters with creatively spelled names. There was a soap opera character named Sierra . . . and another called Ceara. One sitcom character was dubbed Synclaire. What's more, the real live actors whose names rolled in the credits also popularized ever-more outrageous spellings, from Margaux (Hemingway) to Tempestt (Bledsoe) to Khrystyne (Haje).

This kind of thing may get you noticed if you're Cybill Shepherd, but if you're little Briyana (or Baylee or Greggory) Smith, your name will mostly spell trouble. Think of it: "No, that's Briyana, with one *n* and a *y*. No, there's a *y* and an *i*. No, it's pronounced the regular way. Bree-anna. Of course I'm sure."

If you've got a little Briyana of your own, you've doubtless discovered some advantages to counterbalance the problems inherent in an unusual spelling. Your child does stand out from the crowd; the name does feel more "artistic" than the same name with a run-of-the-mill spelling. But we'd wager you'd counsel an expectant parent to hesitate before stepping down your path.

Of course, there are some names that have more than one accepted spelling, such as Catherine, Katherine, and Kathryn, or Anne and Ann. Funny how a few letters can make a difference: Catherine seems gentler somehow than the *K* versions, Anne more substantial than the too-abbreviated Ann.

NAMED FOR SUCCESS

If your name is your destiny, chances are the fates never intended for Uma Thurman, Neve Campbell, Keanu Reeves, Skeet Ulrich, Jada Pinkett, Winona Ryder, Charlize Theron, Mykelti Williamson, and Ving Rhames to see their names on a marquee.

Maybe they would be poets, herbalists, hairdressers, or, in the case of Mr. Ulrich and Mr. Rhames, professional athletes, but movie stars? With those names? You must be kidding.

Stranger things happen. In a time when diversity, ethnicity and individuality are celebrated, it is the weird, one-of-a-kind monikers that are not only accepted but embraced by cutting-edge moms—and Hollywood moguls.

—JILL GERSTON,
THE NEW YORK TIMES

Then there are those names whose spelling variations become accepted over time. The original Caitlin, for instance, is more often these days spelled phonetically as Katelyn, or Katelynn, or Kaitlyn. Michaela has quickly, through association with the popular Kayla, become Mikayla or Makayla.

But there's such a thing as getting too inventive with a spelling. Our advice: Get creative with the name instead. Rather than Anah, consider a foreign variant such as Anika, Annina, Anouk, or even Annabel or Ana—all legitimate names with history and substance. Or you might seek a distinctive name with a similar sound—Anthea or Angelica.

In the end, the thing to remember is that there is a fine line between cute and cumbersome, out-of-the-ordinary and outlandish, and your child will appreciate you for staying on the right side of it.

CREATIVE NAMES

Creative names instantly confer an artistic, exotic image on your child. They also mark you as a parent who prizes originality, who wants to instill a love of the inventive and poetic in your little one. These days, the source of Creative Names has expanded to include everything from surnames to place names to foreign names to names that are literally coined by the parents. But the names here are among those that have both a historical basis and an instantly recognizable creative image.

GIRLS

ABRA	ANDRA
ALESSANDRA	ANTHEA
ALLEGRA	ANYA
ALTHEA	ARAMINTA
ANAÏS	ARDITH

ARIADNE
ARIEL
ARISSA
ASTRA
ATHENA
AUDRA
AURELIA
AURORA
AUTUMN

BIANCA
BLYTHE
BRYONY

CALLA
CALLIOPE
CAMILLA
CANDIDA
CHINA
CLEA
CLEMENTINE
CLIO
COLUMBINE
CRESSIDA

DAMARA
DARIA
DELPHINE
DIANTHA

EBBA
ELECTRA
ESMÉ
EVANGELINE

FEODORA
FLAVIA
FLEUR
FRANCESCA

GELSEY
GENEVRA
GISELLE
GWYNETH

INDIA
IONE
ISA
ISADORA
ISOLDE
IVY

JADE

KAIA
KATYA
KYRA

LARA
LARK
LEILA
LELIA
LIANA
LILITH
LILO
LOLA
LULU
LUNA

MAIA	RAFFAELA
MALA	REINE
MARA	
MARLO	SABINE
MERCEDES	SABRA
MICHAEL	SASHA
MINTA	SILVER
MIRABEL	SINEAD
MIRANDA	SKYE
MIRRA	
	TALIA
NADIA	TALLULAH
NATASHA	TAMARA
NERISSA	TANIA
NESSA	TATIANA
NEVE	TEAL
NICOLA	TESSA
	THEA
	TRESSA
ODELIA	TRILBY
OLYMPIA	TWYLA
OONA	TYNE
ORIANA	
OUIDA	VENETIA
	VIOLET
PALOMA	
PANDORA	WILLA
PETRA	WILLOW
PILAR	
PORTIA	ZANDRA
	ZARA
QUINTINA	ZELIA

BOYS

ADRIAN	ELLERY
ALEXI	EMMETT
ALISTAIR	
AMYAS	FINN
ANATOL	
ANDRÉ	
ANDREAS	GARETH
ANTON	GARSON
ASH	GRAY/GREY
ATTICUS	
	HARDY
BARNABY	HART
BASIL	
BEAU	INIGO
BENNO	IVO
BOAZ	
	JAGGER
CHENEY	JAMESON
CHRISTO	JASPER
CLAY	
COSMO	
CRISPIN	KAI
CROSBY	KILIAN/KILLIAN
	KINGSTON
DAMIAN	
DANTE	LEANDER
DARCY	LEONARDO
DARIUS	LIONEL
DIMITRI	LORENZO
DONOVAN	LORNE
DORIAN	LUCIAN

MARIUS	QUENTIN
MERCE	QUINCY
MICAH	
MILO	
MISCHA	RAFAEL/RAPHAEL
MOSS	RAOUL/RAUL
	REMY
NICO	ROONE
OMAR	
ORION	SEBASTIAN
ORLANDO	
ORSON	
	TARQUIN
	TRISTRAM
PABLO	
PHILO	
PHINEAS	ZENO

FOR NUMBER FIVE, MARY OR ANNE?

Paula Yates, ex-wife of the British rocker Bob Geldof, named her four daughters Fifi Trixiebelle, Peaches, Pixie, and Heavenly Hirani Tiger Lily.

ARE MARGARETS SMARTER?

Margarets cannot help being the best at everything— and catching hell or oblivion for it. Some scholars have observed the phenomenon as early as third grade. A Margaret will invariably be winning spelling bees, while the entire class can be seen mouthing the word, "miss."

—LOIS GOULD, "THE MARGARET FACTOR,"
THE NEW YORK TIMES MAGAZINE

NO-NONSENSE NAMES

*M*aybe you're sick of fashion. Fed up with fads. Perhaps all the creativity and invention with names is beginning to feel like anything but that to you. For your child, you want a straightforward, down-to-earth, no-nonsense name. You want a name with history, but also one that's honest, that's not putting on airs. Some of the names here—let's face it, Hilda—are a little flat-footed. But many sound appealingly simple and fresh compared with the rich diet of Dakotas and Donatellas the world of baby-naming has been feasting on.

GIRLS

ABIGAIL	CORA
AGATHA	
ALICE	DEBORAH
ANNA	DIANE
ANNE/ANN	DOROTHY
	EDITH
BARBARA	ELEANOR
BEATRICE	ELIZABETH
	ELLA
CAROLINE	EMILY
CATHERINE	ESTHER
CHARLOTTE	EVE
CLARA	
CLARE	FAITH
CLAUDIA	FLORENCE
CONSTANCE	FRANCES

GRACE	MARGARET
	MARIAN
HARRIET	MARIE
HELEN	MARTHA
HILDA	MARY
HONOR	MILDRED
HOPE	MIRIAM
	MONA
IRENE	
	NORA
JANE	NORMA
JANET	
JEAN	
JOAN	PATIENCE
JOANNA	PRUDENCE
JOSEPHINE	
JUDITH	RACHEL
JULIA	REBECCA
	ROSE
KATE	RUTH
KATHERINE	
KAY	
	SALLY
	SARAH
LAURA	
LEIGH/LEE	
LOUISE	WILLA
LUCY	WINIFRED

BOYS

ALBERT	KURT
ALFRED	
ARTHUR	MAX
	MOE
BEN	MOSES
CAL	NAT
CARL	NED
CHARLIE	NEIL
	NICK
DAVID	NORMAN
DREW	
	PAUL
ERNEST	PHILIP
FRANK	RALPH
FRED	RAY
	ROBERT
GEORGE	ROGER
GUS	ROY
HAL	SAM
HAROLD	SAUL
HARRY	SIMON
HENRY	SOL
HOWARD	
HUGH	TED
	TIM
JACK	TOM
JAKE	
JAMES	VICTOR
JOE	
JOHN	WALTER
	WILL

THE NICKNAME GAME

Before we even get into the subject, we have to establish the fact that when we talk about nicknames we're not really talking about nicknames. Nicknames are those descriptive, usually derogatory terms like Fatso, Freckles, Four-Eyes, Skinny and Stretch, Bones and Baldie, which, outside the worlds of rap music and organized crime, have pretty much moved off into the well-deserved purgatory of Politically Incorrect cruelty.

When we say nicknames now, we're actually talking about pet names (which itself has a rather unpleasant puppyish connotation) or diminutives, like Bill and Barbie and Ken.

Modern parents usually have strong feelings for or against the use of a nickname for their child. Over the past decade or so, there has been a pervasive trend toward using children's names in full—especially when it comes to the standard classic names—rather than the short forms that have traditionally been attached to them. There are far more baby Elizabeths, for instance, than there are baby Bettys or Betsys or Beths, just as Jameses now tend to outnumber Jimmys and Jims; and Williams, Edwards, and Victorias also reign across the playgrounds of America.

But be warned that this strike for children's dignity can easily be thwarted, despite any resoluteness to stick with the undiluted original. If and when your eight-year-old Susannah gets a phone call from a friend asking for Susie, there's not very much you can do about it, even if you do say, "Hold on, I'll get Susannah."

What's a parent to do? If you really hate nicknames, the best tack may be to choose a name that seems to be nickname-proof. If what you object to is not nicknames in general but a particular nickname, you might try choosing an unusual one, archaic or foreign, off the bat, before the kids in the playground have a chance to turn Edward into Eddie. More guidance and suggestions follow.

Of course, it may be the nickname you're really after, choosing to name a child Joseph to get to the down-to-earth, easygoing Joe, opting for Katherine because you love Kate. Just be warned that even nickname-names tend to morph all on their own, with Joe somehow descending into Joey and Kate turning into Katie. Parents who deliberately give their children an informal name such as Annie or Jamie may find those names buttoning themselves up into Ann and James.

The only certainty with nicknames seems to be that, no matter what you do, they have a life of their own.

SHORT & SWEET

Since there was such a limited supply of first names in past centuries—at one point, for example, 57 percent of the female population of England was named either Mary, Anne, or Elizabeth—and it wasn't unusual to give more than one child in a family the same name, it's hardly surprising that a great diversity of imaginative diminutive names sprang up to make it easier to distinguish among all the same-named people. Over the years, many of these have simply faded away. But some, we think, are worth reconsidering and resurrecting.

SLIM TIM

[Tim Henman] is the first human called Tim to achieve anything at all . . . The name lacks gravity. It's easy enough to see how it happened: the Tims of the world had all their ambitions crushed, all their aspirations dashed, by being called "Timmy" during childhood. The association with "timid" and "timorous" . . . was obviously too strong to bear.

—Martin Amis,
The New Yorker

GIRLS

BARRA	*for*	Barbara
BEAH		Beatrice
BESS		Elizabeth
BETTA		Elizabeth
CARO		Caroline
CASSIE		Catherine
CHARTY		Charlotte
DAISY		Margaret
DEBS		Deborah
DORO		Dorothy
FEENY		Josephine
FRANKIE		Frances
GRETA		Margaret
IBBY		Isabel
IMMY		Imogen
KAT		Katherine
KAY		Katherine
KITTY		Katherine
LETTIE		Letitia
LIBBY		Elizabeth
LISSA		Melissa
LIVVY		Olivia
LOTTA		Charlotte
LOTTIE		Charlotte
LULU		Louise
MAGO		Margaret
MAISIE		Margaret
MALLY		Mary
MAMIE		Mary
MANDA		Amanda
MELLY		Melanie
MINNIE		Mary

MOLL	Mary
NELL	Eleanor, Helen
NESSA	Vanessa
PATIA	Patricia
PIPPA	Philippa
POLLY	Mary
SADIE	Sarah
SUKIE	Susan
TILLIE	Matilda
TORY	Victoria
VITA	Victoria
ZAN	Alexandra

BOYS

BENNO	*for*	Benjamin
BRAM		Abraham
CHAZ		Charles
CHRISTY		Christopher
DEZI		Desmond
DIX		Richard
DUNN		Duncan
GAZ		Gary
GORE		Gordon
GRAM		Graham
HITCH		Richard
JEM		Jeremy
JOCK		John
KIT		Christopher
LAURO		Laurence
LEX		Alexander
NED		Edward
PIP		Philip
RAFE		Ralph

ROBIN	Robert
SEB	Sebastian
SIMS	Simon
TAD	Theodore
TELLY	Theodore
TIP	Thomas
TOLLY	Bartholomew
WILLS	William
ZAN	Alexander
ZANDER	Alexander

MINI MINNIE

My parents actually named me Amelia, but my sister took one look at me in the hospital and said, 'Minnie.' Thanks a lot—my whole future was determined by a two-year-old. I always thought it was kind of a non-name, because there's no identity in it other than a cartoon character."

—MINNIE DRIVER,
INTERVIEW

NO-NICKNAME NAMES

Do you hate nicknames, or just hate the idea that someone other than you is going to decide what your child is actually named by shortening Elizabeth to Lizzie or creating some similarly unwanted short form? Then you might do well to consider choosing a name that doesn't *have* a nickname, one that already is a short form or that's too succinct to be abbreviated further. Here are some no-nickname options:

GIRLS

AMBER	INGRID
APRIL	IVY
AVA	
	JADE
BLAIR	JOY
BLANCHE	
BLYTHE	
BREE	LEIGH
BRETT	
BROOKE	MAEVE
BRYN	MORGAN
CHELSEA	NORA
CLAIRE	
COURTNEY	PAIGE
	PILAR
DAISY	PIPER
DALE	PORTIA
DREW	
	RAE
FAITH	RUBY
FAY	
	SAGE
GAIL	SKYE
GREER	
HEATHER	TIFFANY
HOPE	TYNE

BOYS

AARON	FINN
ADAM	FLYNN
ADRIAN	FRASER
AMOS	
AUSTIN	
	GLENN
	GRANT
BAILEY	GRAY
BEAU	GROVER
BLAKE	GUY
BO	
BRADY	HARRY
BRAM	
BRETT	IAN
BRICE	
	JAY
	JUDD
CARL	JUDE
CHASE	JUSTIN
CLAUDE	
CLAY	
CODY	KENT
COLE	KIRK
	KYLE
DALLAS	LARS
DAMON	LLOYD
DEAN	LUKE
DREW	LYLE
DUANE	
	MARK
ELI	MILES
ETHAN	MORGAN

NEAL	SEAN
NILES	SETH
NOAH	SHANE
NOEL	
	THOR
	TOBY
PALMER	TODD
	TROY
QUINN	
	WALKER
REED	WILEY
REX	WYATT
ROSS	
ROY	ZANE

FITTING IN/STANDING OUT

This is one of our most popular lists, and one that's much more difficult to construct than it seems at first sight. As you probably realize if you've been hunting for the right name for more than a few days, most names fall on one wrong side or another of the golden mean that will allow your child both to fit in with peers, and stand out among them. Scroll down any index of names and the problem becomes instantly apparent: Aba, too weird; Abena, too weird; Abida, too weird; Abigail, too normal! Yet many parents are looking for a name that is right smack in-between, which we hope you will find on this list. Because so many parents are interested in this category, we've tried to be as inclusive as possible—and as a result, you might find some of *these* names too weird or too normal. But there's also a good chance you'll find a choice among them that strikes the perfect note.

GIRLS

ADRIENNE	FELICITY
ALEXA	FRANCESCA
ALICE	
AMELIA	GEMMA
ANNABEL	GEORGIA
ANTONIA	GILLIAN
ANYA	GRACE
AVA	
	HOPE
BERNADETTE	
	INDIA
CAMERON	IVY
CAMILLE	
CAROLINA	JADE
CELESTE	JOCELYN
CELIA	JULIA
CELINE	JULIANA
CHARLOTTE	JULIET
CHLOE	
CLAIRE	KITTY
CLARISSA	
CLAUDIA	LAUREL
	LEAH
DAISY	LILA
DELIA	LILY
DINAH	LOLA
	LOUISA
ELIZA	LYDIA
ELLA	
EMMELINE	MAIA
EVE	MARGARET

MARGOT	SABRINA
MARIANA	SERENA
MARTINE	SIMONE
MAY	STELLA
MERCEDES	SUSANNAH
MEREDITH	
NATASHA	TAMARA
NELL	TESS
NORA	TOBY
PHOEBE	
POLLY	VALENTINA
PRISCILLA	VIOLET
ROSE	WILLA
RUBY	WILLOW

BOYS

ADRIAN	DEREK
AIDAN	DERMOT
	DUNCAN
BAILEY	EMMETT
BARNABY	
	FLYNN
CALEB	FREDERICK
CALVIN	
CARSON	GABRIEL
CLAY	GORDON
COLIN	GRADY
COOPER	GRANT

GRAY	OWEN
GREGORY	
	PATRICK
HARRY	
HAYDEN	QUENTIN
HENRY	QUINN
HOLDEN	
	REED
ISAIAH	REUBEN
	RILEY
JACKSON	
JONAH	
JULIAN	SEBASTIAN
	SETH
	SIMON
LEO	SPENCER
LUCAS	
MALCOLM	THEO
MILES	TREVOR
MILO	TRUMAN
NED	WALKER
NOAH	WYATT
NOEL	
NOLAN	ZANE

CLASS

*A*mericans like to pretend that class doesn't exist. We often designate someone "working class" or "upper-middle class" according to how much money they make, rather than how they behave or how they talk or what they name their children.

Class in names? Never heard of it. That's what we claim,

anyway. Yet, our feelings about names, whether we like them and consider them appropriate for our children, often have more to do with class than we care to admit, even to ourselves.

There are distinct class patterns and tastes in baby-naming in the United States, as detailed by researchers who've examined what parents of different incomes and educational levels name their children and why. Parents who can be defined as middle or upper class, either by profession or education, are more likely to choose traditionally rooted names and to name children after family members than working-class parents.

Sociologist Alice Rossi found in a landmark study that 83 percent of middle- and upper-class parents named at least one child for a relative, versus working-class parents who used a family name only 37 percent of the time. Boys are more likely than girls to get family names and firstborn boys are more likely to be named after relatives than boys born later. In recent years, parents have been more apt to name children after grandparents on both sides of the family tree than after themselves.

Upper-class parents try to disassociate themselves from lower-class parents by choosing different names, say researchers. But the lower class tries to catch up by adopting those names later. And as names become popular among the lower classes, the upper class abandons them and moves on to fresh, higher ground.

According to research by Harvard sociologist Stanley Lieberson, whose work analyzes which names are chosen by mothers of different educational levels, names appear in the top twenty first among highly educated mothers and a few years later among those with less schooling. This pattern stands for both boys' and girls' names, but it's more pronounced for girls' names. Ashley, for example, first entered the top twenty in 1983 for mothers with some college and postcollege educations, then hit the top twenty lists a year later for high school and college graduates, and then in 1985 made the top twenty among moms with less than a high school education.

But mothers with the lowest educational levels are less

likely than those with more education to choose names from the top twenty at all, and more likely to favor unique or invented names. This is true across all races. Among women in Lieberson's study with less than a high school education, 28 percent of daughters and 41 percent of boys received top twenty names, versus 35 percent of the daughters and 49 percent of the sons of all other mothers. And the women with the lowest educations gave 48 percent of daughters and 36 percent of sons unique names, versus unique names for 35 percent of the daughters and 22 percent of the sons of moms with higher educations.

Lieberson studied the name choices of mothers of different education levels in New York State from 1973 to 1985, and found that white mothers with higher education prefer names that end in an *n* sound, biblical names, and those with long-standing historical roots. For their sons, they like Old Testament names. For daughters, they prefer names that connote strength. (Among African-American mothers, education did not make a significant difference in name preferences. For more details, see African-American Names, page 239).

The Top Ten names preferred by mothers with the highest educations, according to Lieberson's sample, are:

GIRLS

1. EMILY
2. ALLISON
3. LAUREN
4. MEGAN
5. CATHERINE
6. ELIZABETH
7. SARAH
8. LAURA
9. RACHEL
10. REBECCA

BOYS

1. ANDREW
2. ADAM
3. MATTHEW
4. JONATHAN
5. RYAN
6. SCOTT
7. MARK
8. JOSHUA
9. BRIAN
10. DANIEL

Mothers with lower educational levels, however, are more apt to like names ending in the "ee" or "a" or "l" sounds, and to choose novel names or those that lack historical roots. Boys names that connote strength are favored by these moms, as are more conventionally feminine girls' names.

The Top Ten choices among the white mothers with the lowest educations in Lieberson's study are:

GIRLS

1. CRYSTAL
2. TAMMY
3. MARIA
4. ANGELA
5. MICHELLE
6. MELISSA
7. NICOLE
8. LISA
9. STACY
10. JAMIE

BOYS

1. ANTHONY
2. JOSEPH
3. RICHARD
4. ROBERT
5. JASON
6. WILLIAM
7. JAMES
8. JOHN
8. THOMAS
10. SEAN

But the issue of names shifting class status over time is a sticky one, and many of the names on these lists have moved up or down the class ladder since 1985. Lauren, Megan, Ryan, Scott, and Mark have faded from fashion and also slipped a few notches in class status, for instance, while the more classic names on the boys' list preferred by mothers with the lowest educational levels—especially William, James, and Thomas—have moved up.

Figuring out the class status of names in a society where nobody likes to talk about class can be difficult at best. A humorous book called *The Distinctive Book of Redneck Baby Names* makes a stab at defining names at the low end. Two nicknames strung together—Joe Bob, say, or Johnnie Mae—makes for a redneck name. So do initial names like J.W. or nickname-names such as Ouisie.

Humorous but too easy. How to peg the class standing of more ordinary names?

One general rule seems to be that names that sound rich—names that signify expensive things such as Tiffany, Bentley, or Crystal, or names that sound like the surnames of the British nobility such as Ashley or Courtney—are in fact downwardly mobile. And more down-to-earth, less pretentious names—Josephine, Patrick, Sophie, Harry—are moving up.

In England, where class informs every aspect of everyday life, British parents inevitably talk about class in the same breath that they discuss baby names. More important than whether a name is in style or out in Britain is whether it's considered upper class or not.

Consistent use by royalty automatically gives a name an upper-class seal of approval: Names such as Charles, Elizabeth, William, Henry, and Anne, conferred consistently on royal babies over the ages, are unimpeachably upper class. Other traditional royal names—Alexandra, Charlotte, Victoria, and James, for example—are also well established on the upper-class roster. Even less traditional names borne by nobility—Beatrice and Eugenie for instance, Marina and Angus and Zara—are now firmly upper class.

Other names are true class nomads: Harry and Abigail, for instance, once undeniably upper, became working class by the end of the nineteenth century, though now both have recovered favor with the upper classes. Samantha, once an impeccably aristocratic name, became tarnished after it was popularized by the television witch—and an American witch at that. Being branded "American"—invented, silly, untraditional—is about as low as a name can sink in status in Britain.

Some of the most thoroughly upper-class names in England are so stodgy—and, some might say, ugly—that they will never be in danger of becoming too widely used. More than one British parent has said that the most upscale name you can give your daughter is Henrietta. For boys, Hugh and Piers are right up there, along with Hamish.

A name can be counted as upper or not depending on niceties (or not) of spelling: Deborah, Geoffrey, and Stephen are upper class; Debra, Jeffrey, and Steven decidedly not. Likewise, nicknames can make the difference in a name's class status: Kitty is an upper-crust nickname for Katherine while Kath is nonupper; Ned is an accepted upper-class abbreviation for Edward, Ed, and Eddie are not. And pronunciation can be significant: Ralph, pronounced Rafe as in Fiennes, is upper, but not when pronounced Ralf as in Kramden.

One well-known British arbiter of class, *The Official Sloane Ranger Handbook*, divided those names appropriate for Sloanes—sort of the English equivalent of Yuppies—from those that were not. Acceptable girls' names, according to the book, include Emma, Lucinda, Sarah, Diana—"almost any name ending in 'a' except Tanya." Harriet, Georgina, Charlotte, and Caroline are Sloane; Jennifer and Jane are not. Daisy, Flora, and Pansy are Sloane; Lily and Heather un-Sloane. For boys, plain English or Scottish names are considered Sloane-worthy: Henry, Charles, Peter, Simon, William, Alistair, Archie.

In the United States, Yuppies as such may be dead, but Yuppie names are not. There are names that are favored by young urban professional parents, parents who are the American definition of upper-middle class. These names have some style or dash, but are not invented; they're traditional, but not boring. Be warned, however. If you're a Yuppie-equivalent yourself, many of these names will be far more popular among your peers than they seem judging from their standing on popularity lists. Emma, for instance, seems to be today's standard-issue girl's name among Yuppie parents.

YUPPIE NAMES

GIRLS

ALEX	CHLOE
ALEXANDRA	CLAIRE
ALICE	
ALLEGRA	ELEANOR
AMELIA	ELENA/ELANA
ANNA	ELIZA
ANNIE	ELIZABETH
ANTONIA	ELLA
	EMILY
	EMMA
CAROLINE	
CATHERINE	FAITH
CHARLOTTE	FELICITY

FLORA	MIA
FRANCES	MIRANDA
FRANCESCA	MOLLY
GABRIELLE	NATALIE
GEMMA	NATASHA
GEORGIA	NELL
GRACE	NINA
	NORA
HALLIE	
HANNAH/HANA	OLIVIA
HILARY	
HOPE	
	PHOEBE
	POLLY
ISABEL	PRISCILLA
ISABELLA	
	RACHEL
JOANNA	REBECCA
JULIA	ROSE
JULIANA	ROSEMARY
JULIET	RUTH
KATE	SARAH
KATHERINE	SOPHIA
	SOPHIE
LAURA	SUSANNAH
LEAH	
LILY	TESS
LOUISA	TESSA
LUCY	
	VIOLET
MADELEINE	VIRGINIA
MARGARET	
MARTHA	ZOE

BOYS

ALEX	JAMES
ALEXANDER	JONATHAN
ANDREW	JOSEPH
	JULIAN
BENJAMIN	
	LEO
CHARLES	LIAM
CHRISTOPHER	LOUIS
COLIN	
COOPER	
	MALCOLM
DANIEL	MATTHEW
DAVID	MAX
	MILES
EDWARD	
EMMETT	
ETHAN	NATHAN
EVAN	NATHANIEL
	NED
GRAHAM	NICHOLAS
GRAY	
	OLIVER
HARRY	OWEN
HENRY	
HUGH	
	PARKER
IAN	PATRICK
	PAUL
JACK	PETER
JACKSON	PHILIP

QUENTIN	THOMAS
	TIMOTHY
	TOBIAS
REID	
	WALKER
SAM	WILL
SEBASTIAN	WILLIAM
SIMON	
SPENCER	ZACHARY

ROYAL NAMES

Where the royals still reign, the question of class and names becomes a bit clearer, for names that are used by the royal families automatically have class. In general, these tend to be old, well-established names, passed down through the family, though in recent years there have been some breaks with tradition: Princess Anne's daughter is named Zara, for instance, while Princess Stephanie's third child, born out of wedlock and fathered by her bodyguard, is Camille. In fact, many of the choices on this list, while time-honored, also have a surprisingly offbeat quality. Consider these—mostly from the British royal family, but with some Scottish and other European royal names mixed in—for your own little prince or princess.

GIRLS

ADELA	ARABELLA
ADELAIDE	AUGUSTA
AGNES	
ALBERTA	BEATRICE
ALEXANDRA	BENEDIKTE
ALICE	BIRGITTE
AMABEL	
AMELIA	CAMILLE
ANNE	CAROLINE

CATHERINE	JANE
CHARLOTTE	JOAN
CHRISTIAN	JULIA
CHRISTINA	JULIANA
CLAUDINE	
CONSTANCE	LOUISA
	LOUISE
	LUCY
DAVINA	
DONADA	
DOROTHEA	MARGARET
	MARINA
	MARY
EDITH	MATILDA
ELEANOR	MAUD
ELIZABETH	MAY
ELLA	
EMMA	OLGA
EUGENIE	OLIVIA
FEODORA	PAULINE
FINNUALA	PHILIPPA
	ROSE
GABRIELLA	
GERTRUDE	
GRACE	SARAH
	SOPHIA
	STEPHANIE
HELEN	
HELENA	VICTORIA
HENRIETTA	
	WILHELMINA
ISABEL	
ISABELLA	ZARA

BOYS

ALBERT	JAMES
ALEXANDER	JOHN
ALFRED	
ANDREW	
ANGUS	LEOPOLD
ANTONY	LOUIS
ARCHIBALD	
ARTHUR	
	MALCOLM
	MICHAEL
CHARLES	
CHRISTIAN	
COLIN	NICHOLAS
CONSTANTINE	
	PATRICK
DAVID	PAUL
DUFF	PETER
DUNCAN	PHILIP
EDGAR	
EDMUND	
EDWARD	RICHARD
ERNEST	ROBERT
FINLAY	STEPHEN
FRANCIS	
FRANKLIN	
FREDERICK	THOMAS
GEORGE	
	VICTOR
HAROLD	
HENRY/HARRY	WALTER
HUGH	WILLIAM

SEX

Gender identity as it relates to names has become an ever-evolving, increasingly delicate subject. Whether you're expecting a girl or a boy, whether you know the sex of your child-to-be or not, the gender implications of names undoubtedly play an important role in your name discussions and will be central to the perception of your child's name for years to come.

In *Naming a Daughter,* we look at how giving a frankly feminine or a gender-neutral name is apt to affect your daughter's self-image. And we analyze the possible reasons behind parents' preferences and choices for their daughters' names—to help you do the same.

In *Naming a Son,* we approach the same subjects from a male angle. Are there any decidedly masculine names left for boys? Can you find a name that breaks free from the conventional male mold, yet isn't drifting into female territory?

And in our section on *Unisex Names,* we investigate the history, the linguistics, and most important the gender identity of unisex names today.

NAMING A DAUGHTER

All gender issues inherent in raising a daughter today present themselves when choosing a girl's name.

Do you want to give your daughter a traditionally female name, and if so, does that mean confining her to a set of conventional expectations? If you call her Lucinda, say, or Allegra, will people stereotype her as a frilly, hyperfeminine girl? And if they do, what exactly is wrong with that?

Many feminist parents today want to give their daughter an androgynous or even frankly masculine name, liberating her with a kind of gender-free image. When Harvard gets the application, when Merrill Lynch surveys the résumé, no one will guess that Campbell or Christopher is a girl—and that can only be to her advantage. Or can it?

Other parents say it's time to leave that girls-must-be-boys thinking behind, and reembrace femininity along with strength, and energy, as well as ruffles. Parents want the world to be opened up to their daughters, but there's an appreciation for success beyond the conventional male model of corporate ladder-climbing. Success is not only money and power, but creativity, individuality, personal satisfaction.

Studies have found that girls' names are more prone to the whims of fashion than boys' names; they're more decorative, less conventional, more likely to be invented or to be based on diminutives. People find novelty more appealing in girls' names than in those for boys. Linguistically, girls' names tend to have more syllables, are more likely to end in a vowel, and to have an unstressed first syllable than boys' names. And according to name scholar Leonard Ashley, while many of the favored girls' names have meanings that relate to appearance and personality, the male names whose meanings relate to looks—Albert, Claude, Augustus—are mostly out of fashion.

These style and linguistic differences carry a deeper meaning. The theory of "phonetic symbolism" holds that the sound and structure of girls' names makes them lighter, weaker, and less threatening than boys' names. "The divergent tastes underlying naming patterns for boys and girls reflect a tendency to assign a lesser role to women," wrote Harvard professor Stanley Lieberson in the *American Journal of Sociology*.

The more popular the girls' name, the more likely it is to embody conventional feminine characteristics. Sociologists rate names on how strong, how intelligent, how good, sincere, and energetic people think they sound, and the gender gap is widest between the most popular boys' and girls' names, which were thirty-two points apart on these qualities, versus eleven points with less popular names. Popular girls' names score higher than less popular ones on goodness, intelligence, and sincerity, but lower on connotations of strength and activity.

Highly educated mothers, according to Harvard's Lieberson, are less likely to give their daughters names in the conventional female mode, and more likely to choose girls' names that connote strength, goodness, activity, sincerity, and intelligence.

And what of dad's preferences in naming a daughter? They're likely to vary from mom's, studies show. Women are more likely than their husbands to choose unusual or fashionable names for girls, and to choose unusual names for their daughters rather than their sons.

The eminent name researcher Edwin Lawson did a study comparing men's and women's reactions to full girls' names—Barbara, Susan, Deborah—versus short forms such as Barb, Sue, and Deb and affectionate names like Barbie, Susie, Debbie. The men and women were asked to rate the various forms on characteristics such as good, strong, active, sincere, intelligent, calm.

Women ranked affectionate names—Barbie and Debbie—lowest in all categories. Men ranked affectionate names lowest in the Strong and Active categories, but *highest* in the Good, Sincere, and Calm categories, and tied with formal names in Intelligence. Formal names were ranked highest by men for strength, highest by women for goodness and sincerity. Women ranked short forms like Deb and Sue as highest in strength, activity, and intelligence.

"Women . . . reject the image of the immature, dependent 'baby doll' female," writes Lawson. "But why do men accept it? We can only speculate that it is more satisfying to the male ego to perceive women in this way. Dependent, immature women may represent less of a threat to male sensitivities."

Now that you know *why* you and your mate seem to be arguing so much over girls' names, perhaps you can move closer to making an enlightened choice for your daughter.

FEMINISSIMA NAMES

If these names were dresses, they would be pale pink, with ruffles and lace and big bows and sprigs of flowers strewn on every available square inch. They are the sweetest of the sweet, the most feminine of the feminine names.

What makes these names Feminissima rather than merely Feminine? Three or more syllables sometimes do it. Soft sounds—*s*'s and *f*'s—can also push a name over the edge from Feminine to Feminissima. Names that by their meaning suggest ultrafeminine qualities, like Allegra and Lacey, are Feminissima. Very exotic names—especially Latin ones such as Raffaela and Gabriella—qualify. And sex-goddess names—from Salomé to Marilyn to Madonna—also connote an exaggerated femininity.

You can hardly give your daughter one of these names without suggesting a little girl with ringlets and rosy cheeks, the kind of child who plays only with dolls (with ringlets and rosy cheeks) and cries if her Mary Janes get scuffed. Her name will make boys want to go out on blind dates with her, and other girls see her as a potential threat even before they meet her.

Does that mean that giving your girl a Feminissima name will automatically make her a spineless jellyfish? Quite the opposite. There is something modern about these hyperfeminine names, something liberating about the possibility of an Angelica being chosen vice-president over an Alix. Just as the notion of a female Tyler with long hair and high heels has the appeal of the unexpected, so has that of a Felicia in a business suit or sweat pants.

FEMINISSIMA NAMES

ADORA

ADRIANA

ALEXANDRA

ALLEGRA

ALYSSA (and
  variations)

ANGELICA

ANGELINA

ANNABELLA

ARABELLA

ARIANA

ARIEL

AURORA

BABETTE

BARBIE

BELINDA

BLOSSOM

CAMILLA

CAROLINA

CASSANDRA

CECILIA

CECILY

CHERIE

CHRISSIE

CHRISTABEL

CICELY

CLARISSA

CRYSTAL

DAWN

DESIRÉE

DOLLY

ELISSA

EMMALINE

EVANGELINE

FAWN

FELICIA

FIFI

FRANCESCA

GABRIELLA

GEORGIANA

GISELLE

HEATHER

HYACINTH

ISABELLA

JOSETTE

JULIANA

LACEY

LANA

LARISSA

LETITIA

LILIANA

LISABETH

LOUELLA	SABINA
LUCIANA	SALOMÉ
LUCINDA	SAMANTHA
	SCARLETT
MADONNA	SELENA
MARCELLA	SERENA
MARIETTA	SUZETTE
MARILYN	
MARTITIA	
MELISSA	TABITHA
MELODY	TAFFY
MERRY	TATIANA
MIRABELLE	TEMPEST
MISSIE	TIFFANY
MONIQUE	TRICIA
ORIANA	VALENTINA
	VANESSA
PRISCILLA	VENUS
RAFFAELA	
ROSALINDA	YVETTE

FEMININE NAMES

By far the largest group of girls' names is made up of Feminine names: names that are clearly feminine without being too fussy, sweet without being syrupy, soft without being limp. Many of the most popular girls' names of recent years can be found on this list. Style has favored these decidedly feminine names, along with androgynous names, over either ultrafeminine or no-nonsense female names.

The advantages of a Feminine name are several. Most of these names are easy to recognize and easy to like: Your child will hear again and again what a pretty name she has, and that's pleasing as well as ego-boosting. Also, kids like names that are sexually unambiguous; they like labels that clearly identify them as a girl or a boy. And most of these names are familiar, either because of their classic status or because they have been popular in recent times.

What of the future for Feminine names? Some, like Katherine and Elizabeth, are vitually timeless, but many of the names in this group have been so fashionable for several years that they verge on the cliché. If you want to stay away from a name that is already too trendy, be sure to cross-reference any you like here with the So Far In They're Out list in the Style section. One general observation: Many of the extremely euphonic feminine names—Jennifer, Christina,

> *Many names are almost gone: Gertrude, Myrtle, Agnes, Bernice, Hortense, Edna, Doris, and Hilda. They were wide women, cotton-clothed, early rising. You had to move your mouth to say their names, and they meant strength, spear, battle, and victory. When did women stop being Saxons and Goths? What frog Fate turned them into Alison, Melissa, Valerie, Natalie, Adrienne, and Lucinda, diminished them to Wendy, Cindy, Suzy, and Vicky?*
>
> —HUNT HAWKINS, *MOURNING THE DYING FEMALE NAMES* FROM *THE DOMESTIC LIFE*

and so on—are on their way out, while more offbeat feminine names, like Annabel, Daisy, and Savannah, sound newer and stronger.

FEMININE NAMES

ABIGAIL	ADRIENNE
ADELA	AILEEN
ADELAIDE	ALANA/ALANNA
ADELINE	ALEXA

ALEXANDRA
ALEXIS
ALICIA
AL(L)ISON
AMANDA
AMBER
AMELIA
AMY
ANDREA
ANGELA
ANNABEL
ANNETTE
ANTONIA
APRIL
ARAMINTA
ARLETTA
AUDRA
AUDREY

BEATRICE
BEATRIX
BECCA
BELLE
BENITA
BERNADETTE
BIANCA
BONNIE
BRIDGET
BRONWYN/
  BRONWEN

CAITLIN/KAITLYN
CAMILLE
CANDACE
CARA

CAROLINE
CATHERINE/
  KATHERINE
CECILE
CELESTE
CELIA
CHARMAINE
CHELSEA
CHLOE
CHRISTA
CHRISTIANA
CHRISTINA
CHRISTINE
CLARICE
CLAUDETTE
CLEMENTINE
COLETTE
COLLEEN
CORDELIA
CORNELIA
CYNTHIA

DAISY
DANIELLA
DAPHNE
DARLA
DARLENE
DEANNA
DEBORAH
DEIRDRE
DELIA
DELILAH
DENISE
DIANA
DINAH

DOMINIQUE	HALEY/HAYLEY
DONNA	HELENA
DOREEN	HELENE
DORIA	HENRIETTA
DOROTHEA	HIL(L)ARY
	HOLLY
EILEEN	IMOGEN(E)
ELAINE	INGRID
ELENA	IRIS
ELISE	ISABEL
ELIZA	
ELIZABETH	JACQUELINE
ELOISE	JANICE
EMILY	JANINE
ESMÉ	JASMINE
EVA	JEANETTE
EVELYN	JENNA
	JENNIFER
	JESSA
FERN	JESSICA
FIONA	JOANNA
FLORA	JOCELYN
FRANCINE	JULIA
	JULIET
GABRIELLE	JUSTINE
GAY	
GELSEY	KATHLEEN
GEORGIA	KEZIA(H)
GILLIAN	KIMBERLY
GINA	KIRSTEN
GLORIA	KRISTIN
GLYNIS	
GRETCHEN	LAILA
GWENDOLYN	LARA

LAURA	MELANIE
LAUREL	MELANTHA
LAUREN	MERCEDES
LEATRICE	MIA
LEILA	MICHELLE
LEONORA	MIRANDA
LIA	MOLLY
LIANA	MONICA
LILA	
LILIAN	NANCY
LILY	NANETTE
LINDA	NAOMI
LISA	NATALIE
LIZA	NESSA
LOLA	NICOLA
LORETTA	NINA
LORNA	NOELLE
LORRAINE	NOREEN
LOUISA	
LUCIA	ODELIA
LUCY	ODETTE
	ODILE
MADEL(E)INE	OLIVIA
MARA	OPHELIA
MARCIA/MARSHA	
MARGO	PALMA
MARGUERITE	PALOMA
MARIA	PAMELA
MARIEL	PANDORA
MARINA	PANSY
MARLENE	PATRICE
MARYA	PATRICIA
MAURA	PAULETTE
MAUREEN	PAULINA
MEGAN	PAULINE

PEGEEN	SERENA
PENELOPE	SHANA
PETRA	SHANNON
PHILIPPA	SHARON
PHOEBE	SHEENA
PIA	SHEILA
PILAR	SHERRY
POLLY	SIMONE
	SONDRA
QUINTINA/	SONIA
QUINTANA	SOPHIA
	STELLA
RAMONA	STEPHANIE
REBECCA	SUSANNAH
REGINA	SUZANNE
RENATA	SYLVIA
RENÉE	
RHEA	TALIA
RITA	TAMAR
ROCHELLE	TAMARA
ROSA	TANYA
ROSALIE	TARA
ROSALIND	TESSA
ROSAMOND	THEODORA
ROSANNA	T(H)ERESA
ROSEMARY	THOMASINA
ROWENA	TINA
ROXANNE	
RUBY	VALERIE
	VENICE/VENETIA
SABINE	VERONICA
SABRA	VICTORIA
SANDRA	VIOLET
SAVANNAH	VIRGINIA
SELENA	VIVIAN

WENDY	ZANDRA
	ZARA
	ZELIA
YASMINE	ZENA
YOLANDA	ZOE
YVONNE	ZORAH

NO-FRILLS NAMES

These are the denim skirts of girls' names: clearly not fit for boys, but as straightforward, down to earth, and—sometimes—blunt as you can get while still being female.

One readily apparent difference between these and the more feminine girls' names is that they are shorter: fewer letter and syllables, fewer embellishments. Many end in consonants rather than vowels, which gives them a stronger sound. They're almost like generic labeling: Yes, they say, this is a girl, but that's all we're going to tell you.

The No-Frills names here fall into two groups: those with a straightforward sound—direct and to-the-point names like Jean, Lynn, Ruth—and those with a no-nonsense image: Constance, Gladys, Mildred.

NO-FRILLS NAMES

ADA	BETH
ADELE	BLANCHE
AGATHA	
AGNES	
ALICE	CARLA
ANNA	CAROL
ANN(E)	CASS
	CEIL
	CHARLOTTE
BARBARA	CLAIRE
BERNICE	CLAUDIA
BESS	CONSTANCE

CORA	HANNAH
CORINNE	HARRIET
	HAZEL
DELLA	HEIDI
DIANE	HELEN
DORA	HESTER
DORCAS	HILDA
DORIS	HONOR
DOROTHY	HOPE
	HORTENSE
EDITH	
EDNA	
ELEANOR	IDA
ELLA	INA
ELLEN	INEZ
EMMA	IRENE
ENID	
ESTELLE	
ESTHER	JANE
ETHEL	JANET
ETTA	JEAN
EUNICE	JILL
EVE	JOAN
	JOANNE
	JOSEPHINE
FAITH	JOY
FAY	JOYCE
FRANCES	JUDITH
FREIDA	JULIE
	JUNE
GAIL	
GERALDINE	
GLADYS	KAREN
GRACE	KATE
GRETA	KAY
GWEN	KIM

LEAH

LEIGH

LENORE

LESLIE

LOIS

LOUISE

LUCILLE

LYNN

MADGE

MAE/MAY

MAEVE

MARGARET

MARIAN

MARIE

MARTHA

MARY

MAUD(E)

MAVIS

MAXINE

MEG

MILDRED

MIRIAM

MONA

NELL

NOLA

NORA

NORMA

OLIVE

PATIENCE

PAULA

PAULINE

PEARL

PHYLLIS

PRUDENCE

RACHEL

RHODA

ROBERTA

ROSE

RUTH

SALLY

SARA(H)

SELMA

SOPHIE

SUSAN

SYBIL

THELMA

TRUDY

VELMA

VERA

VERNA

WANDA

WILLA

WINIFRED

ZELDA

NAMING A SON

It's a fact: Parents name boys differently from the way they name girls.

Boys are more likely than girls to be named after family members, to be given more traditional names, as well as less apt to be given names that are currently fashionable, found the eminent sociologist Alice Rossi in her landmark study of middle-class naming patterns. As evidenced by their names, said Rossi, boys are expected to be the symbols of family continuity and prestige.

Things have changed in the few decades since Rossi's study, but not entirely. More boys than girls are still given the top-ranked names, and fewer boys get unconventional or invented names. We're more serious when we name our sons, and we tend to give them more serious names.

Why? Well, partly because even the most liberal among us are still a little bit sexist. We may bear our sons' future career success and earning power more closely in mind than we do our daughters', and so give them more straightforward traditional names. And we might shy away from newer names as a tad androgynous, with only the conventional male names carrying the requisite masculine punch. Dads tend to take this consideration especially seriously. Moms push harder for less traditional names, but men are more likely to prefer widely used, historically based names, especially for sons.

The trouble is, as any parent who's searched for a boy's name soon discovers, there simply are not that many old-fashioned, down-to-earth, no-frills masculine names. And the ones that do exist tend to be used for so many thousands of males, decade after decade after decade, that they begin to feel like generic brands. There's Michael, the number-one boy's name for four decades, David and Joseph and John, William and James and Robert, Thomas and Charles.

The boys' names that straddle the boundary between the old-line men's club and hipper, more nouveau choices tend to get very popular indeed. These include Jacob and its short form Jake, which is taking a serious shot at Michael for the number-one spot. Christopher is another longtime favorite that blends traditionalism with style. Many other boys' names well-used in recent years tend to offer this same combination: Matthew, Nicholas, Zachary, Daniel, Jonathan, Ryan, Justin, Alexander, Benjamin.

Over the past several decades, we've kept changing our minds about how masculine and traditional we want our sons' names to be. The fifties and early sixties were strict Bobby-Billy-Johnny territory. Then, with the antiestablishment, "down with male chauvinist pigs" era, we turned to names that symbolized a softer, less aggressive brand of masculinity, to androgynous nickname-names such as Jody and Jamie, and to Victorian gentleman names such as Lindsay, Whitney, and Morgan—yes, for boys.

And increasingly, for girls too, which seemed to cause a sort of backlash in tastes in boys' names. As more girls took over names formerly reserved for boys—Shannon and Shawn, Casey and Taylor—parents began to turn back to the male names that were unequivocably identifiable as such. Yuppie parents in the eighties "rediscovered" such old-time masculine favorites as Andrew and Henry, and also turned once more to old sources for names that were clearly male, yet carried some originality.

One ever-more-popular source has been the Bible, particularly the Old Testament, for names ranging from Caleb to Nathaniel to Noah. And the formerly fusty grandpa names, brought out of mothballs, have also been major hits, with Max and Sam leading the pack.

Now there seems to be yet another swing, this time back to less conventional boys' names, though most of them are rooted firmly in male territory. For now, that is: Any boy's name, even the old-timers like Thomas and Christopher, seems to be fair game for girls these days. And the most stylish new boys' names share something—a flavor, a sensibility—with their female counterparts. It may seem clear, to the modern American ear, that Tyler and Tanner are boys' names and Taylor is primarily a girls', that Mason is for boys yet Madison and Mackenzie are for girls, but linguistically these names are all joined at the hip.

This is a real divergence from times past, when linguists analyzed boys' and girls' names as being very different from one another. The cultural origins of the most widely used traditional boys' names, for instance, were more likely to be Greek, Hebrew, and English, while several of the leading girls' names had latinate roots.

And then there are the sounds themselves. One linguistic analysis showed that 87 percent of the top one hundred boys' names ended in a consonant. Favorite girls' names are also much more likely than boys' to end with the "ee" sound, which tends to make the name sound like a more childlike diminutive.

These linguistic investigations confirm what most of us assume: That traditional boys' names "sound" stronger than girls' names. And other studies show that boys' names, particularly popular boys' names, rate higher in such qualities as strength, intelligence, and energy than girls' names. Still another study showed that for whites, less educated mothers were most likely to favor boys' names that connote strength, while more educated mothers choose names rooted in history. And African-American mothers of all educational levels are more likely to give their sons unusual or invented names than are white mothers. What does all this mean for naming your son? It always helps, especially when dealing with an issue as powerful and complicated as gender identity, to try to untangle your feelings and prejudices when you discuss names. These are likely to differ from one partner to another, and to clash with the opinions of people from another generation, such as parents who are offering name advice, solicited or not.

A boy with a less-than-conventional male name will certainly feel at home in today's more liberal atmosphere. Compared with even a decade ago, boys' names are becoming decidedly less macho and more adventurous. Top-fifty lists are crowded with such gentle choices as Tristan and Elijah, Gabriel and Cameron.

If you like this sort of bordering-on-androgynous name,

the one caveat we offer is that you consult the text and list in the Unisex section on the gender status of the names you like. Several names have recently crossed the border from mainly boys' to mainly girls' choices, and female-ward is the direction in which names tend to move, bad news for the boys' camp. Your son will definitely not like sharing his name with his female classmates, and we advise you to beware of using a name that's becoming popular for girls.

The traditionally male and borderline names are easy choices. You can't go wrong with one of these old stand-bys—unless you hate the idea of giving your son a standard-issue name. As we said before, there are relatively few of these names, and those that exist tend to be extraordinarily popular. So if it's fresh ground you want to till, you'll have to look elsewhere.

Like where? Foreign rosters are an increasingly popular choice, for new variations on the conventional names. Alejandro, Marco, Kristof: these are fresh twists on familiar material. Surname-names, especially ones that authentically spring from your family tree, are another good source.

It is somewhat dicier, in the end, to give your son an unusual or unique name than it would be to give one to a girl. There's some evidence that boys have a more difficult time fitting in with unusual names, and are less likely than girls to feel good about those names. But attractiveness is the bottom line: Choose a likable name that, unusual or popular, your son will have an easy time carrying through life.

ALL-BOY NAMES

While some cutting-edge parents may be starting to use conventionally male names for their daughters, these traditionals are still firmly in the boys' camp. There have long been girls named Michael, for instance, yet that hasn't stopped Michael from being the number-one boys' name for nearly half a century. The names here are the standard, classic male names, perhaps not wildly exciting but always reliable. Boys tend to fare well with these sturdy, classic names. No one ever gets teased for being called David, and no little Frank is ever mistaken for a girl on the basis of his name. Here is the all-boy selection:

ADAM	HARRY
ALAN/ALLAN/ALLEN	HARVEY
ALBERT	HENRY
ALEC	HUGH
ALEX	
ALEXANDER	JACK
ALFRED	JACOB
ANDREW	JAMES
ANTHONY	JEFFREY
ARTHUR	JEREMY
	JOHN
BENJAMIN	JONATHAN
	JOSEPH
CARL	JOSHUA
CHARLES	JUSTIN
CHRISTOPHER	
	LAWRENCE
DANIEL	LEO
DAVID	LEWIS/LOUIS
DOUGLAS	LUCAS/LUKE
EDWARD	MARK
ERIC	MARTIN
	MATTHEW
FRANK	MAX
FREDERICK	MICHAEL
GEORGE	NATHAN
GERALD	NATHANIEL
GORDON	NEAL/NEIL
GREGORY	NED

NICHOLAS	SAMUEL
NORMAN	SEBASTIAN
	SIMON
	STEPHEN
OLIVER	STUART/STEWART
PATRICK	
PAUL	THEODORE
PETER	THOMAS
PHILIP	TIMOTHY
	TOBIAS
RALPH	VICTOR
RAYMOND	VINCENT
RICHARD	
ROBERT	WALTER
ROGER	WARREN
RONALD	WILLIAM
ROY	
RUSSELL	ZACHARY

THE TWO-SYLLABLE SOLUTION

There is a popular new genre of boys' name that has a surname-name feel, a distinctly masculine flavor, and that also has, inevitably, two syllables. These choices seems to be an alternative to both the traditional males' names—William, Henry, and others—as well as the newer names that might seem a tad girlish. These hot two-syllable boys' names include:

AIDAN	BRANDON
AUSTIN	BRENDAN
	BRENNAN
BAILEY	
BRADEN	CALEB
BRADLEY	CARSON
BRADY	CARTER

CASEY	JORDAN
CHANDLER	JUSTIN
CODY	
COLIN	KADEN
COLTON	KIERAN
CONNOR	
COOPER	LIAM
CORBIN	LOGAN
DALTON	MASON
DEREK	
DEVIN	NATHAN
DUNCAN	
DUSTIN	OWEN
DYLAN	
	PARKER
EMMETT	
ETHAN	QUENTIN
EVAN	
	RILEY
GARETH	RORY
GARRETT	ROWAN
GRADY	RYAN
GRIFFIN	
	SAWYER
HAYDEN	SCHUYLER
HOLDEN	SPENCER
HUNTER	
	TANNER
JACOB	TAYLOR
JARED	TRAVIS
JAREN	TREVOR
JARON	TRISTAN
JARRETT	TRUMAN
JONAH	TUCKER

TYLER   WALKER
TYSON   WYATT

UNISEX NAMES

You've got to peek into the diaper to determine the sex
of many a baby these days, because their names are not
going to give you a clue. Dylan, Dakota, Morgan, Bailey,
Jordan, Alex, Taylor—any of these trendy-named kids
could be either a boy or a girl.

In Germany, a name code dictates that the gender of a
child has to be recognizable based on the first name. But
in the United States, anything goes, and this sort of one-
name-fits-all unisex naming grows only more popular every
year.

According to the 1998 Social Security statistics on over
three million babies' names, male Jordans outnumber females about two to one—but there were plenty of each.
Nearly twelve thousand boys were named Jordan to almost
six thousand girls. With Cameron, the balance tips further
toward the boys, with just over nine thousand male Ca-
merons to about twelve hundred females. With Taylor, the
balance tips in the other direction, with fifteen thousand girl
Taylors to three thousand boys. And girl Morgans outnumber boys more than ten to one, at over eight thousand to
just 762.

Dakota has four times as many male bearers as female,
while Bailey claims more than twice as many girls—and
that's not counting popular feminized spellings such as
Baylee and Baileigh. Casey seems to be the sole name that
is absolutely ambisexual, with 1617 boys called Casey to
1709 girls. Yet the growing legion of Kaycee's and Kaci's
may tip the name more to the girls' side.

Many states have begun tracking how many girls and
how many boys receive each name. In Kansas in 1997, in
what surely must be a name history first, Jordan stood exactly even in the count, with 19 boys and 19 girls given
the name. In Kentucky the year before, there were 296 boy

Jordans versus 133 girls, 371 female Taylors versus 90 males, 259 female Morgans versus 24 boys, and 187 boy Logans versus 16 girls.

Over time, most androgynous names move to the girl column. One study that compared unisex names in 1960 and 1990 from Pennsylvania records found that in those thirty years, none shifted from a majority of girls to boys, but ten moved the other way: Morgan, Noel, Jaime, Kendall, Casey, Taylor, Shannon, Kerry, and Jan. Names that were officially boys' names in 1960 but girls' names by 1990 include: Morgan, Noel, Kendall, Casey, Taylor, Angel, Shannon, Kerry. Names that had been designated boys' names in the 1940s but girls' by 1960 were Alexis, Robin, Jamie, Kim, Lynn, Kelly, Dana. None shifted the other way.

One linguistic study showed that people's preferred names—the names they like to be called as opposed to those they were given—are moving in the direction of male names, which are more likely than female ones to be monosyllabic, end in a consonant, and stress the first syllable. But another study analyzing most popular names over the years says names in general are becoming more feminine, with more syllables and softer sounds.

Linguists say names have gender markers, even when they're invented. The *a* ending usually signals a girls' name, though recent favorites Joshua, Noah, Elijah, and Jonah are evidence of the softening trend in boys' names. Androgynous geographic names such as Dakota, Montana, and Sierra also often end in an *a*. The *d* ending—David, Richard—is almost always a boys' name, while the *sh* beginning is most often used for girls.

Since androgynous names are about gender identity, if you're interested in this kind of name, it makes sense to think about what this says about who you hope your child will become. Parents who favor unisex or masculine names for their daughters may want to encourage their girls to take on characteristics once thought of as male: strength, ambition, athleticism. And giving a son an androgynous name may signal that you don't want your boy to be a traditional male, that you would prefer that he be sensitive and creative rather than aggressive and macho.

Why today's boom in androgynous names? The new generation of feminist parents and working mothers is one reason. The fashion for surname-names, family names, place names, and names with personal meaning is another. Plus androgynous names fit in with the burgeoning search for ever-more-unusual names. Naming your daughter Thomas or your son Avery will definitely make him or her stand out in a crowd, though perhaps not as positively as you wish.

The sexual shifts names are undergoing today are not unprecedented. Alice, Anne, Crystal, Emma, Esmé, Evelyn, Florence, Jocelyn, Kimberly, Lucy, and Maud all were originally male names. Christian was a feminine name in the Middle Ages, as was Douglas in the seventeenth century and Clarence in the eighteenth. A king of East Anglia in the seventh century was named Anna.

There is a long history of appealing heroines with boyish names: from Jo in *Little Women* to Lady Brett in *The Sun Also Rises*. Irene Dunne played a Ray in one movie, and Audrey Hepburn a Reggie; Bette Davis, Stanley; Olivia de Havilland, Roy; Janet Leigh, Wally; and Jane Russell, Nancy Sinatra, and Anne Baxter all Mikes.

Today, the stars themselves are more likely to have the boyish names: witness Glenn Close, Jodie Foster, Drew Barrymore, Meryl Streep, Sean Young, Whitney Houston, Daryl Hannah, and Jamie Lee Curtis.

Sometimes, a name that sounds tired for a boy, like Sydney, becomes fresh and crisp when applied to a girl. Names that can be wimpy for a boy, such as Brooke or Blair, can confer a brisk kind of strength on a girl.

But androgynous names often appeal more to parents than to children themselves. Little boys dislike having the same name as female playmates, and often find the androgynous name even more troublesome down the road. Little girls likewise tend to dislike unisex names in early childhood, when most children seem to prefer all things sexually distinct, from their clothing to their toys to their names. However, most grown-up women with androgynous

names say that once they reached adolescence they began
to appreciate the sexual ambiguity as well as the sex appeal
of their names.

In the sixties, the big trend was toward cute nicknames
that sounded just as right for boys as girls: Jody, Toby,
Jamie. In the eighties, unisex nicknames for more sexually
distinct proper names took center stage: Chris, Nicky, Alex.
Today, the field has widened to include surname-names of
all ethnicities, place names, and all-boy names—Gregory,
Zachary—for girls. Below are some categories of unisex
names.

THE TRUE UNISEX NAMES
These names—and there aren't that many of them, nor are
they necessarily compatible in style—truly work as well
for boys and girls.

ALEX	HUNTER
BAILEY	JAMIE
BRETT	JESSIE
	JO/JOE
CAMERON	JORDAN
CASEY	
CHRIS	
	KAI
	KEIL
DALE	KYLE
DARYL	
DREW	
DYLAN	LANE
	LEE/LEIGH
EVAN	
FRANCES/FRANCIS	MICKEY
GENE/JEAN	NICKY
GERRY/JERRY	
GLENN	PAT

QUINN	SAM
	SCHUYLER
	SEAN/SHAWN
RAY/RAE	SKY
RICKI/RICKY	SPENCER
RILEY/REILLY	
RORY	TERRY

BOYS TO GIRLS

Many girls' names are feminized versions of male names: Carol, Caroline, and Charlotte (not to mention Carla, Charla, and Charlene) all derived from Charles, for instance. We've heard some pretty bad male-to-female inventions (Davette comes to mind) but the names on this list are gently old-fashioned and may be a good way to name a daughter after a male ancestor or lend a masculine note to her name without going all the way to David.

ALANA/ALANNA	CLEMENTINE
ALBERTA	CORNELIA
ALEXANDRA	
ALFREDA	DANIELLE
ANDREA	DAVIDA
ANTONIA	DENISE
AUGUSTA	DOMINICA/
	DOMINIQUE
BERNADETTE	
	EDWINA
	ERICA
CARLA	ERNESTINE
CAROL	EUGENIA
CAROLINE	
CHARLOTTE	
CHRISTINE	FRANCES/FRANCINE
CLAUDIA	FREDERICA

GABRIELLE	MARCELLA/MARCIA
GEORGIA/GEORGINA	MARTINA
GERALDINE	MAXINE
	MICHAELA
	MICHELLE
HARRIET	
HENRIETTA	
	NICOLE
ISIDORA	PATRICIA
	PAULA
	PAULINE
JACOBA	
JACQUELINE	
JESSICA	ROBERTA
JOHANNA	
JORDANA	SIMONE
JOSEPHINE/JOSEPHA	STEPHANIE
JULIA/JULIANA	
JUSTINE	THEODORA
	VALENTINA
LAURA	VICTORIA
LAUREN	
LEONA	WILHELMINA/WILLA
LOUISE	
LUCY	YVONNE

THE GIRLS ARE WINNING

It seems to be a law: Unisex names, over time, tend to become more feminine. Not that long ago, there were hardly any female Blairs, Blakes, or Glenns. There were as many little boy Ashleys, Jordans, and Morgans as there were girls. Today, those names and the rest of the list here have either established themselves firmly in the female camp, or are headed inexorably that way. The message? Beware of using any of these names, however adorable, for

a son. Your boy may find it difficult to share his moniker
with a girl (or two) in his class.

ASHLEY	MACKENZIE
AVERY	MALLORY
	MEREDITH
BLAINE	MERLE
BLAKE	MERRILL/MERYL
	MORGAN
CHEYENNE	
COURTNEY	
	REGAN
DAKOTA	ROBIN
DEVON	
JODY	SHELBY
	SIERRA
KELSEY	STACY
KENDALL	SYDNEY
KERRY	
KIM	
	TAYLOR
LESLIE	TRACY
LINDSAY	WHITNEY

ANDROGYNOUS STARBABIES

AUGUST *(girl)*	*Garth Brooks*
AUGUST *(boy)*	*Lena Olin*
BAILEY *(boy)*	*Anthony Edwards*
BAILEY *(girl)*	*Melissa Etheridge*
DAKOTA *(girl)*	*Melanie Griffith & Don Johnson*
DAKOTA *(boy)*	*Melissa Gilbert*
DYLAN *(girl)*	*Robin Wright & Sean Penn*
DYLAN *(boy)*	*Pierce Brosnan, Pamela Anderson & Tommy Lee, Joan Cusack*

ELIOT *(girl)*	Sting
ELLIOT *(boy)*	Robert De Niro
JORDAN *(girl)*	Leeza Gibbons
JORDAN *(boy)*	Robert De Niro
SATCHEL *(girl)*	Spike Lee
SATCHEL *(boy)*	Woody Allen
SCOUT *(girl)*	Demi Moore & Bruce Willis
SCOUT *(boy)*	Tai Babilonia
SPENCER *(girl)*	Debbie Dunning
SPENCER *(boy)*	Cuba Gooding, Jr.

THE TROUBLE WITH TAYLOR

Androgynous names abound: Ashley used to be a boy's name, as fans of Gone with the Wind remember. (Ashley Wilkes was played by Leslie Howard; now even Leslie is a girl's name.) Taylor, Cameron, and Madison can be borne by male or female. This means it is harder for prospective employees to tell a job applicant's sex when reading a résumé, a possible reason for the choices.

—WILLIAM SAFIRE, "WELCOME BACK SARAH," *THE NEW YORK TIMES MAGAZINE*

TRADITION ☆

I t may seem ironic that, in the face of all the new adventurousness in choosing children's names, Tradition is one of the fastest-growing sections of this book. But for many parents, the quest for novelty and creativity is coupled with a search for personal meaning—for history and ethnic identity. And these qualities are anything but mutually exclusive, with many of the most exciting new names coming from our own pasts or cultural backgrounds.

There's much that's new in this section.

We delve into American naming history from Colonial times to the present. And we take a new look at the often-separate African-American naming traditions, tracing today's African-American name choices back to roots in slavery and early naming practices that blended customs from Africa with the developing American culture to produce a name lexicon that's distinctive and unique.

We offer here a greatly expanded selection of ethnic names, hundreds of selections from European cultures as well as African, Arab, and Hebrew names. Here also is information on Jewish naming traditions, as well as a wide range of saints' names.

A CONCISE HISTORY OF AMERICAN BABY-NAMING

In the few centuries since the earliest colonial settlements were established in this country, our stock of names has grown from the limited number of Anglo-Saxon standards that came over on the *Mayflower* and other early vessels to a vast stewpot composed of flavors from different cultures and of names created on our native soil. A look back at our naming history can provide inspiration to today's baby namer as well.

COLONIAL PERIOD & EIGHTEENTH CENTURY

As you may remember from fourth-grade history, the first English-speaking settlement, called the Raleigh Colony, was established on the mid-Atlantic coast in 1587, and although it soon vanished, we're lucky enough to have some of its name records. Of the ninety-nine men who settled there, twenty-three were named John, fifteen Thomas, and ten William, plus a sprinkling of biblical names as well. On the *Mayflower,* there was a similar proportion of Johns, Williams, Edwards, and Richards, but also men named Resolved, Love, and Wrestling. (A boy born midvoyage was appropriately called Oceanus Hopkins.) In the later Massachusetts Bay Colony, 21 percent of the females were called Mary, 17 percent were Elizabeth, and 15 percent Sarah.

When it came time for the settlers to name their own children, a lot of these old traditional standards faded in favor of biblical names, from both the Old and New Testaments. The Good Book was scrutinized in the search for names of admirable figures, parents believing that such names could shape the character of their children. It was not unusual to find really extreme examples, like Eliphalet and Bezaleel, but the most commonly used by the Puritans and other colonists—most of which still sound righteous today—were:

GIRLS	BOYS
ABIGAIL	AARON
	ABIJAH
DEBORAH	
	BENJAMIN
ELIZA	
	DANIEL
HANNAH	DAVID
JEMIMA	EBENEZER
	ELIHU
LYDIA	ELIJAH
	EZEKIAL
MARTHA	
	GIDEON
RACHEL	
REBECCA	IRA
RUTH	ISAAC
SARAH	JEDEDIAH
SELAH	JONATHAN
SUSANNAH	JOSHUA
	MOSES
	NATHANIEL
	SAMUEL
	SETH
	SOLOMON

In their pursuit of ever-more upright, upstanding names, the Puritans went even further, choosing meaningful "virtue" names (for the most currently viable, see page 26), especially for girls. Some of the more radical names (to modern ears) were Desire, Love, Increased, Renewed, Silence, Humility, Fear, Experience, Hopewell, Mindwell, and Thankful—the last being among the commonest names given to New England girls before 1750.

Of course names varied from colony to colony. In Virginia, the settlers continued to follow British patterns, with two-thirds of the girls being called either Mary, Elizabeth (often recorded as Eliza), Sarah, or Anne. In New England it became a very common practice to name children after their parents—in one town 74 percent of firstborn daughters shared their mothers' names and 67 percent of the boys bore their fathers'.

Toward the end of the seventeenth century, there was an influx of European immigrants, who brought their native favorites with them, adding still more diversity to the pot. Among the German and Dutch contributions were Frederick, Johann, Mathias, and Veronica, while the Scots added a multitude of Andrews, Archibalds, Alexanders, and Duncans, the Welsh brought over such names as Owen and Hugh and the Irish imported Patrick and Patricia, among others.

One of the most significant developments of this time was the increased use of a middle name—by the turn of the eighteenth century, one in four Harvard students had one, whereas previously this had been a rarity. After the Revolutionary War, the wave of biblical names began to recede, replaced by such newly popular names as Charles, George, Frederick, Francis, and Augustus, and such imported royal names as Charlotte, Caroline, and Sophia, as well as a revival of the Robert-Henry-Edward breed.

The distinctively American custom, which continues to thrive today, of using surnames as first names, also took firm hold. Not only were family names moved into first place, but there was an expanded use of the surnames of both historical and contemporary notables for newborn boys. Some that came to the fore in the eighteenth and nineteenth centuries were:

BRADFORD	LEE
BRYAN	LINCOLN
CALHOUN	MARSHALL
CLAY	MASON
CLEVELAND	MAXWELL
CLINTON	MONROE
CORNELL	MORRIS
CURTIS	
	NELSON
DEXTER	
	OTIS
EVERETT	
	RANDOLPH
FRANKLIN	
	WARD
GRANT	WARREN
	WASHINGTON
HAYES	WAYNE
	WEBSTER
JACKSON	WESLEY
JEFFERSON	WINTHROP

Another trend of this time was the legitimizing of pet forms. Whereas boys and girls had for centuries been called by nicknames (in order to separate the large numbers of Johns, Marys, Margarets, etc. from one another), now those diminutives became the names with which they were christened. This led to an explosion of new girls' names, helping to even out the previously unbalanced numbers—between 1700 and 1750 there had been twice as many boys' names as girls', and three times more biblical names for boys. Among the newly sanctioned girls' names were:

ABBY	LUCY
ANNIE	LULU
BESS/BESSIE	
BETSY	MAISIE
BETTY	MAMIE
	MILLY
	MINNIE
CARRIE	MOLLY
DAISY	
	NANCY
ELSIE	NELL
HATTIE	PEGGY
	POLLY
JENNY	
JESSIE	
	SADIE
	SALLY
KITTY	
LETTY	WINNIE

The eighteenth century also saw upper-class parents taking an interest in Latinized forms of women's names. Mary was now as apt to be Maria, and names like Sophia, Anna, Juliana, and Cecilia came into widespread use.

NINETEENTH CENTURY

From the end of the eighteenth century, and into the nineteenth, parents began to favor boys names drawn from the classics (Homer, Horatio, Horace) and chivalrous-sounding Anglo-Saxon and Arthurian names (Arthur, Alfred, Harold, Edmund), with corresponding girls' names such as Enid, Elaine, Edith, Audrey, and Vivian. The Scottish names discovered in the novels of Sir Walter Scott also enjoyed a surge of popularity, heroic names like Kenneth, Donald, Ronald, Roland, Guy, Quentin, Roy, Douglas, and Bruce. Girls were often named after other romantic literary characters, including Beatrice, Agnes, Julia and Juliet, Lavinia, Rosalind, Clarissa, Gwendolyn, and Maud. Flower and other nature names began to come into fashion, such as Rose, Violet, Lily, Iris, Hazel, and Myrtle, as well as gem names like Pearl, Opal, and Ruby, not to mention the months April, May, and June. Another route to a broader base of girls' names was the feminization of male names. Enter Henrietta, Harriet, Georgia, Charlotte, Edwina, Josephine, Theodora, and others (for a more complete list, see page 218).

This was a period of increasingly widespread immigration, a fact reflected in the foreign input and influences on American names—although if a name became anything resembling a stereotype of a certain group, it soon tended to be avoided, as in the Irish examples of Pat and Mick (Patrick and Michael). This resonated in class distinctions as well—names considered to belong to servants, such as Nora and Bridget, were shunned by middle- and upper-class parents.

Other trends of the nineteenth century: Sons continued to be named for fathers, and there was a greatly accelerated use of the "Junior" form, as well as an even more prevalent use of middle names. This led to the flourishing of combined girls' names such as Marianne, Rosemary, Annabel, Pollyanna, and so on. Expanding populations, urban living, and a turning away from biblical names created a need for new names. For boys, one rich source proved to be the surnames of English and Scottish nobility, some examples of which were:

BARRY	CLARK
BRENT	CLIFFORD
	CRAIG
CHESTER	
CLARE	GRANT

HARVEY	SIDNEY
HERBERT	STANLEY
HOWARD	STUART
PERCY	

At this time, children had achieved an elevated importance in society and, consequently, more attention was now given to their names, with a decreased use of repeating the parents' or grandparents' name in favor of one that would be uniquely chosen for that child, a trend that would come into full bloom in our own century. The names that were most popular in the third quarter of the nineteenth century showed a variety of sources for the girls' names, while the boys' remained the old classics. These were, in order of popularity:

GIRLS	BOYS
MARY	WILLIAM
ANNA	JOHN
ELIZABETH	CHARLES
EMMA	HARRY
ALICE	JAMES
EDITH	GEORGE
FLORENCE	FRANK
MAY	ROBERT
HELEN	JOSEPH
KATHERINE	THOMAS

TWENTIETH CENTURY

All the movements mentioned above gradually coalesced in the present century to form an almost infinite number of names available to the prospective parent. At the turn of the century, the most popular list for males was virtually the same as it had been twenty-five years before, with the addition of Samuel and Arthur, but for girls there were several changes. Mary remained in first place, as it would until 1950, but there were new entries on the scene: Ruth, Margaret, Dorothy, Mildred, and Frances had now entered the Top Ten.

The 1920s and 1930s saw major shifts in the naming landscape. One of the hottest trends of this period was what can be thought of as freckle-faced-kid names, for both girls and boys. These were "Our Gang" comedy names that came complete with button noses and overbites. Many of them were nicknames for perennial favorites—Billy or Willie for William, for example, or Margie, Maggie, or Peggy for Margaret. For the first time, media stars were affecting baby naming, as in Jean, Marion, Norma, Myrna, Shirley, and Virginia. Other female fads included names ending in the letter *s* (Doris, Phyllis, Iris, Lois); and names with the suffix "een" or "ine"—Irish ones like Eileen, Pegeen, Maureen, Noreen, Kathleen, and Colleen, and more Gallic specimens such as Arlene, Nadine, Maxine, Pauline, and Marlene. Even more fashionably French were Annette, Paulette, Claudette, Jeanette, Georgette, and Nanette, not to mention Rochelle, Estelle, and Isabel.

In 1925, although the official top names for girls were Mary, Barbara, Dorothy, Betty, and Ruth, a more colloquial list of popular choices would be:

BETSY	PATSY
BINNIE	PEGGY
	PENNY
DOLLY	POLLY
GWEN	
	SALLY
KATHLEEN	
KITTY	TRUDY
MARY ANN	WINNIE

For boys, the usual Anglo-Saxon stalwarts still ruled the official popularity lists, but more representative of the period were:

BARNEY	FRANKLIN
	HAL
CALVIN	HOMER
CHESTER	
CLEM	MICKEY
DEXTER	NED
	WILBUR
ELMER	WILLIS

During the mid-thirties through the forties, some of the fustier-feeling names like Dorothy, Shirley, Ruth, George, Frank, Edward, and Clarence fell off the Top Ten, to be replaced by Carol, Judith, Joan, Ronald, David, and Linda, which, in 1948, would finally topple Mary from first place. Other new names were moving in as well, more sophisticated names for kids whose parents envisioned them triumphing over the Depression and growing up to wear glamorous gowns, drink martinis and use cigarette holders, and live in elegant Hollywood-inspired mansions. Television was still in a neonatal state, so no one could foresee that these would become the sitcom mom and dad names of the next generation:

GIRLS

ANITA	BERNICE
ARLENE	BEVERLY
AUDREY	

CYNTHIA	MARILYN
	MARJORIE
DEBORAH	
DIANE	NANCY
	NATALIE
ELAINE	NORMA
ELLEN	
	PAMELA
GAIL	PAULA
HELENE	RENEE
	RHODA
JANET	RITA
JILL	
JOANNE	SANDRA
JOYCE	SHEILA
	SUSAN
LOIS	SYLVIA
LORRAINE	
LYNN	ZELDA

BOYS

ALAN	GERALD
BARRY	HAROLD
	HARVEY
CARL	HOWARD
CHRISTOPHER	
	IRA
ELLIOT	
EUGENE	JOEL

KENNETH	PAUL
	PETER
	PHILIP
LAWRENCE	
	ROGER
	RUSSELL
MARTIN	
MICHAEL	STANLEY
MITCHELL	STEVEN
	VINCENT
NEIL	
NORMAN	WARREN

Post–World War II America was a time of bubbling optimism and a major baby boom that spawned a whole new generation of cuter, younger, glossier names for kids who would play with Betsy Wetsy dolls and watch *Howdy Doody*, oblivious to the treacherous times just past. These names reflected a collective lust for a new way of life, the good life in the sprawling suburbs. In 1948, Linda had leaped into the number-one spot for girls and Sharon and Karen were neck-and-neck at numbers nine and ten. The boys' list still showed Robert in top place, but Michael, a biblical name that had been out of favor for two hundred years, catapulted to second place, with other new names appearing including Gary, Dennis, Douglas, and Bruce.

The above were representative of what we call Beach Boy names, cool monikers that hit the shores in the late fifties and early sixties and were the personification of surfer machismo. These righteous dudes included:

BRAD	DARREN
BRIAN	DARRYL
	DEAN
	DENNIS
CHAD	
CRAIG	

DOUG	LANCE
DUANE/DWAYNE	
	RICK
GARY	
GLENN	
GREG	SCOTT
JEFF	TERRY
	TODD
KEITH	TROY
KEVIN	
KIRK	WAYNE

Some of the newly popular girls names of the fifties, many of which remained in vogue through the Kennedy administration, were:

AMY	JANICE
	JULIE
BRENDA	
	KIM
CHARLENE	LISA
CHERYL	
CHRISTINE	MICHELLE
	ROBIN
DARLENE	
DENISE	
DONNA	TERRY
	TINA
HEIDI	
HOLLY	WENDY

It was in the fifties that television began to have a great impact on names, first of all introducing a whole posse of long-forgotten western names like Jason, Joshua, and Jeremy (see page 104), and helping to make the American name supply ever-less regional in scope. An even greater name revolution came during the Age of Aquarius, when sexual stereotypes were being reexamined and dispelled as men grew their hair to their shoulders and women abandoned their bras, and names became equally androgynous. In deference to the then-current credo of "Do your own thing," new names were invented, familiar forms of old names became perfectly acceptable, and the spelling of traditional names became a contest of creativity: the Karens and Craigs gave way to Caryns and Chastitys, Kellys and Clouds. The ultimate trendy name of the sexually liberated sixties was actually a relaxed nickname name, preferably ambigender. We saw a lot of the following:

CANDY	MANDY
CAREY	MARCY
CASEY	MARNIE
CINDY	MINDY
COREY	
	RANDI
	RICKI/RICKY
JAMIE	
JESSE	
JODY	SHARI
JONI	SHELLY
	SHERRY
	STACY
KELLY	
KERRY	
	TAMMY
	TAWNY
LORI	TRACY

The sixties was also the era of invented hippie names, not so different from the people, place, nature, and word names that seem to be making a comeback right now (see page 36). Among those that seemed the grooviest for flower children were:

AMERICA	PEACE
	PHOENIX
BREEZE	
	RAIN
CHE	RAINBOW
CHINA	RIVER
CLOUD	
DAKOTA	SEAGULL
	SEQUOIAH
GYPSY	SKY
	SPRING
HARMONY	STAR
	STARSHINE
LEAF	SUMMER
LIBERTY	SUNSHINE
LIGHT	
	TRUE
MORNING	
OCEAN	WELCOME

The seventies saw not only a revival of pioneering American names (Annie, Becky, Jenny, Jessie, Katie, Maggie, Molly, Ethan, Jed, Jesse, Luke, Shane, Zane), but also biblical names like Adam, Aaron, Benjamin, Jacob, Samuel, Jonathan, Rachel, Rebecca, and Sarah were born again, even if the parents choosing them weren't. Those who didn't want to reach back to the frontier or the Bible for their roots looked to their own or other people's ethnic backgrounds for inspiration. Names derived from the Irish or French became particularly popular, even for parents who had no connection to those countries. Thus were born thousands of Erins, Kellys, Kevins, Megans, Ryans, Seans, Shannons, and Taras. For girls, the French twist was the rage, with names such as Danielle, Michelle (given a huge boost by the Beatles song), and Nicole.

Other little girls were liberated from female stereotypes with names previously reserved for effete upper-class gentlemen: Ashley, Blake, Brooke, Courtney, Kimberly, Lindsay, and Whitney. Similar in tone, though they had always been girls' names, were Tiffany and Hayley. At the opposite end of the scale was a group of girls' names as purely feminine as lavender sachet. These were the wildly popular Victorian valentine names, many of which would remain popular through the nineties, which included Alexandra, Alyssa, Amanda, Jennifer, Jessica, Melissa, Samantha, Vanessa, and Victoria, along with their male counterparts Justin, Brett, Alexander, and Nicholas.

And then came the eighties, the era of Yuppie-Gekko-greed, Reaganomics, Cabbage Patch Kids, and Calvins. It was also the decade of a new baby boomlet and of the first generation of mothers more likely to work outside the home than to stay home with their kids. Feminism made concrete, upward mobility, and a strong emphasis on image all conspired to influence naming trends of the era.

In 1980, Jennifer still reigned supreme. The Top Ten girls' names of that year formed a transitional bridge between the soul-searching seventies and the neoconservative Reagan-Bush era. They were:

1. JENNIFER

2. AMY

3. MELISSA

4. KIMBERLY

5. SARAH

6. MICHELLE

7. HEATHER

8. AMANDA

9. ERIN
10. LISA

By the middle of the decade, most of these names vanished from the Top Ten list. At decade's end, only the two most timeless—Sarah and Amanda, would remain. Other classic names, which evidenced the refined taste and traditional values prized in the decade, were restored, with legions of eighties babies named Katherine, Elizabeth, Emily, William, Daniel, Andrew, and Christopher. Working mothers and feminist dads sought in the eighties a different kind of naming equality from the previous decade's, giving both daughters and sons upwardly mobile androgynous names such as Jordan and Morgan and Alex and Blake. Ashley, one such name that emerged for children of both sexes during the seventies, enjoyed a meteoric rise for girls throughout the eighties, reigning at number one for much of the decade.

When the eighties and some of its more superficial values ended with a crash, several of its naming trends survived, with a decidedly nineties twist. The veneer of old money was replaced by a more solid emphasis on genuine family histories, with names that honored real ancestors rather than those that conjure up phony WASP pedigrees. Ethnic names and surnames, as well as place names and nonglitzy family names, became more fashionable than the slick choices of the eighties, directions we see continuing well into the millennium.

AFRICAN-AMERICAN NAMES: HISTORY AND TRADITION

Consider LaKeisha.

LaKeisha is a quintessential African-American name, one well-used by African-American parents for their children, but by virtually no one else, not white Americans, not Africans, not Europeans. It doesn't exist in any conventional naming dictionary, and many people, including name experts, believe it is made up. "Created," decrees one popular name book. Another incorrectly declares it a combination of "the popular La prefix" with Aisha, the name of Muhammad's favorite wife and one that's often used, in many variations, by African-American parents.

But most name books simply disregard LaKeisha, along with the entire subject of African-American names, as well as the thousands of names favored by African-Americans. Why? Ignorance plays a major role in the issue, with everyone from name scholars to African-American parents—and of course, most especially the general public—largely unaware of the history and traditions of African-American names. Not much has been written on the subject, and research has been spotty, confined to slave names, for instance, or modern African-American naming practices, but rarely considering the entire sweep of black naming history.

Thus, the misunderstanding of LaKeisha, a name that embodies many of the primary influences that have shaped African-American names over the centuries.

Take that "La" at the beginning. Hundreds of African-American names, male as well as female ones, start with "La," a practice that can be traced back to the vigorous Free Black community in nineteenth-century Louisiana, where the French "La" prefix was affixed to many names, first as well as last.

Keisha derives not from Aisha but from Keziah, a biblical name. Keziah was one of the daughters of Job—Jemima was another one—whose name was popular among slaves who adopted Christianity and favored Old Testament names. Although Puritans used the name Keziah, it was not widely used by Southern whites, which made it fair game for blacks.

This is key: The black naming tradition has always, in America, been separate from the white one, distinct in its references and choices. It is a tradition influenced by Africa, influenced by Europe and American whites, and, more recently, influenced by the Muslim culture. But it is, most dramatically, a tradition unto itself, uniquely African-American.

At the core of the African-American naming culture are

variety and invention. You can see that in LaKeisha: It takes something from here, something from there, shakes the spelling up a bit, to arrive at a name that's new and special. This diversity can be traced to the first Africans to arrive as slaves in America in the seventeenth and early eighteenth centuries. They arrived with African names but were immediately renamed by their new white masters. The first generation of African-American infants also tended to be named by the slave owners. Whites endeavored to give each of their slaves a unique name, one borne by no other slave on the plantation, in order to simplify work assignments and provision distribution. And they also looked for names that were not, by and large, used by the white community.

Some of the favorites of these early times were names from classical Greece and Rome. Southern plantation owners admired those ancient cultures, and fancied their own as being similar. Before 1800, classical names accounted for 20 percent of those given to slaves. While these are certainly noble names relating to heroic characters, the attitude of the slave owners in bestowing them, according to one scholar, may have been "whimsical, satiric or condescending in intent." Following are some of the most widely used classical names:

FEMALE

CLEOPATRA	MINERVA
DAPHNE	PHOEBE
DIANA	
DIDO	SAPPHO
FLORA	THISBE
JUNO	VENUS

MALE

ADONIS	JUPITER
AUGUSTUS	
	NERO
BACCHUS	
	POMPEY
CAESAR	PRIMUS
CATO	
CICERO	
CUPID	SCIPIO
HANNIBAL	TITUS
HECTOR	
HERCULES	VIRGIL

Because the slave owners needed a large pool of names, they allowed the continuation of some African names and naming practices, even though many accounts suggest they tended to be threatened by African names and traditions. In Colonial times, as many as 15 to 20 percent of slaves in the two Carolinas bore African names, most notably day names, which relate to the day of the week on which the person is born. Prior to 1750, according to the scholar John Inscoe, 14 percent of African-American babies were given pure African names at birth and 25 percent were given names influenced by African names. The West African day names were:

	Female	*Male*
SUNDAY	QUASHEBA	QUASHEE
MONDAY	JUBA	CUDJOE
TUESDAY	BENEBA	CUBBENAH
WEDNESDAY	CUBA	QUACO
THURSDAY	ABBA	QUAO

| FRIDAY | PHEBE/PHIBBI | CUFF/CUFFEE |
| SATURDAY | MIMBA | QUAME/KWAME |

Some of these names were changed to English cognates: Cudjoe to Joe, Quaco to Jack, Juba to Judy, Abba to Abby, Phebe to Phoebe. And then the entire day-naming tradition was translated into English, by slave owners and slaves alike. Names were chosen that signified days of the weeks, months of the year, and special holidays. Some Anglicized day names that were used, primarily for boys but for girls as well, include Monday, Friday, Christmas, Easter, March, and July.

Place names were also commonly used in early days for slaves, often signifying a site of importance to the slave owner but sometimes relating to a place meaningful to the African-American parents. Sometimes, in keeping with the African tradition of using an event of the day of the child's birth to inform the name choice, the place an important ship arrived from might dictate the name. Between 1720 and 1740, as many as one in four male slaves were given place names. The only ones noted for females were Carolina, Angola, and Cuba. The male choices from that time include:

ABERDEEN	GLASGOW
AFRICA	
ALBEMARLE	LONDON
AMERICA	
BALTIMORE	NORFOLK
BARBARY	
BOSTON	RICHMOND
CAROLINA	
CONGO	WILLIAMSBURG
CURRITUCK	WINDSOR
DUBLIN	YORK

Most avant-garde, to our twenty-first-century ears, were the word names used for and by African-Americans, signifying everything from virtues à la the Puritan naming tradition to weather. The use of these kinds of names relate to the African belief in the power of a name to shape personality or influence fate or impart a desirable quality, although some of them sound distinctly pessimistic. Some virtue and word names that have been recorded among early African-Americans are:

FEMALE

CHARITY	MOURNING
DIAMOND	OBEDIENCE
EARTH/EARTHA	
	PATIENCE
HONOR	PROVIDENCE
HOPE	
JEWEL	QUEEN
LOVE	TEMPERANCE

MALE

CALIFORNIA GOLD	HARDTIMES
DUKE	JUSTICE
FORLORN	KING
GOODLUCK	LOWLIFE

MAJOR	SQUIRE
MISERY	SUFFER
PLENTY	
PRINCE	VICE

EITHER

CHANCE	PLEASANT
FORTUNE	RAINY
FREEZE	STARRY
LIBERTY	STORMY

After 1800, two changes significantly altered African-American naming patterns. One was that many slaves had been in the United States for a generation or two, and began naming their own children, often using names of kin. This served to shrink the pool of names used as well as to reinforce family ties among African-Americans. Interestingly, blacks tended to name babies after grandparents, an African tradition, and also a way to extend a family's roots back to African forebears, while whites of the same period tended to name after parents first. Grandparents sometimes chose an infant's name, another African custom. The other major nineteenth-century change was the conversion of many blacks to Christianity, and their subsequent adoption of biblical names. For males, the use of biblical names doubled from 1720 to 1820, from 20 to 40 percent. Popular choices for both sexes included:

FEMALE

DELILAH	ESTHER
DORCAS	

HAGAR	RACHEL
HANNAH	REBEKAH
	RHODA
JEMIMA	
	TAMAR
KEZIAH	
LEAH	ZILPAH

MALE

ABEL	LAZARUS
CAIN	MOSES
ELIJAH	
EPHRAIM	NOAH
EZEKIEL	
	SAMSON
HEZEKIAH	SHADRACH
	SOLOMON
ISAAC	
ISAIAH	
ISHMAEL	ZACHARIAH

This move toward biblical names meant that blacks and whites now shared the same names more often than ever before, although African-American choices still tended to diverge from white ones. The use of the older "slave names"—the day names, place names, classical names—declined as biblical names rose to the fore, and when they were used it was as a kin name. After 1865, blacks often dropped names too closely identified with slavery, Pericles becoming Perry, Willie formalizing to William.

By the early part of the twentieth century, black and white names in America were as closely related as they would ever be. There were some similarities as well as some differences in popularity lists, but most significantly, roughly the same proportion of black and white children received one of the top names. During this period, in other words, African-Americans stayed as close to convention and chose from as narrow a selection of names as whites did.

Still, there were variations. A detailed survey of the most popular names given to black females in Augusta, Georgia, in 1937, shows many overlaps with the white popularity list of that time, but with more informal and familiar forms—Lillie instead of Lillian, for example, and Janie not Jane. These short forms reflect the black's subordinate position in society, according to more than one expert:

1.	MARY	12.	LOUISE
2.	ANNIE	13.	ELIZABETH
3.	MATTIE	14.	ELLA
4.	CARRIE	15.	JULIA
5.	ROSA	16.	LULA
6.	LILLIE	17.	LIZZIE
7.	EMMA	18.	MARIE
8.	MAMIE	19.	SUSIE
9.	HATTIE	20.	ALICE
10.	SARAH	21.	JANIE
11.	FANNY		

Black and white naming patterns began to widely diverge during the 1960s with the rise of Black Nationalism and ethnic identity. While for decades black parents had been more likely than whites to choose unique names for their children, in the sixties everyone's taste for individual names rose—but African-American parents' desire for one-of-a-kind names increased even more. During this period black parents began looking to Muslim and African names for their children, but also took the roots of those native names and made them their own. Perhaps more significantly, for names if not for black culture, this is when the full-blown trend toward invention began.

From 1973 to 1985 in New York, 31 percent of black girls and 19 percent of black boys were given unique names—names that were not used for any other child of their sex and race in that state and that year—according to data collected by Stanley Lieberson, a sociology professor at Harvard. Similarly, in 1989 in Illinois, 29 percent of African-American girls and 16 percent of boys received unique names, according to another study by Lieberson. Although no newer data have been published, our guess is that those numbers have only increased with time.

For whites, the tendency to choose unique names drops off as the child's mother's education rises, according to Lieberson. But for blacks, the mother's education does not affect the chances that she'll choose an individual name for her child. African-American mothers of varying educational levels, says Lieberson, tend to choose names more similar to each other than do white mothers of the same education level. "Race," says Lieberson, "is a more powerful influence than class on the naming of children." The race effect is strongest on girls' names: roughly twice as significant as on boys' names, which tend to overlap more in popularity.

POPULAR AFRICAN-AMERICAN NAMES

Many African-American parents draw from the general pool of names for their children, and indeed many of the same names—Taylor and Ashley for girls, for instance, and Christopher and Michael for boys—are most popular for children of all races. Some African-American parents give their children African or Muslim names, or at least names that have their roots in those cultures: The enormously popular Ayeesha in all its variations, for instance, comes from Aisha, the name of Muhammad's favorite wife.

But there is another group of names that can be considered truly African-American, names that spring uniquely from the tradition and culture of blacks in America and that are widely used by black parents today. Among these are names with historical antecedents in the African-American community: Keisha, for instance, embodies both the biblical slave and New Orleans Free Black traditions as detailed earlier. Malik, a stylish boy's name, relates to the Muslim name and also bears a phonetic resemblance to the extraordinarily popular (for all races) Michael as well as to Malcolm. Some African-American names relate to black pride: Ebony and Raven, for instance. Others are associated with black celebrities: Jada, for example, as in Pinkett Smith, and Tyra, as in supermodel Banks. Nia relates to one of the days of Kwanzaa.

Then there are names that are used differently by African-American parents than by those of other races. Among whites, for instance, Jordan is more popular for girls than for boys, but for black parents in Texas Jordan was the number-three name for *boys*, certainly due to the popularity and masculine appeal of Michael Jordan. Educator Marcus Garvey has inspired thousands of namesakes, making his first name one of the most popular for boys in the African-American community. Other names more popular for boys among black parents than white parents include Xavier, Cameron, Darius, Isaiah, Elijah, Jeremiah, Derrick, Adrian, André, and Desmond.

For girls, the list is longer. Jasmine is the number-one name for African-American girls in Texas, for example, but much further down on the list for white girls. Other names black parents like more than white parents do: Dominique, Brianna/Breanna, Destiny, Asia, Mariah, Desirée, Felicia, Alexandria (as opposed to Alexandra), Andrea, and Angel.

And then there are names that white parents favor that African-American parents reject. For girls, notable examples in this category include Emily, Sarah, Hannah, Samantha, Madison, Elizabeth, and the Katelyns. For boys, they include Austin, Andrew, Alexander, Benjamin, and Thomas.

One interesting thing about the differences between the white and black popularity lists is that, in many ways, African-Americans start the naming trends that whites adopt much later. Because creativity is more accepted among African-Americans for baby names, several trends only now clicking in among white parents—toward invented names, for instance, and place names and more unusual Old Testament names—have been well-established among black parents for years.

But the most widespread and enduring overall African-American naming tradition is diversity and invention. Many names that might be considered African-American are, by their very definition, unique, and so difficult to corrall onto a list. But here is a selection of African-American favorites:

GIRLS

AALIYAH	EBONY
ALEXANDRIA	
ALEXIA	
ALONDRA	IMANI
ANDREE	INFINITY
ANGEL	IVORY
ASIA	
	JADA
CAMIKA	JAKEISHA
CHANDRA	JALEESA
CHANELLE	JAMAICA
CHANTAL	JAMEEKA
CHARISMA	JASMINE
CHARLAYNE	
CHARLISE	
CHARMIAN	KALINDA
CHERISE	KATIAH
	KATRINA
DANICA	KENDRA
DASHAY	KESHIA
DEJA	KIANA
DESIREE	KIARA/KIERA
DESTINY	KIERRA
DIAMOND	KYESHA

LaKEISHA
LaSHAUNA
LaTEISHA
LaTOYA
LETONYA

MARQUISHA/
  MARKEESHA
MIATA
MISHAYLA

NAKARI
NASHIRA
NIA
NIARA

PRINCESS

RASHANDA
RASHIDA
RAVEN

SABRIELLE
SAMISHA
SARONDA
SHAKEISHA

SHAKIRA
SHALISA
SHANAY
SHANIQUA
SHANISE
SHEVON/CHEVONNE

TAISHA
TAMIKA
TAMISHA
TANISHA
TASHAWNA
TAWANNA
TIA
TIARA
TYRA

VALETTA

XAVIERA

YASMIN

ZELEKA
ZORA

BOYS

ALIKA
ANDRÉ
ANTAWN/ANTON
ANTWON

ARIES
ASHANTE

BRAWLEY
BRYANT

CLAYTON	KADEEM
	KAMAR
DAMON	KENDRICK
DANTE	KESHAWN
DARION	KYAN
DARIUS	
DARNELL	LAMAR
DASHAWN	
DEION	MALIK
DENZEL	MARCUS
DERRICK	MARIUS
DESMOND	MARQUIS
DEVIN	MONTEL
	MORGAN (for boys;
	whites use this more
ELIJAH	often for girls)
GERMAINE/	
JERMAINE	NILE
GERVAISE	
	ORION
HARLEM	ORLANDO
	OTIS
IMARI	
ISAAC	PRINCE
ISAIAH	
ISHMAEL	QUINCY
JAHAN	RASHAUN
JALEEL/JALIL	REGINALD
JAMAD	
JAMAR	SHAMAR
JAMEL	SHAQUILLE
JARREL	SHAUN/SHAWN
JAYLON	SHEMAR
JUWAN	STERLING

TARIQ	TEVIN
TARON	TYRONE
TARRYL	
TAUREAN	
TERRIL/TYRELL	XAVIER

MUSLIM/ARABIC NAMES

Muslim names usually derive from those of the Prophet Muhammad, his descendants or immediate family. There are five hundred variations of the name Muhammad itself; taken together they become the most common boy's name in the world. Other popular Arabic names, such as Karim and Kamil, represent the ninety-nine qualities of God listed in the Koran.

Many African-Americans have adopted the Muslim religion and taken Arabic or Muslim names. Notable examples include Muhammad Ali, Kareem Abdul-Jabbar, and playwright Imamu Amiri Baraka. But even non-Muslim blacks sometimes use Arabic names, in their original form or as the basis for an invented variation.

GIRLS

ABIDA	ATIFA
ABIR	AYASHA
ADARA	AZA
ADIVA	AZIZA
AISHA	
AKILAH	
ALAIA	BARAKA
ALIYA	BATHSIRA
ALMIRA	
ALTAIR	CALA
AMINA	
AMIRA	FAIZAH
ARA	FATIMA

GHALIYA

HABIBAH
HAFSAH/HAFZA
HAMIDA
HANIFA
HATIMA
HINDA

IAMAR
IMAN

JAMILA
JENA
JINAN

KALIFA
KALILA
KAMILAH
KARIDA
KARIMA
KHADIJA
KHALIFA

LAILA
LEILA
LOELIA
LUJAYN

MAJIDAH
MARIAM
MOUNA

NABILA
NAILA
NAIMA
NEDIRA
NIMA
NUMA
NUR

OMA

RADIAH
RAJA
RAZIYA
RIDA
RIHANA
RIMA

SABA
SADIKA
SADIRA
SAFIA
SAHAR
SAHARA
SALIHA
SALIMA
SALMA
SAMIRA
SAMYA
SANA/SANNA
SHADIYA
SHAFIQA
SHAHAR
SHARIFA

TABINA	YAMINA
TALIBA	YASMEEN
TAMASHA	
	ZADA
	ZAHIRA
ULIMA	ZULEIKA

BOYS

ABDUL	HAMID
ABDULLAH	HANA
AFIF	HANIF
AHMAD/AHMED	HASHIM
AKBAR	HASSAN
AKIL	HUSAIN
ALI	
ALLAH	IBRAHIM
AMIR	
ARNAN	JAFAR
AZIZ	JAMIL
	JUMAH
BAHIR	
BILAL	KADAR
	KAMALI
DAWUD	KAMIL
	KARIM
FARID	KASIM
FARRAN	
FAYSAL	MALIK
	MEHMET
HAKEEM	MUHAMMAD
HALIMA	
HAMAL	NURI

OMAR	TAHIR
RAFI	YASIR
RAHMAN	YAZID
RAMI	
RASHID	ZAKI
SADIK	
SALIM	
SHARIF	

AFRICAN NAMES

African names used by black American parents are drawn from a wide range of languages and cultures, from Swahili to Bintu, from Ethiopian to South African. Here is a selection of names that fit well into the American culture:

GIRLS

ABBA	AYANA
ABEBA	AZMERA
ABEBI	
ABINA/ABENA	
ADA	BINTA
AFRIKA	
AFYA	CAMISHA
AKINA	CHINAKA
AKUA	CHINARA
ALITASH	
AMARA	DALILA
AMINATA	DAURA
ARUSI	DAYO
ASHAKI	
ASMINA	
ASURA	EFIA

FANA	NADIFA
FAYOLA	NANTALE
	NAYO
HASINA	NEEMA
	NIA
IMAN	NKEKA
ISSA	NOBANZI
JAHA	ONI
JANI	OZORO
KAHINA	PANYA
KAMARIA	
KANIKA	RAMLA
KATURA	
KAYA	
	SALAMA
LATEEFAH	SANURA
LISHAN	SHANI
LULU	SUMA
MAKINA	TABIA
MARIAMA	TARANA
MARJANI	TISA
MASIKA	
MONIFA	ZUWENA

BOYS

ABASI	ATSU
ADOM	AZIBO
AKONO	AZIZI
ANKOMA	

BENO	MANU
BOMANI	MAZI
	MONGO
	MUSA
CHUMA	
	OBASI
EBO	ODION
	OJO
HANISI	OMARI
	PAKI
JABARI	
JAHI	
JELANI	RAFIKI
JIMIYU	RAJABU
JUMA	ROBLE
	RUNAKO
KALEB	SIMBA
KALUME	
KAMUZU	
KITO	TABAN
KOJO	TANO
KWAMI	
KWASI	YULISA
	ZAHUR
LABAAN	ZANI
LEBNA	ZURI

ERICA TO ERYKAH

Long before Afrocentric R&B chanteuse Erykah Badu made a big name for herself . . . she was known as Erica Wright. "I didn't want to have the slave name anymore," says Badu . . . "So I changed the spelling of my first name because the 'kah' is Kemetic [ancient Egyptian] for 'the inner self.' "

—PEOPLE

NAMES FROM ACROSS THE OCEAN

Let's say your roots are Italian and you'd like to give your child a name that reflects your ethnic heritage, but want to go beyond names like Maria and Mario to find others that reflect the expressive beauty of the Italian language. What we offer here is a greatly expanded, much wider variety of choices from primarily European cultures, ranging from names that have long been familiar in this country, such as the French Madeleine and Marguerite, say, to bolder, more original choices like Manon and Musette. For lists of names that are currently most popular in these countries, see pages 268 and 278.

CELTIC NAMES

Celtic names are, as a group, among the most appealing to parents today. But pronunciations can be pesky. Here, we offer wide-ranging lists of names native to Ireland, Scotland, and Wales, with pronunciation guides where pertinent.

SCOTTISH NAMES

GIRLS

AILSA (*AYL-sa*)

AINSLEE

ALEXINA

AMABEL

AMILIA

ANNELLA

BARABAL

BETHIA

BEVIN

CAIT

CAITRIONA, CATRIONA
 (*Ka-TREE-nuh*)

DAVINA

EILIDH (*I-lee*)

ELSPETH

EUNA

FINELLA/FENELLA

FLORA

GREER

IONA

ISLA

ISOBEL/ISHBEL

JACOBINA

JAMESINA

KEITHA

KENNA

KIRSTY

KYLA

LILEAS/LILIAS

LORNA

MAIRI (*MAH-ree*)

MAURA

MOIRA (*MOY-ra*)

MUIREALL (*MOOR-uh-yel*)

NAIRNE

NESSA

ROWENA

SEONA (*SHAW-nuh*)

SHEENA

SHONAH

SILE (*SHEE-luh*)

SINE (*SHEE-nuh*)

SORCHA (*SOHR-ra*)

THEODOSIA

TRIONA

BOYS

ADAIR
ALASDAIR
ANGUS
ARCHIBALD

BAIRD
BLAIR

CALUM/CALLUM
CAMERON
CAMPBELL
COLIN
CONALL
COSMO
CRAIG

DOUGAL (*doo-UHL*)
DUFF
DUNCAN

EWAN/EUAN

FARQUHAR
FERGUS
FIFE
FINLAY
FRASER

GAVIN
GEORDIE
GILLEAN (*GILL*-yan)

GORDON
GRAHAM
GREGOR
GUINN

HAMISH

IAIN (*EE-ayn*)
INNES
IVAR/IVOR

JOCK

KEIR
KEITH
KYLE

LACHLAN
LAIRD
LENOX
LOGAN

MACAULEY
MacDONALD
MAGNUS
MALCOLM
MANIUS
MUIR
MUNGO
MUNRO

NAIRNE	SEAMUS *(SHAY-muhs)*
NIALL	SIM
NINIAN	STEWART/STUART
PADRUIG *(PA-trik)*	TAVIS/TAVISH
ROSS	UILLEAM

IRISH NAMES

GIRLS

AILIS *(AY-lish)*	LAOISE *(LEE-sha)*
AINE *(AWN-ya)*	
AISLING *(ASH-ling)*	MAEVE *(MAYV)*
AOIFE *(EE-fah)*	MAIRE *(MAH-ree)*
AUGUSTEEN	MAJELLA
	MAOLIOSA *(Ma-LEE-sah)*
BIDELIA	MELLA
	MUIREANN *(MEER-an)*
CATRIONA *(Kat-REE-na)*	
CIARA *(KEER-ra)*	
CLODAGH *(KLOH-da)*	NIAMH *(NEE-av)*
DARINA	ORLA
DEIRDRE	
	ROISIN *(Roh-SHEEN)*
EABHA *(AY-va)*	
EITHNE *(ETH-na)*	SAOIRSE *(SEER-sha)*
	SILE *(SHEE-la)*
FIONNUALA *(Fin-NOO-la)*	SINE *(SHEEN-ah)*
	SINEAD *(Shin-AID)*
GRANIA *(GRAW-nyah)*	SIOBHAN *(Shi-VAUN)*
	SORCHA *(SOR-ra)*
ISEULT *(EE-sult)*	
JUNO	TALULLA

BOYS

AENGUS, AONGHUS *(EYN-gus)*

AIDAN *(AY-dan)*

ALASTAR

AODH *(AY)*

BRAN *(Brawn)*

CHRISTIE

CIAN *(KEE-an)*

CIARAN *(KEER-an)*

COLM, COLUM *(KUHL-uhm)*

CONNERY

CONNOR, CONOR

DIARMAID *(DEER-mit)*

DONAGH *(DUN-a)*

EAMON *(AY-mun)*

ENEAS *(Ey-NEY-as)*

EOIN *(OH-in)*

FAOLAN *(FEH-lan)*

FARQUHAR *(FAR-har)*

FARRY

FINN

FINNIAN

IVAR

JARLATH

KEIR *(Care)*

KIERAN

KILLIAN

LIAM

LORCAN

MICHEAL *(MEE-haul)*

NIALL *(NEE-al)*

ORAN *(OH-ran)*

OWNY

PADRAIG *(PAWD-rig)*

QUINLAN

RIAN *(REE-an)*

RIORDAN *(REER-dawn)*

SEANAN *(SHAW-nawn)*

SEARLAS *(SHAR-las)*

SEOIRSE *(SHORE-sha)*

SIVNEY

SORLEY

TIERNAN *(TEAR-nan)*

UILLIAM *(OOL-yuhm)*

UINSEANN *(IN-sun)*

WELSH NAMES

GIRLS

AELWYN, AYLWYN
AERON (AY-ron)
ANEIRA
ANWEN
ARDDUN
ARIANELL (ah-ree-AHN-elh)
ARIENWEN (ah-ree-AHN-wen)
AURON (AYR-on)

BETHAN (BETH-an)—a
popular Welsh nickname
for Elizabeth
BRANWEN, BRONWEN,
BRONWYN
BRIALLEN
BRYN, BRYNN

CATRIN (KAHT-rin)
CORDELIA

DELYTH
DILYS (DIL-iss)
DWYN

ELERI (EL-eh-ree)

FFION, FFIONA (Fee-on, fee-OH-nah)
FFLUR (FLEER)

GLENYS, GLYNIS
GWENIVERE
GWENLLIAN
GWYNETH

IOLA (YOH-lah)

LLEULU (HLYOO-loo)
LLINOS

MARGED (MAHR-ged)
MORWENNA

NERYS (NER-iss)
NESTA
NIA

OLWEN (AHL-wen)

RHIAN (RHEE-an)
RHIANNON (Rhee-AHN-nun)
RHONWEN

SIAN (SHAN)

TEGAN (TEG-ahn)

VENETIA

WALLIS
WINNE

BOYS

AED *(AYD)*
AEDDON *(AYD-un)*
ALUN

BEVAN
BRAN

CADOC *(KAHD-oc)*
CAI *(kay)*
CELYN *(KEL-in)*
CIAN *(KEE-an)*
COLLEN

DAFYDD *(DAH-vith)*
DEWI

ELIAN
EMLYN
EVAN

GARETH
GLYN
GRIFFITH
GWILYM *(GWIL-im)*

HEW *(HYOO)*

IAGO
IEUAN *(YAY-un)*
IOLO *(YOH-loh)*
IVOR

JEVAN

LLEWELLYN, LLYWELYN
LLIO

MORGAN

NYE

OWAIN, OWEN, EWAN

PADRIG *(PAHD-rig)*
PRYS *(PREES)*

RHYS

SIARL *(Sharl)*
SION *(SHON)*
SULIEN *(SIL-yen)*

TEILO *(TAY-loh)*
TREFOR *(TREV-ohr)*

DUTCH NAMES

GIRLS

ANNEKE
ANOUK

BEATRIX

DEMI

ELINE
ELISABETH
EVA

FEMKE
FRANCISCA

GERDA
GREET/GRETA

IRIS

JOHANNA
JULIANA

KATRYN
KLARA/KLAARTJE

LOTTE

MARGARETE/MARGRIET
MARIEKE

NAOMI

ROMY

SANNE
SASKIA
SOFIE

TESSA

VALENTYN

WILHELMINA

BOYS

ADRIAAN/ADRIAEN
ANDRIES
ANTON
ANTONIUS

BART
BAS
BENEDIKT
BRAM

CASPAR

CLAUS

COOS

CORNELIS/CEES

DAAN

DIDERIK/DIEDERIK

DIRK

FLORIS

FRANS

FREDERIK

GASPAR

GEERARD

GEERD

GERRIT

HANS

HENDRIK

IZAAK

JAAP

JACOBUS/COBUS

JAKOB

JAN

JEROEN

JOHANNES

JOOP

JOOST

JOREN

JORIS

JURGEN

JUSTUS

KAREL

KEES

KLAAS

LARS

LAURENS

LUCAS

MAARTEN/MARTIJN

MATHYS

MAX

MENNO

NIELS

NIKOLAAS/NICOLAES

OTTO

PIETER/PIET

REIGNIER

ROBIN

RUBEN

RUTGER

SANDER

SEBASTIAAN/BAS

SIMON

TON

WILLEM

FRENCH NAMES

France has a strict name law instituted under Napoleon, which calls for Christian children to get saints' names, Jewish children to receive Old Testament names, and all children to receive names that will not make them the subject of ridicule. But things seem to be getting somewhat lax of late. Two of the trendiest names: Oceane (yes, like Ocean) for girls and Zinnedine, after the hottest 1998 World Cup soccer player, for boys.

GIRLS

ABELIA
ADELINA
ADRIENNE
AIMÉE
ALAINE
ALBANE
ALEXANDRINE
ALIZÉE
AMANDINE
AMÉLIE
ANABELLE
ANAÏS
ANGE
ANGÉLIQUE
ARABELLE
ARIANE
ARLETTE
AUDINE
AURÉLIE
AURORE

BERNADETTE
BERNADINE

BERTHILDE
BERTILLE
BIBIANE
BLANCHE/BLANCHETTE
BRIGITTE

CAMILLE
CECILE
CELESTE
CERISE
CHANTAL
CHRISTIANE
CLAIRE
CLARICE
CLAUDE
CLÉMENTINE
CLOTHILDE
COLETTE
COLOMBE
CORINNE

DELPHINE

DOMINIQUE

DYNA

EDWIGE

ELIANE

ELODIE

ELOISE

ELORIANE

ÉMILIE

EUGÉNIE

EULALIE

FABIENNE

FELICITÉ

FERNANDE

FLEUR

FRANCE

FRANÇOISE

GABRIELLE

GENÈVE

GENEVIÈVE

GEORGETTE

GERMAINE

HÉLOISE

INDRA

ISABELLE/ISABEAU

JOËLLE

JOSETTE

JULIENNE

LAURE

LAURENCE

LÉA

LÉONIE

LIANNE

LILIANE

LISETTE

LOURDES

LUCIENNE

LYDIE

MADELEINE

MAELYS

MAEVA

MANON

MARGUERITE

MARINE

MARJOLAINE

MARTHE

MARTINE

MATHILDE

MAUDE

MAXIME

MELICE

MELISSANDE

MICHELINE

MIGNON

MIRABELLE

MIREILLE

MONIQUE

MORGANE

MUSETTE

NICOLETTE

NOËLLE

NOEMIE

OCEANE
ODETTE
ODILE
ORIANNE
ORLEANE

PATRICE
PHILIPPINE

RACHELLE
RÉBEQUE
REINE
ROMAÏNE

SABINE
SALOMÉ
SANDRINE

SÉRAPHINE
SIDONIE
SIMONE
SOLANGE
SOLENE
SYLVIE

TENILLE
THOMASINE

VANINE
VENISE
VÉRONIQUE
VIOLETTE

ZÉNOBIE
ZOÉ

BOYS

ADALARD
ADRIEN
ALAIN
ALEXANDRE
ALUIN
AMBROISE
AMÉDÉE
ANATOLE
ANDRÉ
ANSELME
ANTOINE
ANTONIN
APPOLINAIRE
ARISTIDE

ARMAND
AUBERT
AUGUSTE

BAPTISTE
BARDIOU
BARTHÉLMY
BASILE
BASTIEN
BAUDIER
BELLAMY
BENOÎT
BLAISE

CÉSAR	JACQUES
CHRISTOPHE	JÉRÉMIE
CLAUDE	JOURDAIN
CLÉMENT	JULIEN
CONSTANTINE	
CORENTIN	LAURENT
CORNEILLE	LAZARE
	LÉO
DAMIEN	LUC
DENYS	LUCIEN
DIDIER	
DION	MARC
	MARIUS
ÉMILE	MATHURON
ÉTIÉNNE	MATTHIEU
	MAXIME
FABIEN	MELCHIOR
FABRICE	MICHEL
FÉLIX	
FLORIAN	ODILON
FRANÇOIS	OLIVIER
FRÉDÉRIC	
	PASCAL
GASPARD	PATRICE
GASTON	PHILIPPE
GAUTIER	PIERRE
GEORGES	PROSPER
GERMAIN	
GRÉGOIRE	QUENTIN
GUILLAUME	
GUY	RAINIER
	RAOUL
HENRI	RAPHAEL
HERVÉ	REMI/REMY
HONORÉ	ROMAIN

SÉBASTIEN	VIRGILE
SERGE	
SILVAIN	
	YANIS
TANCRÈDE	YOHAN
TANGUY	YVES
THÉOPHILE	
THIBAULT	
THIERRY	ZINNEDINE

GERMAN NAMES

GIRLS

AGNA	ELKE
ALOISA/ALOISIA	EMELIE
AMALIA/AMALIE	EVA
ANGELIKA	
ANJA	
ANNELIESE	FLORENTIA
ANTONIA	FRANZISKA
	FREYA
	FRIDA
BERTITA	FRITZI
BIANKA	
BIRGITTE	
BRIGITTA	GERDA
	GERTA
CAROLA	GISELA/GISELLE
CHRISTA	GRETA
CONSTANZA	GRETCHEN
CORINNA	
	HANNE/HANNI
EBBA	HEIDI
ELEONORE	HELGA

ILSA/ILSE	MATHILDE
IMMA	MINA
INGE	MINNA
	MITZI
JACOBINE	MONIKA
KÄETHE	OTTILIE
KAMILLA	
KARLOTTE	RENATE
KATJA	ROLANDA
KLARISSA	
KLEMENTINE	STEPHANINE
KORINNA	SYBILLA
KORNELIA	
KRISTIANA	TILDA
	TRINE
LENI	
LILI/LILLI	ULLA
LIN	URSULA
LORELEI	UTA
LUCIE	
LUISE	VERONA
LUZI	VERONIKE
MAGDA	WILHELMINA
MAGDALENE	
MARGRETE	ZELLA
MARTHE	ZITA

BOYS

ABALARD	FRANZ
ALARIC	FRIEDERICH
ALBRECHT	FRITZ
ALOIS	
ANDREAS	
ANSELM	GEORG
ANTON	GOTTFRIED
ARIUS	GREGOR
ARNO	GÜNTHER/GÜNTER
AUGUST	GUSTAV
AXEL	
	HANS
BALTHASAR	HASSO
BENEDIKT	HEINRICH
BENNO	HELMUT
BRUNO	HORAZ
	HORST
CASPAAR	HUGO
CLAUS	
CLEMENS	
	JAKOB
	JOHANN/JOHANNES
DIETER	JOSEF
DIETRICH	JURGEN
DOMINIK	JUSTUS
EGON	
EMIL	KASIMIR
ERICH	KASPAR
	KLEMENS
FABER	KONRAD
FELIX	KONSTANTIN
FLORIAN	KURT

LORENZ
LOTHAR
LUKAS

MAGNUS
MARIUS
MARKUS
MATTHAEUS/MATHIAS
MAX
MELCHIOR

NIKOLAUS

OSKAR
OTTO

RAINER
ROLF
RUPERT

SANDER
STEFAN

THADDAUS
THEOBOLD
TOMAS

ULF

VALENTINE
VIKTOR
VINCENS

WALDO
WERNER
WILHELM
WOLFGANG/WOLF

ZEPHYRIN

GREEK NAMES

GIRLS

ACACIA
ACANTHA
ADELPHA
AEOLA
ALETHIA
ALIDA
ALPHA
ALTHAIA
ALYSIA

ANATOLA/ANATOLIA
ANEMONE
ANTHEA
ARIADNE
ARTEMIS
ASTA
ATHENA

BASILA

CALANDRA	LALIA
CALANTHA	LARISSA
CALISTA	LEANDRA
CALLA	LELIA
CASSIA	LYDIA
CHLOE	
CLIO	MAIA
COSIMA	MELANTHA
CRESSIDA	MELINA
CYNARA	
	NEOLA
DAMARA/DAMARIS	NEOMA
DELIA	NERISSA
DELPHINE	
DEMETRIA	ODESSA
DIANTHA	OLYMPIA
DORCAS	
	PALLAS
ECHO	PANDORA
ELECTRA/ELEKTRA	PENELOPE
ELENA/ELENI	PHAIDRA
EUDOCIA	PHOEBE
EUDORA	
EUGENIA	RHEA
EULALIA	
	SABA
GAEA	
	THADDEA
IANTHE	THALASSA
IOANNA	THALIA
	THEA
KALLIOPE	THEODORA
KORA	THEODOSIA
KOREN	THEONE

XANTHE
XENIA

ZELIA
ZENOBIA
ZITA
ZOE

BOYS

ALEXANDROS
ALEXIOS
ANDREAS
ARGOS
ARISTEDES
ARSENIOS
ARTEMAS

BARNABAS
BASIL

CHRISTIANO
CHRISTOS
CLAUDIOS
CLETUS
CONSTANTINE
COSMO/KOSMOS
CYRIAN

DAMIANOS
DARIUS
DEMETRI/DEMETRIOS

ELIAS

GEORGIOS
GREGORIOS

HOMER

ILIAS
IONNES

KRISTIAN

LEANDER
LOUKAS

MARKOS
MATTHIAS
MAXIMOS

NEMO
NICO/NIKO/NIKOS
NIKODEMUS

ORION

PERICLES
PETROS
PHILO
PLATO

SANDROS
STAMOS

STAVROS	VASILIS
STEPHANOS	
	ZENO
THANOS	
THEODOROS	
TITOS	

ITALIAN NAMES

Italian baby-naming books do not merely offer a list of names and root meanings. Rather, each name comes with a detailed character analysis as well as lucky days, numbers, colors, and gems. Names are almost like minihoroscopes. Name your son Enzo, for instance, and you're sure to get a boy who's sweet and romantic, who loves music and art; a Martino will be prudent and economic.

GIRLS

ALESSIA	FABRIZIA
AMALIA	FLAVIA
AMBRA	
ANTONELLA	
ARIANNA	GIANNA
	GIOIA
	GIOVANNA
CANDIDA	GRAZIANA
CHIARA	
CLELIA	
	ILARIA
	ISOTTA
DANILA	
DONATA	
	LIA
	LILIANA
ELETTRA	LUCA
EMILIANA	LUCIA

MADDALENA	PALMA
MARCELLA	PETRONILLA
MARZIA	PIA
	RAFFAELA
NICOLETTA	RENATA
NOEMI	ROMANA
	ROSARIA
ODILIA	
ORIANA	VIOLETTA

BOYS

ADAMO	GIACOMO
ALDO	GIANNI
AMEDEO	GIORGIO
ANSELMO	GIUSEPPE
ARTURO	GUIDO
AURELIO	
	LEONARDO
BERNARDO	LORENZO
CARLO	
CESARE	MARCO
COSIMO	MARIO
	MATTEO
DOMENICO	
	ORAZIO
ELIO	OTTAVIO
ENZO	
ERASMO	
	PAOLO
FRANCESCO	PIETRO

RAOUL	UMBERTO
ROCCO	
RUGGERO	VITO

TEO

SCANDINAVIAN NAMES
GIRLS

AGATA	EBBA
AGNA	EDDA
AGNETHE/AGNETA	ELISABET
AMMA	ELKE
ANNELI	ELSE
ANNELIESE	ESTER
ANNIKA	
ANTONIA	FREJA/FREYA
ARNA	
ASA	GALA
ASTA	GERDA
ASTRID	GUDRUN
AUDNY	GUNILLA
	GUNN
BARBRO	
BENEDIKTA	HANNA
BERIT	HEDDA
BIRGIT	HEDVIG
BRITT	HELGE
	HJORDIS
CARINA	
	IDONY
DAGMAR	INGA/INGE
DAGNY	INGER
DISA	INGRID

JAKOBINE

JANA

JANNIKE

JENSINE

KAREN/KARIN/
  KARENA

KARITA

KAROLINA

KERSTIN

KLARA

KOLINA

KRISTINA

LAILA

LENA

LINNEA

LIS

LIV

LOVISA

MAI

MAJ

MAJA

MALENA

MARGIT

MARGRETA

MARIT

MARKETTA

MARNA

MÄRTA

MERETE

META

MIA

MONIKA

NANNA

NEA

ODA

OLA

OLEA

PELLA

PERNILLA

PETRINE

PIA

RAGNA

RAKEL

RUNA

SANNA

SIGNY

SIGRID

SILJA

SIV

SOFI/SOFIA/SOFIE

SOLVEIG

SONJA

SUNNIVA

SVANNI

SVEA

TEKLA

THORA

TILDA/TILDE

TYRA

ULLA

ULRIKA

URSULA

VALESKA

VANJA

VERONIKA

VIKTORIA

VILMA

VITA

VIVEKA/VIVECA/
 VIVICA

VOR

BOYS

AKSEL

ALVIS

ANDERS

ANDOR

ANDREAS

ANTERO

ARI

ARNE

ARVID

ASMUND

AUDUN

AXEL

BARDO

BARTHELEMY

BASILIUS

BENEDIKT

BJØRN

BO

BORJE

CHRISTER

CLAES/CLAUS

DAG

EDVARD

EERO

EETU

EILIF

EIRIK

ELOF/ELOV

EMIL

ERIK

ESAIAS

EYOLF

FINN

FREDERIK/FREDRIK

GEORG

GERD

GJORD

GORAN

GREGER/GREGERS

GUNNAR/GUNDER

GUNTHER

GUSTAV

HAAKON/HAKAN/
HAKEN
HAGEN
HALLE
HALSTEN
HANNU
HARALD
HEMMING
HENRIK
HILLEVI

IB
INGEMAR/INGMAR
ISAK
IVAR/IVOR

JAKOB
JARL
JENS
JOHAN
JORAN
JØRGEN
JORN
JOSEF

KAARLE
KAI/KAJ
KALLE
KARL
KLEMENS
KNUT/KNUTE
KONRAD
KONSTANTIN
KORT
KRISTOFFER

LARS
LASSE
LAUNO
LAURIS/LAURITZ
LEIF
LENNART
LORENZ/LORENS

MAGNUS
MIKKEL
MIKKO
MORTEN

NELS
NIELS
NIILO
NILS
NJORD

ODIN
OLAF/OLOF
ORJAN
OSKAR
OVE

PAAVO
PEDER
PELLE
PER

RIETI
RIKARD
ROALD
ROLF

SOREN	TOR
STAFFAN	TORSTEN
STEN	TRYGVE
STIAN	TYR
STIG	
SVANTE	ULF
SVEN	
SVERRE	
	VALDEMAR
	VALENTIN
TAIT	VERNER
THOR	VIGGO

SLAVIC NAMES

GIRLS

ADELINA	CELINA
AGATÁ	
ALENA	
ALIDA	DANIKA
ALINA	DASHA
ALINKA	DOROFEI
ALZBETA	DOSIA
AMALIA	
ANASTASIA	ELZBIETÁ
ANASTAZIE	ESTZER
ANEZKA	EWÁ
ANIELA	
ANTONINÁ	
	FANYA
	FEODORA
BARA	FILIPA
BASIA	FRANZISKA
BRONYA	FYODORA

GALA	LIDIA
GALINA	LIDMILA
GIZELA	LILLÁ
	LUBA
HALINA	LUDMILA/
HANÁ	LUDMILLA
HEDVIG	LUIZA
ILKA	MAGDÁ
ILONA	MARGIT
IRINA	MARIKA
IVANNA	MARINÁ
IZABELLÁ	MASHA
	MAVRA
JAGÁ	MILDA
JANÁ	MILENA
JELENA	
JONNA	NADYA
JOZEFINA	NASTASIA
JUDITA	NATALYA
	NATASHA
KAMILÁ	NINA
KAROLINÁ	
KASIA	OKSANA
KATERINA	OLÁ
KATINKA	OLENA
KATYA	OLEXA
KILINA	OLGA
KIRA	OTILIE
KLAUDIA	
	POLINA
LARA	
LARISA	RADA
LICIA	RAINA
LIDÁ	RAISA

ROZA	VALESKA
RUZENA	VARVARA
	VERA
SARI	
SASHA	
SIBILIA	WANDA
SONYA	
STEFANIÁ	
SVETLANA	YELENA
TALYA	
TAMARA	ZANETA
TANYA	ZINA
TATIANA	ZOFIA
TEODORA	ZUZANNA

BOYS

AKIM	BARTO/BARTOS
ALEKSANDER	BAZYLI
ALEXEI	BÉLA
ALEXEJ	BENEDYKT
ALYOSHA	BORIS
AMBROZ	BORYS
ANATOLI	
ANDRAS	
ANDREI	CEZAR
ANDREJ	
ANTON	
ANTONIN	DARIUSZ
ANZELM	DIMITRI/DMITRI
ARKADI	DMITRO
ARSENI	DOBRY
ARTEMI	DOMINIK

EELIA

EVGENI/EUGENI

FABIAN

FERENC

FILIP

FLORIAN

FYODOR

GÁBOR

GASPAR

GEORGI

GREGOR

GRIGORI

GYORGY

HAVEL

IAKOV

IDZIO

IGOR

ILYA

IMRE

IVAN

IZYDOR

JAKUB

JALU

JAN

JÁNOS

JAREK

JAZON

JENŐ

JERZY

JIRI

JOSEF

KÁLMÁN

KAMIL

KÁROLY

KAZIMIR

KOLYA

KORNEL

KRYSTOF

LAJOS

LÁSZLÓ

LAVRO

LECH

LEONTI

LEOS

LEV

LÓRÁNT

MAKSIM

MAREK

MIKLOS

MIKHAIL

MIKOLAS

MILOS/MILOSZ

MISHA

MORIZ

NIKITA

NIKOLAI

NOE

ŐDŐN

OLEG

PAVEL	VADIM
PIOTR	VALENTIN
	VANYA
RODION	VASILI
ROMAN	VENEDIKT
	VIDOR
SÁNDOR	VILEM
SASHA	VILMOS
SAVVEL	VLADIMIR
SEMYON	VLAS
SERGEI	
SEVASTIAN	
STASIAK	YAKOV
STEPAN	YEGOR
SZYMON	YURI
TIBOR	
TIMOFEI	ZAREK
TOMAS/TOMASZ	ZOLTÁN

SPANISH NAMES

GIRLS

ADELA/ADELINA	AMALIA
ADRIANA	ANA
AFRICA	ANTONIA
AIDA	APOLONIA
ALEJANDRA	AQUILINA
ALETA	AURELIA
ALIDA	
ALITA	
ALMA	BEATA
ALOISIA	BEATRIZ/BEATRIX

BELIA

BELICIA

BENICIA

BIBIANA

BLANCA

CALIDA

CAMILA/CAMELIA

CARLOTA

CARMELA

CARMEN

CATALINA

CATARINA

CELESTINA

CHARA/CHARO

CHELA

CINTIA

CLARITA

CLELIA

CLIO

CONSTANZA

CONSUELO

CORAZON

DALILA

DAMIANA

DAMITA

DAVINA

DELFINA

DEMETRIA

DOLORES

DOMINGA

EDITA

ELECTRA

ELEONORA

ELOISA

EMELIA

ENRIQUA

ESMERALDA

ESPERANZA

ESTRELLA

EULALIA

FABIANA

FABIOLA

FAUSTA/FAUSTINA

FELICIA

FELIXA

FERNANDA

FILIPA

FILOMENA

FRANCISCA

GENOVEVA

GIANINA

GRACIA

GRACIELA

GUADALUPE

IDALIA

IDONIA

ILEANA

IMELDA

INÉS/INÉZ/YNÉZ

ISABELA

ISOLDA	MILENA
IVONNE	MIRANDA
JACINDA/JACINTA	NADIA
JADA	NARDA
JAZMIN	NATALIA
JUANA/JUANITA	NELIA
JULIETA	NEVA
JUSTINA	NIDIA
	NOEMI
LAUREANA	NUELA
LAURENCIA/	
LAURENTIA	OCTAVIA
LELIA	ODELIA/ODILIA
LETICIA	OLIMPIA
LIA	
LIANA	PALMA
LIDIA	PALOMA
LILIA	PAOLA
LILIOSA	PAULINA
LOLITA	PAZ
LORENZA	PIA
LOURDES	PILAR
LUCELIA	
LUCIA	RAFAELA
LUCINDA	RAMONA
LUISA	RAQUEL
LUPE	RÍA
LUZ	
	SABANA
MAGDALENA	SABINA
MANUELA	SAMARA
MARISOL	SANCHA
MERCEDES	SARITA
MIGUELA	SERAFINA

SOLANA

SOLEDAD

YNEZ

YOLANDA

YSABEL

TAMAR

TIA

TIANA

ZAIDA

ZAIRA

ZITA

VALERIA

VIOLETA

VIVIANA

BOYS

ACACIO

ADAN

AGUSTIN

ALEJANDRO

ALEJO

ALONZO

ÁLVARO

AMADEO

AMADO

AMANDO

ANDRÉS

ANSELMO

ANTÓNIO

AQUILINO

ARCINIO/ARSENIO

ARLO

ARMANDO

AUGUSTO/
  AUGUSTINO

AURELIO

BARNABUS

BASÍLIO

CALIXTO

CALVINO

CARLOS

CELESTINO

CELIO

CLAUDIO

CLEMENTE/
  CLEMENTO

CLETO

CONRADO

CORNELIO

CRISPO

CRISTÓBAL

CRUZ

DANILO

DEMETRIO

DIEGO

DOMINGO

DONATO

EDMUNDO

EDUARDO

ELIGIO

ELIO

ELVIO

EMILIO

ENRIQUE

ESTEBAN

ESTEVAO

EUGENIO

FABIO

FEDERICO

FELIPE

FÉLIX

FERNANDO

FIDEL

FILIPE

FRANCISCO

FREDERICO

GABINO

GALO

GREGORIO

GUILLERMO

GUTIERRE

HECTOR

HELIO

HUGAN

IBAN

ÍÑIGO

ISIDORO

JACINTO

JACOBO

JAIME

JANDINO

JAVIER

JENARO

JOAQUIN

JORGE

JOSÉ

JULIO

JUSTO/JUSTINO

LAUREANO

LÁZARO

LEANDRO

LEONARDO

LIBORIO

LISANDRO

LOPE

LORENZO

LUCIO

LUIS

MANUEL

MARCOS

MARINO

MATEO

MAXIMO

MIGUEL

NARNO	REY/REYNALDO
NATALIO	RICARDO
NEREO	RODRIGO
NICASIO	RUBEN
NILO	
NOÉ	SALVADOR
	SANCHO
OCTAVIO	SANTIAGO
ORILIO	SEVASTIÁN
ORLANDO	SEVERINO
ÓSCAR	SILVANO
OTILIO	
	TABO
PABLO	TADEO
PACO	TAJO
PASQUAL	TEODORO
PATRICIO	TITO
PAULO	TOMÁS
PAZ	TULIO
PEDRO	
PLÁCIDO	VALERIO
	VASCO
QUINTILIO/QUINTO	VENTURO
	VIDAL
	VIVIANO
RAFAEL	YAGO
RAIMUNDO	
RAMÓN	
RAUL	ZENOBIO

MADONNA & CHILD

Lourdes, the shrine of miracles, fit this tiny wonder better, Madonna decided, than Lola, who what she wants she gets . . . it seems entirely appropriate to name this child for a tiny French mountain village that no one would have ever heard of if not for its association with that other Madonna, the Immaculate Girl.

—NEW YORK

VARIAZIONI ON A THEME

Sometimes a good way to find a slightly unusual and exotic name is to consider foreign variations on what otherwise might be considered a fairly prosaic English name. Some of those we particularly like—with their English cognates—are:

GIRLS

ADETTE (*French*)	*for*	**ADELINE**
ADRIANA (*Italian*)		**ADRIENNE**
AINE (*Irish*)		**ANNA**
ALEJANDRA (*Spanish*)		**ALEXANDRA**
ALEKA (*Hawaiian*)		**ALICE**
ALESSANDRA (*Italian*)		**ALEXANDRA**
ALESSIA (*Italian*)		**ALEXA**
ALEXANDRINE (*French*)		**ALEXANDRA**
ALIDA (*Hungarian*)		**ADELAIDE**
ALIZ (*Hungarian*)		**ALICE**
AMALIE (*German*)		**EMILY**
AMANDINE (*French*)		**AMANDA**
ANAÏS (*Hebrew*)		**ANN**
ANIELA (*Polish*)		**ANGELA**

ANIKA (*Czech*)	ANNA
ANNELLA (*Scottish*)	ANNE
ANNIK/ANNIKA (*Slavic*)	ANN
AVRIL (*French*)	APRIL
BARBRO (*Swedish*)	BARBARA
BERTILLE (*French*)	BERTHA
BLANCHETTE (*French*)	BLANCHE
CAITRIONA (*Irish*)	KATHERINE
CARO (*Spanish*)	CAROL
CATIA (*Portuguese*)	CATHERINE
CHIARA (*Italian*)	CLAIRE
DAEL (*Dutch*)	DALE
DASHA (*Russian*)	DOROTHY
EDDA (*Polish*)	EDITH
ELSBETH (*German, Scottish*)	ELIZABETH
EMILIA (*Italian*)	EMILY
ENRICA (*Spanish*)	HENRIETTA
EVVA (*Russian*)	EVE
FEODORA (*Russian*)	THEODORA
FIONNULA (*Irish*)	FLORA
FLANN (*Irish*)	FLORENCE
GINEVRA (*Italian*)	GENEVIEVE
GRANIA (*Irish*)	GRACE
ISABEAU (*French*)	ISABEL
JANICA (*Czech*)	JANE
JENICA (*Romanian*)	JANE
JENSINE (*Scandinavian*)	JANE
KASIA (*Polish*)	KATHERINE
LILIA (*Spanish*)	LILLIAN
LILIJANA (*Slavic*)	LILLIAN
LISETTE (*French*)	ELIZABETH
LORENZA (*Italian*)	LAURA
LUCIENNE (*French*)	LUCY
MAIRE (*Irish*)	MARY
MAIREAD (*Irish*)	MARGARET

MALIA (*Hawaiian*)	MARY
MANON (*French*)	MARY
MARGIT (*Hungarian*)	MARGARET
MARIT (*Scandinavian*)	MARGARET
MARITZA (*German*)	MARISA
MARZIA (*Italian*)	MARCIA
MELISANDE (*French*)	MELISSA
MIGUELA (*Spanish*)	MICHAELA
MOIRA (*Irish*)	MARY
NICOLA (*Italian*)	NICOLE
NOEMI (*Italian*)	NAOMI
OONA (*Irish*)	AGNES
PAOLA (*Italian*)	PAULA
PAVIA (*Russian*)	PAULA
ROZA (*Slavic*)	ROSE
SINEAD (*Irish*)	JANE
SIOBHAN (*Irish*)	JOAN
SORCHA (*Irish*)	SARAH
VARVARA (*Russian*)	BARBARA
VERONIQUE (*French*)	VERONICA
VITTORIA (*Italian*)	VICTORIA
XUXA (*Brazilian*)	SUSANNAH
YNEZ (*Spanish*)	AGNES
ZARITA (*Spanish*)	SARAH
ZOIA (*Slavic*)	ZOE
ZUSA (*Czech/Polish*)	SUSAN
ZUZI (*Swiss*)	SUSAN

BOYS

ABRAN (*Spanish*)	*for*	ABRAHAM
ADRIANO (*Italian*)		ADRIAN
ALASTAIR/ALASDAIR (*Scottish*)		ALEXANDER

ALEJANDRO/JANDO (*Spanish*)	**ALEXANDER**
ALESSANDRO/SANDRO (*Italian*)	**ALEXANDER**
ALEXANDRU (*Romanian*)	**ALEXANDER**
ALEXIOS (*Greek*)	**ALEXANDER**
ALLESIO (*Italian*)	**ALEXANDER**
ALUN (*Welsh*)	**ALAN**
ANDERS (*Swedish, Danish*)	**ANDREW**
ANDREAS (*German, Greek*)	**ANDREW**
ARAM (*Armenian*)	**ABRAHAM**
ARNO (*Italian*)	**ARNOLD**
ARRIGO (*Italian*)	**HENRY**
BARDO (*Danish*)	**BARTHOLOMEW**
BARTO (*Spanish*)	**BARTHOLOMEW**
BAZIL (*Czech*)	**BASIL**
BENOÎT (*French*)	**BENEDICT**
BJØRN (*Scandinavian*)	**BERNARD**
CHARLOT (*French*)	**CHARLES**
CLAUDIO (*Spanish/Italian*)	**CLAUDE**
CLOVIS (*French*)	**LOUIS**
COLIN (*Irish*)	**NICHOLAS**
DANO (*Czech*)	**DANIEL**
DEWI (*Welsh*)	**DAVID**
DUARTE (*Portuguese*)	**EDWARD**
EAMON (*Irish*)	**EDMUND**
EDO (*Czech*)	**EDWARD**
EERO (*Finnish*)	**ERIC**
ELIA (*Italian*)	**ELIJAH**
ESTEBAN (*Spanish*)	**STEPHEN**
ETIENNE (*French*)	**STEPHEN**
EWAN (*Scottish*)	**EVAN**
FRANCHOT (*French*)	**FRANCIS**
GERRIT (*Dutch*)	**GERALD**
GRAEME (*Scottish*)	**GRAHAM**
GWILYM (*Welsh*)	**WILLIAM**
HEW (*Welsh*)	**HUGH**

ILIE *(Romanian)*	ELIAS
JAAN *(Estonian)*	JOHN
JACO *(Portuguese)*	JACOB
JENO *(Hungarian)*	EUGENE
JENS *(Danish)*	JOHN
JORGEN, JOREN *(Danish)*	GEORGE
LARS *(Swedish)*	LAWRENCE
LEV *(Russian)*	LEO
LIAM *(Irish)*	WILLIAM
LORCAN *(Irish)*	LAURENCE
LUC *(French)*	LUKE
LUCIANO *(Italian)*	LUCIAN
MARCOS *(Spanish)*	MARCUS
MATTEO *(Italian)*	MATTHEW
MIGUEL *(Spanish)*	MICHAEL
MOZES *(Dutch)*	MOSES
NIALL *(Scottish, Irish)*	NEIL
NICOLO *(Italian)*	NICHOLAS
NIELS *(Danish)*	NEIL
NILO *(Finnish)*	NEIL
OLIVIER *(French)*	OLIVER
ONDRO *(Czech)*	ANDREW
ORLANDO *(Italian/Spanish)*	ROLAND
PABLO *(Spanish)*	PAUL
PADRAIC/PADRAIG *(Irish)*	PATRICK
PAOLO *(Italian)*	PAUL
PHILIPPE *(French)*	PHILIP
PIERO/PIETRO *(Italian)*	PETER
PIET *(Dutch)*	PETER
RAOUL *(French)*	RUDOLPH
REDMOND *(Irish)*	RAYMOND
ROBINET *(French)*	ROBERT
SAMO *(Czech)*	SAMUEL
SAMU *(Hungarian)*	SAMUEL
SEAMUS *(Irish)*	JAMES

SIMEON (*French*)	SIMON
TADEO (*Spanish*)	THADDEUS
TAVISH (*Scottish*)	THOMAS
TOMAZ (*Portuguese*)	THOMAS
UILLIAM (*Irish*)	WILLIAM
VASILIS (*Greek*)	BASIL
VITTORIO (*Italian*)	VICTOR
WILLEM (*Dutch*)	WILLIAM
YOEL (*Hebrew*)	JOEL
ZAKO (*Hungarian*)	ZACHARIAH
ZAMIEL (*German*)	SAMUEL

JEWISH NAMES

Only a few short years ago, we felt perfectly comfortable saying that there was no such thing as a "Jewish" first name anymore; now we're not so sure. For although large numbers of Jewish parents continue to follow national trends, and there are as many Kyle Cohens as there are Kyle Culhanes, a growing percentage are now, like members of other ethnic and religious groups, looking back into their own heritage, at less common Old Testament names, at Hebrew names, and at names that have become popularized in Israel.

From the early biblical period on, first names have held a powerful, often symbolic significance for Jews. In the beginning, names were given that reflected some momentous event—either public or within the family—which had taken place around the time of the baby's birth. Later, with the taking of the Jews into Babylonian captivity, Palestinian Jews appropriated the Egyptian practice of naming children after deceased family members.

A dichotomy in this matter developed between the Ashkenazi Jews from Central and Eastern Europe and the Sephardim from Spain and the Balkan countries, North Africa, and the Middle East. The former believed in honoring deceased parents and grandparents in order to preserve their name and memory, also holding the superstition that naming a baby after an older living relative might confuse the Angel of Death, while the latter had no such strictures. In fact, Sephardic Jews evolved a fixed convention for baby naming: the oldest grandson was named for his paternal grandfather, the oldest granddaughter for her father's mother, whether the grandparents were living or not. Subsequent offspring would be named for their maternal grandparents, followed by uncles and aunts.

Contrary to widespread belief, there are no Jewish laws pertaining to the subject of naming a baby after a deceased relative, and no reference to it in the Bible. Actually, names borrowed from the Bible did not come into use until the sixteenth century—prior to that each Old Testament personage, from Adam and Eve on, was thought to have exclusive title to his or her name.

When masses of Jewish immigrants arrived at Ellis Island at the end of the nineteenth century, most of them held on to a somewhat transliterated version of their own names. It was with their children, the first American-born generation, that the nomenclature suddenly changed. Following the old tradition of using the same initial letter for the English name as for the Hebrew one, and in an effort at instant assimilation, these newcomers were determined to bestow on their sons and daughters the most elegant-sounding, non-ethnic Anglo names they could find. Thus, the descendant of Moishe might be called Murray (a Scottish surname), Morton or Milton (British surnames), Myron (a Classical Greek name), or Marvin (Old Welsh). The strategy backfired, however, when these names were adopted in such prodigious numbers that Milton, Marvin, and so forth began to be thought of as "Jewish" names.

The names Milton and Marvin and their generational peers, such as Seymour, Stanley, and Sheldon, are rarely given to babies now, and the reason for this can be explained by the theory we call the Kosher Curve. As we said, first-generation immigrants typically try to renounce any hint of their ethnicity by choosing the most mainstream names of their new country. It isn't until the third or fourth generation that there is a resurgence of ethnic identity and pride, plus sufficient psychological distance, for the original names to sound fresh and youthful enough to be bestowed on a baby. By the 1970s, for instance, the world was ready for a new era of Maxes, Sams, Bens, Jakes, Mollys, and Annies, while the eighties and nineties saw a rebirth of Annas, Hannahs, Henrys, Harrys, Jacks, Sarahs, Rachels, and Rebeccas. The big question: Are we ready to bring back Shirley and Sherman? Not quite yet.

THE KOSHER CURVE

The following chart tracks some representative American-Jewish given names and their permutations from the turn of the century to the present.

ABE	ARTHUR	ALAN	ADAM	AUSTIN
ANNIE	ANN	ANITA	ANNIE	ANNA
BEN	BERNARD	BARRY	BEN	BENJAMIN
CLARA	CLAIRE	CAROL	CARLY	CLARISSA
DORA	DOROTHY	DIANE	DEBBIE	DAKOTA
FANNY	FRANCES	FRANCINE	FERN	FRANCESCA
HANNAH	HELEN	HELENE	HEATHER	HANNAH
HARRY	HENRY	HARRIS	HARRISON	HENRY
ISAAC	IRVING	IRWIN	IRA	ISAIAH
JAKE	JACK	JAY	JASON	JACOB
JENNY	JEAN	JEANETTE	JENNIFER	JENNA
LILY	LILIAN	LINDA	LORI	LILY
MAX	MARVIN	MITCHELL	MICHAEL	MAX
MOLLY	MARIAN	MARSHA	MARCY	MADISON
NELLIE	NORMA	NANCY	NICOLE	NELL
RACHEL	RUTH	RENEE	RANDI	RACHEL
ROSE	ROSALIE	RHODA	RHONDA	ROSIE
SADIE	SYLVIA	SUSAN	STACY	SADIE
SAM	SHELDON	STEVEN	SAM	SAWYER
SARAH	SALLY	SHEILA	SHELLY	SARAH
SOPHIE	SHIRLEY	SHARON	SHERRY	SOPHIE
TESSIE	THELMA	TERRY	TIFFANY	TESSA

JEWISH NAMING CEREMONIES

For several generations, it has been traditional to name a male child at the time of his circumcision, the eighth day after his birth. At that time the mohel (circumciser) recites a Hebrew prayer for the child, incorporating his name ("Let his name be called in Israel as——, the son of——.").

The naming ceremony for girls is of much more recent origin. Called brit bat, brit banot Yisrael, or simchat bat, it became prevelant in the 1960s and 1970s, with the advent of feminism. Because the ceremony is so new, there are no precise rituals and the celebration is open to the creativity of the family, but there is usually a ceremonial pronouncement of the child's name, as well as stories and reflections on the relative whose memory the baby honors.

HEBREW & ISRAELI NAMES

According to an Israeli friend, only the most Orthodox Jewish families in Israel use the kind of traditional Old Testament names—Rebecca, Noah—favored by American Jews. Instead, they turn to choices like these:

GIRLS

ABIAH	ALIYAH
ABIRA	ALIZA
ADAH	AMALYA
ADAYA	AMMA
ADIAH	ANINA
ADINA	ARIELA
AHLAI	ARIZA
ALIMA	ASHRA

ATARA

AVIVAH

AZUBAH

BAARA

BAT-SHEVA/
  BATHSHEBA

BETHE

BINA

BITHIA

BLUMA

CARMA

CARNIA

CHANIA

CHARNA

CHAYA

CHIBA

DALYA

DEVORAH

DORIT

DOVEVA

ELIANA

ELIEZRA

ELIORA

ELISHEBA

ELULA

GALIA

GAVRIELA

GITEL

GOLDA

HADASSAH

IDRA

ILANA

INBAR

JETRA

JORDANA

JOSEFA

KANARA

KELILA

KETURAH

KETZIAH

KHANNAH

KIRIAH

LEEONA

LEVIAH

LILIT

LINIT

LIORA

LIVYA

MAHALIA/
  MAHALAH

MARAH

MENORAH

MIKA/MICAH

MIRYAM

NAAMAH

NAARAH

NATANIAH

NEDIVA	SHOSHANNAH
NEILA	SHUA
NEVONAH	SHULAMIT/SHULA
NIMA	
NISSA	TALMA
NOAH	TALYA
NOOMI/NAOMI	TAMAR
	TAVORA
OFFIR	TIRZAH
OPHIRA	TOVAH
ORPAH	TZAHALA
	TZILA
PAZIAH/PAZ	TZINA
PENINA	TZOFI/TZOFIA
RAANANA	VARDA
RAISA	
RAKHEL	YAEL/JAEL
RAYNA	YAFA
RAZIELA/RAZ	YASMIN
RENANA	YEMIMA
RIVKA	
	ZAAVA
SAMIRA	ZAHARA
SANSANA	ZARA
SAPHIRA	ZAVIDA
SARAI/SHARAI	ZEMORAH
SHAI	ZILLAH
SHIFRA	ZIRAH

BOYS

ABBA	ADAEL
ABIEL	ADIN

ADIR	BINYAMIN
ADLAI	BOAZ
ADON	
ADRIEL	CHAGAI
AHAB	CHAI
AHARON	CHAIM
ALON	CHALIL
AMAL	CHAZON
AMIDOR	
AMIEL	DEVIR
AMIR	DIVON
AMIT	DORAN
AMOZ	DOV
ARIAV	DOVEV
ARIEL	
ARLES	EFRON
ARON	EITAN
ASA	ELAN
ASAEL	ELAZAR
ASHER	ELIAM
ASSAF	ELIAZ
AVIAH	ELIHU
AVIEL	ELISHA
AVIV	EPHRAIM
AVRAHAM	ETAN
AZ	EZRI
AZAI	
AZIEL	GAAL
	GAHAM
	GALIL
BARAQ	GAMALIEL
BARUCH	GAVRIEL
BENAIAH	GEDALIAH
BENONI	GERSHOM
BENZION	GERSON

GILEAD

GURIEL

HILLEL

HODIAH

HOSEA

IDAN

IDO

ILAN

ISHMAEL

ITAI

ITHRO

ITZAK

KALIL

KEMUEL

KENAN

KOLAIAH

LABAN

LAEL

LAVI

LEV

LEVI

MACABEE

MALACHI

MALKAM

MALUCH

MAON

MAOZ

MEIR

MENAHEM

MICHA

NAOR

NEHEMIAH

NOAM

NOAZ

OMAN

ORAN

OREN

OZ

RAPHAEL

RAVIV

RAZ

RENON

REUEL

SAMAL

SELIG

SETH

SHALLUM

SHAMIR

SHAVIV

SHILOH

SHIMON

SION

TABEEL

TALMAI

TEVYE

TOBIYAH

TOVIEL

TZEVI

URI	YOAV
URIEL	YOEL/JOEL
UZIAH	YONAH/JONAH
	YOSHA
YAAKOV	YOSSI
YAAL	
YABAL	ZAKAI
YABIN	ZALMAN
YAMIN	ZAMIR
YAOSH	ZAN
YARED	ZARED
YASHIV	ZAVACHIAH
YEDIDIYAH	ZAVID
YEHUDAH/JUDAH	ZEBEDEE
YITZCHAK	ZIV
YOAB/JOAB	ZVI

CONAN, PATRON SAINT OF LATE-NIGHT TV, AND OTHER UNUSUAL, LIVELY, AND SURPRISING SAINTS' NAMES

If because of tradition or religion you want to give your child a saint's name, you don't have to settle for obvious choices like Anne, Cecelia, Anthony, or Joseph. Yes, there really is a Saint Fabian, as well as Saints Chad, Benno, Phoebe, Susanna, and Colette. What follows is a selective list of unexpected saints' names:

FEMALE

ADELA	AGATHA
ADELAIDE	ALBINA

ANASTASIA	EMILY
ANGELA	EMMA
ANGELINA	EUGENIA
ANTONIA	EULALIA
APOLLONIA	EVA
AQUILINA	
ARIADNE	FABIOLA
AUDREY	FAITH
AURIA	FELICITY
AVA	FLORA
	FRANCA
BEATRICE	
BEATRIX	GEMMA
BIBIANA	GENEVIEVE
BRIDGET/BRIGID	
	HEDDA
CANDIDA	HYACINTH
CHARITY	
CHRISTINA	IDA
CLARE	ISABEL
CLAUDIA	
CLEOPATRA	JANE
CLOTILDA	JOANNA
COLETTE	JOAQUINA
COLUMBA	JULIA
CRISPINA	JULIANA
	JUSTINA
DARIA	
DELPHINA	LELIA
DIANA	LEWINA
DOROTHY	LOUISA
	LUCRETIA
EBBA	LUCY
EDITH	LYDIA

MADELEINE	SABINA
MARCELLA	SALOME
MARINA	SANCHIA
MARTINA	SERAPHINA
MATILDA	SILVA
MAURA	SUSANNA
MELANIA	
MICHELINA	
	TATIANA
NATALIA	THEA
	THEODORA
ODILIA	THEODOSIA
OLIVE	
PAULA	VERENA
PETRONILLA	
PHOEBE	
PRISCILLA	WINIFRED
REGINA	
RITA	ZENOBIA
ROSALIA	ZITA

MALE

AARON	ALEXIS
ABEL	AMBROSE
ABRAHAM	AMIAS
ADAM	ANSELM
ADOLF	ARNOLD
ADRIAN	ARTEMAS
AIDAN	AUBREY
ALBERT	AUSTIN
ALEXANDER	

BARDO	EDMUND
BARNABAS	EDWIN
BARTHOLOMEW	ELIAS
BASIL	EPHRAEM
BENEDICT	ERASMUS
BENJAMIN	ERIC
BENNO	ERNEST
BERTRAND	
BLANE	FABIAN
BORIS	FELIX
BRENDAN	FERDINAND
BRICE	FERGUS
BRUNO	FINNIAN
	FLAVIAN
	FLORIAN
CASSIAN	
CHAD	
CLEMENT	GERARD
CLETUS	GILBERT
CLOUD	GILES
COLMAN	GODFREY
CONAN	GREGORY
CONRAD	GUNTHER
CORNELIUS	GUY
CRISPIN	
CYPRIAN	HENRY
CYRIL	HERBERT
	HILARY
	HUBERT
DAMIAN	HUGH
DANIEL	HUMBERT
DECLAN	
DIEGO	ISAAC
DONALD	ISIDORE
DUNSTAN	ISRAEL

JASON	OTTO
JOACHIM	OWEN
JONAH	
JORDAN	PIRAN
JULIAN	
JULIUS	QUENTIN
JUSTIN	
	RALPH
KEVIN	RAYMOND
KIERAN	REMI
KILIAN	ROCCO (Italian version
	of Saint Roch)
LAMBERT	RODERIC
LEANDER	RUFUS
LEO	RUPERT
LEONARD	
LINUS	SAMSON
LLOYD	SEBASTIAN
LUCIAN	SILAS
LUCIUS	SIMEON
	SIMON
	SYLVESTER
MALACHY	
MARIUS	THEODORE
MAXIMILIAN	TITUS
MEL	
MILO	VIRGIL
MOSES	
	WILFRED
NARCISSUS	WOLFGANG
NOEL	
NORBERT	YVES
OLIVER	ZACHARY
OSWALD	ZENO

SOME CELTIC SAINTS

FEMALE

AIDEEN	GWENN
AINE	
ALMA	INA
	JENIFRY
BERYAN	
BREACA	
BRIGID	MARGARET
	MORGANA
	MORWENNA
CEARA	
CIAR	
COLUMBA	ORNA
CONNA	
	RIONA
	RIVANON
DOMINICA	
	TALULLA
EITHNE	TARA

MALE

AENGUS	BRAN
AIDAN	BRAZIL
ALAR	BRECCAN
ALOR	BRENDAN
AUSTELL	BROGAN
BARRI	
BECAN	CADOC
BLANE	CASS

CELLACH	IVAR
CIARAN	
COLM	JARLATH
CONALL	
CONAN	KADO
CONLEY	KILIAN
CONRAN	
CORCAN	LORCAN
CORMAC	
	MALACHY
DAVID	MALCOLM
DECLAN	MEALLAN
DENIEL	
DEWI	ORAN
DONAN	
	PADRAIG
EOAN	
EWEN	RIAN
	RONAN
FALLON	RUADAN
FAOLAN	
FERGUS	SAMZUN
FINNAN	
FINNIAN	TIARNAN
	TOLA
GARMON	TUDI

FAMILY

Family is a central consideration when choosing names, both in wrestling over individual choices to finding names from the family tree to keeping everyone in the family from trying to dominate your name decision.

In this section, we offer advice on how to reconcile your name tastes with your mate's, how to deal with your family's name advice and opinions, and what to do if your sister wants to give her baby the same name you want to give yours.

Also, here are thoughts on how to construct a family of names for siblings, what to do about naming twins, and whether or not you should make your son a junior.

And what to do if you can't decide on a name, or if two months later you still can't quite get used to the one you picked? Hint: Don't panic unless truly desperate.

YOU SAY MARIA, I SAY MARIAH: WHEN COUPLES DISAGREE ABOUT NAMES

*M*ost couples agree on whether they want kids. They often reach an easy accord on *when* they want them. Many even are like-minded on such sticky issues as where they'd prefer to raise their children, how they'd like to educate them, and what style of discipline they believe in.

Choosing a name can prove more problematic than any of the above.

Names are one of those subjects that summon up all kinds of hopes and fears, desires and secrets that you might otherwise never have guessed about your mate. How else, but on the hunt for the perfect name, would you discover that your husband once got his nose bloodied on the playground by a red-haired she-bully named Kelly, and ever since cannot abide the name? When might you have occasion to confess that you dated not one but, um, *three* guys named Michael, so he might not want to push that one for your firstborn son?

Such individual associations are par for the baby-naming course. Conceiving your child may have made you feel, more than any other step you've taken together, as if you had finally and truly become one. Choosing its name can remind you that, nope, you're still actually two.

There are all those people with all those names that each of you knew and loved or hated before you met each other. Those ancient experiences and emotions are key determinants of whether you like a name or loathe it. If you and your spouse retreat to separate corners and draw up individual lists of your favorite names, then exchange your lists, chances are you'll cross off half of each other's picks because you went to third grade with an Elizabeth whose nose was always running, or had a college roommate named Daniel who told terrible jokes.

Then there are your individual families and backgrounds

to consider. Couples who successfully negotiate religious difference and complicated family holidays sometimes find themselves stymied by conflicting name ideas and requirements. One couple we know, for instance, compromise his Jewish and her Catholic backgrounds by attending a Unitarian church, but when naming their baby hit a deep divide when he wanted to follow religious tradition and give their child a name that started with the same letter as that of his recently deceased grandmother, and she bucked against being pinned down to only names beginning with *s*.

Another factor that can make for difficult name negotiations between prospective parents is that, in most cases, one of you is a man and the other is a woman. A study by Charles Joubert of the University of Northern Alabama demonstrated that men and women often have very different tastes in and ideas about names.

Joubert asked his male and female subjects to choose a name for a hypothetical child from a list he provided. Men, he found, were more likely to choose common or old-dated names for children of either sex, but less likely to propose recently popular names. Women were more likely to propose a common name for a boy than for a girl, less likely to elect unusual names for boys than for girls.

Another issue: men and women often have very mixed ideas on the child's gender identity and on the signals a name sends out. Many moms, for example, like boys' names that sound

---

THE ART OF COMPROMISE

Niki, the name we finally gave to my younger daughter, is not an abbreviation; it was a compromise I reached with her father. For paradoxically it was he who wanted to give her a Japanese name, and I— perhaps out of some selfish desire not to be reminded of the past—insisted on an English one. He finally agreed to Niki, thinking it had some vague echo of the East about it."

—KAZUO ISHIGURO, *A PALE VIEW OF THE HILLS*

creative and nontraditional, but some dads are fearful of giving their son a name that might label the boy as a wimp.

"There are two kinds of boys' names," one father told us, "the kind that makes you sound like you can hit a baseball and the kind that makes you sound like you'd sit in the outfield looking at the clouds. I was the type of kid who looked at the clouds, but I want my son to be a ball-hitter." A Bob, in other words, or a Dave, a Steve, or a Charlie. Not a Miles or a Jasper.

On the other hand, moms tend to be more comfortable with girls' names that are androgynous or even decidedly masculine, while dads seem to like frillier, more traditional girls' names. Mom campaigns for Alix, for example, while Dad favors Alicia; Mom likes Sydney, Dad opts for Samantha.

Why the gender gap? Some mothers may be more sensitive than their spouses to sexism and stereotyping. And for girls, moms tend to think about names they would have liked to have had themselves, while dads are looking at the issue from the outside in. Of course, when it comes to naming boys, the situation is reversed, and it's the father who can imagine firsthand what it might be like to be a Cyril when teams are being picked.

What of gay couples? There, the associations to names might be more similar, but the gender issues may get more complicated. A gay male couple we know who were adopting a baby daughter, for instance, wanted to give her the family name Carson. But, they worried (as did we), was it unfair to give a girl who was sure to face complex gender issues in her upbringing a name that further muddied the gender waters? Maybe, and yet this was probably the only child they would have and they dearly wanted to use a name that had been in the family for generations. The solution: They named her Carson, and call her the more conventional (and feminine) Carrie.

How to resolve any naming problems you and your spouse might be having? Here are some tips:

TALK ABOUT ISSUES LIKE IMAGE AND GENDER BEFORE YOU TALK ABOUT NAMES. What do you each hope for in a child? Is your fantasy child energetic or studious, "all-boy" or gentle, feminine or tomboy? Coming to agreement on these matters, or at least getting them out in the open, can help when you're choosing a name, not to mention raising your child.

RULE OUT ALL NAMES OF EX-GIRLFRIENDS AND EX-BOYFRIENDS. No matter how much you like the name Emily, do not proceed with it if your husband had a long, torrid affair with an Emily way back when. Do not tell yourself you'll forget: You won't, and neither will he.

MAKE A "NO" LIST AS WELL AS A "YES" LIST. Most couples only make lists of the names they like; it can help to make lists, too, of the names that are absolutely out for each of you. Include those you'd rule out for personal reasons (the roommate who stole all your clothes) as well as names you simply hate. Agree that neither of you will bring up the names on each other's "absolutely not" lists, no matter how much you like them or how neutral they may be for you.

AVOID USING THE NAME-SELECTION PROCESS AS AN OPPORTUNITY TO CRITICIZE EACH OTHER'S LOVED ONES. When he campaigns for naming your son Morton after his father, this is not an excuse to tell him how much you dislike his father, no matter how much you detest the name Morton.

INVESTIGATE THE REASONS FOR EACH OTHER'S CHOICES. Let's say you love a name your spouse hates. Instead of fighting over the name itself, explore what it is about the name that appeals to you. Figuring out whether you like a name because it's classic, or feminine, or stylish can lead you to other names with the same characteristics that both of you like.

REMEMBER THAT PARENTHOOD IS A JOINT VENTURE. Just as your child will be a unique blend of characteristics from both of you, so should you endeavor to arrive at a name that combines each of your sensibilities and tastes. If you absolutely can't find a name you both love, agree that one of you will choose the first name, the other one the middle.

Or one will name this child, the other will name the next. Such enlightened negotiation and compromise is what marriage is all about.

FAMILY NAMES

Parents today are shaking the family tree in an energetic attempt to come up with names that are personally significant as well as stylish. One satisfying benefit of a family name is that it conveys the essence of a loved one, bestowing his or her best qualities on your child. Even if you never knew the forebear for whom you name a child, family stories about the person—his heroism during the Civil War, her solo flight over the mountains of Peru—come alive again through the name, granting your child an instant and noble legacy.

Of course, the power of names is not to be taken lightly. While you may love the melody of Grandpa Malachy's name, will you be able to hear it without thinking of his sour disposition? Or maybe it's the name itself that hits a wrong note: Great Aunt Mildred may be a saint and a millionaire, but could you really burden your adorable baby with her unfashionable moniker?

In Colonial America, most children were named after relatives. In one extended Southern clan whose naming patterns were analyzed, 90 percent of the families used father's name, 79 percent used paternal grandfather's name, and 40 percent used maternal grandfather's name for a son. Girls were named for kin less often than boys, but family names were still widely used: 72 percent of families named a daughter for her mother, 44 percent for paternal grandmothers, and 52 percent for maternal grandmothers.

Many Latin countries have strict family-naming protocols that are followed even today. The first son is named after the father's father, the first daughter after father's mother, second son and daughter after the mother's parents, and subsequent children after aunts and uncles first on the paternal and then on the maternal side of the family. In some traditions, this pattern deviates so that boys are more often named after the father's side of the family, and girls after the mother's side.

Historically, family names were important because they helped consolidate kinship ties and family wealth. Today, the motivation for choosing a family name may be more generally to strengthen family ties and imbue the child with a sense of history. Who you name your child after, and how you do it, is less rigid, more creative.

There are, in fact, several ways to honor terrific family members with less-than-terrific names or to mollify a difficult yet prominent relative without clouding the everyday existence of your child. Mildred might make a fine middle name, which can always be shorted to the letter *M*. Or you might choose a variation such as Millie or Millicent, which both have an old-fashioned sweetness that Mildred lacks. And if you have two grandpas battling for name superiority, why not use both as middle names, as the royals do? Prince William's full name, for instance, is William Arthur Philip Louis Windsor.

There may also be some great names hiding deeper in the family vault. Look to

CALL ME CALVIN

Among European Jews it's traditional to name a child in memory of someone. People like my parents tended to fulfill that obligation loosely by giving the child the same Hebrew name as the person being memorialized and an English name that had the same first sound. Like my cousin Keith and my cousin Kenneth, I was named in memory of my father's father—whose own name eventually acquired a consistent spelling of Kusel . . . Honoring some other departed relative, my father came up with the rather tony middle name of Marshall. ("It's an old family name," I've sometimes explained. "Not our family, but still an old family name.")

—CALVIN TRILLIN, *MESSAGES FROM MY FATHER*

ancestors' middle names, which may be maiden names or the names of their ancestors. Collecting family records and birth certificates is a valuable exercise that can yield family names that might otherwise be forgotten.

Transforming last names into first names is another way to resurrect family names. Politicos James Carville and Mary Matalin pulled an innovative switch when they named their daughter Matalin Mary Carville.

Be open-minded about the names you unearth. Many choices may not seem consistent with today's fashions, but if you give names time—or focus on the people you love who held them first—they may start to sound better to you. A friend who gave her daughter her mother's name of Margaret rather than the faddier version Megan finds that she loves the authentic version more and more over time.

If you don't find a name you like in your family tree, consider a new name with the same meaning as a family original: Grandma Gloria, for instance, might be honored by a child named Abigail, Felicity, or Hilary, as all four names mean happiness or joy. Or look to a name that symbolizes a characteristic of a much-loved family member: One mother we know called her son Reid, which means "red-haired," to honor her red-tressed father.

The one forbidden practice when it comes to family names is to cave into family pressure and name your child after someone you don't like, or whose name you can't stand. This pressure can be considerable at times, and can really rob you of a lot of the pleasure that can go into choosing a name. The only solution is to ward off the suggestions from the outset by saying something gentle and direct: "I know you'd love to see Grandma Helen's name live again, but we really have to insist that this be our decision." And then drop the subject of names—forever.

PUTTING THE NAME BEFORE THE BABY

In this age of amniocentesis and ultrasound, many parents have the option of knowing their baby's sex—thus making a firm decision on a name—long before his or her arrival.

While these medical advances have been a boon for mothers and babies alike, and knowing your child's sex can cut the work of choosing a name in half, we nevertheless caution against telling the world your child's gender and name months before his or her actual arrival.

Announcing in midpregnancy that a boy named Dawson is waiting to be born can have a dampening effect on his entrance into the world. For one thing, other people tend to draw a more or less complete picture of little Dawson's looks and personality, based on his name and their knowledge of his parents, long before they get a chance to meet him! For another, you may find that other people are actually less eager to meet him. Instead of waiting by the phone for news of your baby's sex and name, they may receive your announcement with a bored, "Oh, Dawson's finally here."

The only real advantage we can cite for sharing your child's name before his birth is not really that much of a plus: People can give you shower gifts of little T-shirts with Dawson spelled out on the back.

BAD ADVICE?

What are you going to name the baby?

That's the question of the hour, or rather, the question of the entire nine months leading up to your baby's birth. Everyone from your family and friends to the woman selling newspapers at the corner will want to know. The problem is that all those people will have opinions, too—contradictory, confusing, often debilitating.

Let's say you and your mate have agreed that, if the baby is a boy, you will name him Ned. You tell your mother-in-law.

"I had a great-uncle Ned," she says. Pause. "He drank."

You tell your best friend.

"Have you noticed," she says, "how so many nerdy movie characters are called Ned?"

You tell your brother.

"Sounds like a seventy-year-old," he says.

You tell your ten-year-old, who makes gagging noises. "All the kids will hate him!" she cries.

Your four-year-old agrees with his sister. "I hate him," he says.

Before all these outside opinions, you thought Ned was a fine name; now you're not so sure. And even if you still like the name Ned, you don't want your child's grandmother to associate him with the family alcoholic, your friends to gossip about how bad your taste is, or your children to reject the baby because of his name.

So you and your husband come up with a new idea. Let's say it's Jack. This time, your mother-in-law approves, your best friend thinks it's too groovy, your brother thinks it's bland, and your kids still hate it.

All right: How about Omar? Your mother-in-law, brother, and best friend all think it's too bizarre; the ten-year-old thinks it's cool; the four-year-old stands fast in his dislike.

At this point, you may be catching on to the fact that the four-year-old might be having problems with the idea of the baby beyond choosing its name. And it also might be dawning on you that, no matter what name you set forth, there's going to be someone who doesn't like it. How do you decide which naming advice you take to heart, which you disregard?

The first step might be to consider your sources. People who've never had kids may be ignorant of swings in style and may also be out of touch with how names affect kids.

> ## IT TAKES TIME TO FIND THE RIGHT NAME
>
> *People are horrified we haven't come up with a name yet,"* said mom Maria Shriver in one of her first public outings since the debut of Schwarzenegger No. 4 two weeks ago. ... *"We want to find a name that fits the child,"* Shriver said.
>
> —IRENE LACHER, *LOS ANGELES TIMES*

Other children in your family may have a very good idea of how a name will be perceived by fifth graders, but no long-range take on a name's viability. A friend or relative who's had children in the past five years, however, may be able to give you an educated opinion on a name's popularity as well as advise you on how the choice of a name feels to a parent over time.

The next step may be to review the general taste of those offering their opinions. Would you let these people choose what color you paint your house? Would you let them pick out your clothes? Their tastes in other matters are a good indication of the validity of their taste in names.

The final step—which often proves to be very enlightening—is to ask those who offer their opinions for name suggestions of their own. You may well find that your mother-in-law loves the name John, too basic for your tastes. Your best friend suggests Homer and Jethro, which you find too offbeat. Your brother likes Darryl and Curtis, too declassé. The ten-year-old offers Max and Sam, the names of the most popular boys in her class, but too popular for you. And the four-year-old's idea of a good name? Rainbow Boy.

Despite all those negative opinions, you may find Ned sounds better by the minute.

BABY, JR.

The easiest solution to the question of what to name a baby boy is simply to repeat the father's name, appending to it the letters *Jr.* Although this practice is fading out of fashion, it does have certain advantages: a direct link with a progenitor, the pride that goes with carrying on a family name.

But the disadvantages can outweigh the benefits. The child may well feel he's inheriting an identity along with a name, that he's merely a paler shadow of his father, that he will always be number two.

In addition, if a boy is actually addressed by the same

name as his father, countless confusions will arise, from the most obvious, such as "Which Donald do you want, Big Donald or Little Donald?" on the phone, and fathers and sons opening (and reading) each other's mail, to subtler ones, like mother having to call the two most important males in her life, husband and son, by the same name.

On the other hand, if the child is actually called Junior, he is somewhat dehumanized, almost like being referred to as a number, and a lesser number than his father at that. More common is for the child to be known by the familiar, childish form of the name, a practice that spawns its own perils. Dad is Don and junior is Donny, forever locked by his name into an adolescent (or younger) image of himself that persists long after he leaves home. Or, even worse, he might be known to the world as Bud, Buster, Butch, Sonny, Skip, or Chip.

Giving a boy the same name as his father and grand-father—making him a III—is a somewhat different issue. On the positive side, it could be argued that you're carrying on a family tradition rather than purely indulging in ego-tism. And honorable WASP nicknames for IIIs—Tripp, Tre, or Trey—are not quite as humiliating as the ones many juniors are saddled with. On the down side, little Frederick or Albert the third has the image of not one but two grown-up men to live up to, with a fairly strong (and potentially overwhelming) mandate to carry on the family tradition.

Only one president in the history of the United States has been a junior—James Earl Carter, Jr., who, as we all know, insisted on being known by his childhood nickname of Jimmy. Gerald Ford was born Leslie Lynch King, Jr., but his name was changed when he was adopted by his stepfather. Vice President Al Gore is a junior, and the man we know as Bill Clinton was born William Jefferson Blythe IV. Relatively few juniors are to be found among high achievers in sports or the fine arts. However, there are lots of military men, junior grade.

How to avoid the pitfalls or juniordom and still name your son after his father? You could go the royal route and name him Donald Dalton Duckworth II. Or the child could be given a different middle name, say Donald Duncan Duckworth, be called Duncan by the family, and later sign his memos D. Duncan Duckworth. But before taking this approach, remember the old saying, "Don't trust anyone who parts his name on the side."

BIG TROUBLE WITH JUNIOR

In a study ominously titled "The Trouble with Junior," researcher Catherine Cameron comes to the conclusion that boys named after their fathers do tend to run into more trouble down the line than those with individual names—they encounter more child abuse and later are more delinquent. The reason? Cameron says that although all sons carry their father's surnames through life and thus add luster or tarnish to that name, since juniors replicate their fathers' entire names, they may therefore be more susceptible to parental expectations, becoming a focus for pride or a target for abuse.

Among the results cited were: a higher rate of juniors was found in a hospital psychiatric ward than in the general population and a higher percentage of parental abuse was in the histories of those boys. Statistically, 21 percent of the institutionalized boys were juniors, while only 10 percent were found in a regular high school; and 37 percent of the juniors had been abused as children, as opposed to 15 percent of those not father-named.

SOME JUNIORS WHO MADE NAMES FOR THEMSELVES

KAREEM ABDUL-JABBAR *(Ferdinand Lewis Alcindor, Jr.)*

MUHUMMAD ALI *(Cassius Marcellus Clay, Jr.)*

ED BEGLEY, Jr.

MARLON BRANDO, Jr.

WILLIAM F. BUCKLEY, Jr.

JIMMY CARTER *(James Earl Carter, Jr.)*

TOM CLANCY *(Thomas L. Clancy, Jr.)*

HARRY CONNICK, Jr.

BILL COSBY *(William H. Cosby, Jr.)*

WALTER CRONKITE *(Walter Leland Cronkite, Jr.)*

ROBERT DE NIRO, Jr.

JOHN DENVER *(Henry John Deutschendorf, Jr.)*

JOHNNY DEPP *(John Christopher Depp, Jr.)*

ROBERT DOWNEY, Jr.

CLINT EASTWOOD *(Clinton Eastwood, Jr.)*

CUBA GOODING, Jr.

AL GORE *(Albert Arnold Gore, Jr.)*

LOUIS GOSSETT, Jr.

KEN GRIFFEY, Jr.

DON IMUS *(John Donald Imus, Jr.)*

RICK JAMES *(James A. Johnson, Jr.)*

MAGIC JOHNSON *(Earvin Johnson, Jr.)*

QUINCY JONES, Jr.

ELMORE LEONARD *(Elmore John Leonard, Jr.)*

BILL MAHER *(William Maher, Jr.)*

ED McMAHON *(Edward Leo Peter McMahon, Jr.)*

RONALD REAGAN, Jr.

ROBERT REDFORD *(Charles Robert Redford, Jr.)*

BURT REYNOLDS *(Burton Leon Reynolds, Jr.)*

MICKEY ROONEY *(Joe Yule, Jr.)*

MICKEY ROURKE *(Philip André Rourke, Jr.)*

NOLAN RYAN *(Lynn Nolan Ryan, Jr.)*

ANTONIO SABATO, Jr.

WILLARD SCOTT *(Willard Herman Scott, Jr.)*

RIP TORN *(Elmore Torn, Jr.)*

GERALD FORD *(Leslie Lynch King, Jr.)*

GORE VIDAL *(Eugene Luther Vidal, Jr.)*

DENZEL WASHINGTON, Jr.

FRANK ZAPPA *(Francis Vincent Zappa, Jr.)*

EDWARD ALBEE *(Edward Franklin Albee III)*

ALEC BALDWIN *(Alexander Rae Baldwin III)*

BEAU BRIDGES *(Lloyd Vernet Bridges III)*

BILL CLINTON *(William Jefferson Blythe IV)*

TOM CRUISE *(Thomas Cruise Mapother IV)*

TED DANSON *(Edward Bridge Danson III)*

MILES DAVIS *(Miles Dewey Davis III)*

LAURENCE FISHBURNE III

JACK LEMMON *(John Uhler Lemmon III)*

TRINI LOPEZ *(Trinidad Lopez III)*

LUKE PERRY *(Coy Luther Perry III)*

RICHARD PRYOR *(Richard Franklin Lennox Thomas Pryor III)*

TED TURNER *(Robert Edward Turner III)*

SIBLING NAMES
(FOR FIRST-TIME PARENTS ALSO)

If you're having your second, third, fourth child, or beyond, you have probably already experienced the inherent difficulties and dilemmas involving sibling names. Ideally, the names you choose for later children should "go with" the name you picked for your first child: They should be harmonious in rhythm and style. At the same time, names of later children should be different enough from the first child's name to avoid confusion. Yes, there are families with a Jane and a Jean, a Larry and a Harry, an Ellen and an Eleanor, but the resulting mix-ups do not seem worth the cuteness.

The real problem with sibling names arises because most parents don't consider later names when they choose the first. But the first choice sets the pattern, narrowing future options. Here's how it works:

Because we have personal experience with this one, let's say you decided to name your first child, a girl, Rory. Good enough, but now you're about to have your second. Names that rhyme are out: Good-bye Laurie, Corey, Glory, Maury, Tory, and so on. So too with similar-sounding names: everything in the Rose family, the Mary family, the Doria group, the Lauras, Coras, Noras, and Floras, not to mention Larry, Gerry, Terry; Rowen, Rourke, Rollo. You get the idea.

Also, because Rory is such a distinctively Celtic name, it would sound odd with a name from a different ethnic background. Rory and Francesca won't do, for example. In terms of image, Rory is clearly a high-energy name. Would it be fair to pair her name with one from the No-Nonsense group? Would a little sister named Ruth, for example, always feel bookwormish by contrast; would Rory, conversely, feel flighty in comparison? Another consideration is the name's ambisexuality. Choosing a sister's name from the Feminine or Feminissima group—Angelica, for instance, or Melissa—might not only sound discordant but could make the two girls feel differently about their sexuality. And if the sibling is a boy, giving him a unisex name could make matters even more confusing. A girl named Rory with a brother named Ashley? It just wouldn't work. Finally, Rory is a somewhat unusual name, and a more classic choice for a brother or sister could also strike the wrong chord. Rory and Jane? Rory and John? Somehow they just don't belong together.

Further complications set in if you have changed your ideas about names after living with your real live first choice for a few years. You may regret choosing a unisex name like Rory because of all the confusion over whether the child was a boy or a girl, and may also wish you had chosen a more common name that was easier for the child to pronounce and for others to understand. You may really want to name your second child Jane or John, yet not feel comfortable with those choices.

The point of all this is to encourage you to consider future possibilities when you're choosing the name of your first child. If your two favorite names are Anna and Hannah, for example, realize that picking one now rules out the other forever. When you're deciding among several names, consider the future implications of each. Imagining which names might follow for other children may help you narrow the field.

What, in particular, works and what doesn't? Without

taste or value judgments on the specific names, we can tell you some instances of sibling names we're familiar with that do work. Jane and William, for instance, or Sam and Lily. Both pairings are good because, for one, the girls' names are clearly feminine and the boys' names are clearly masculine. The style is consistent: fashionable, but not to the point of cliché. And the names sound harmonious but not confusingly alike. Another good brother-and-sister combo is Elizabeth and Charles, called Libby and Charley. Both are classic names that happen to be in style now, and both nicknames are gently old-fashioned, more compatible than, say, Liza and Chuck would be.

Two brothers whose names catch the right rhythm are Felix and Leo. Both are traditional names—saints' names in fact—that, because they havn't been widely used for some years, have an appealingly offbeat quality. The *x* and the *o* endings provide different but equally unusual sounds for the two names, and they are further related by both being feline.

We know a family of three girls named Melissa, Danielle, and Lauren. Their mother wanted to name the third daughter Patricia. But the classic Patricia—or Pat or Patti—simply did not sound like the sister of the trendier Melissa and Danielle, so Lauren she became.

When the name of a fictional character breaks rank with those of his or her siblings, there's usually some symbolism involved. The classic case is *Little Women*'s Meg, Jo, Beth, and Amy. Even if you haven't read the book, guess which one was the tomboy with ambitions greater than her sisters?

So too in real life, where the child with a name that is "different" from those of his brothers and sisters may also feel different in spirit. We know of a family with four children named Mary, Christopher, Nicole, and Alexandra. It's clear here too which one considers herself the odd child out.

If you already have your first child and are choosing a name for a sibling, keep the following guidelines in mind:

DON'T BE CUTE: No rhymes, sound plays, precious pairings. Resist the temptation, for example, to name Daisy's sister Maisie, Darcy, or Hyacinth.

DON'T FALL INTO THE SAME-INITIAL TRAP: A trend of the fifties and sixties was to choose sibling names all starting with the same letter. Sometimes, parents didn't consider the consequences if they had chosen to start with the letter *E* and happened to have, say, five boys. Edward was fine for the first, Eliot okay for the second, but by the birth of their fifth son they were stuck with choices like Earl, Elmer, and Egbert. While few parents have five children today, the same-initial trend should be avoided as dated and overly precious.

DO MAINTAIN CONSISTENCY OF STYLE, IMAGE, SEX, AND TRADITION: This rule is to be interpreted loosely, but, as detailed in the example of Rory, sibling names should ideally stay in the same, well, family.

BE CAREFUL ABOUT SEXUAL DISTINCTIONS: If you choose a boyish name for your daughter, and later have a son, go with a boy's name that is clearly masculine. So too if you give your boy a unisex name; both he and his little sister will fare better if her name is distinctly feminine. The names of same-sex children should not have widely divergent sexual images: Bruno's brother shouldn't be named Blair, for instance; nor should Belinda's sister.

AVOID USING TWO NAMES WITH THE SAME NICKNAME: This problem usually crops up when parents, hoping for a junior, despair at the third girl and name her Roberta or Christina or Geraldine. She then becomes Bobbie or Chris or Gerry. When her long-awaited little brother is born five years later, he is named Robert or Christopher or Gerald. Try as the parents might to prevent it, they may end up with a Bobbie and a Bobby, Chris and Chris, or Gerry and Gerry, in addition, of course, to Bobby, Chris, or Gerry, Sr. The trend toward smaller families has headed off most occurrences of this problem in recent years, but it still happens. If you're entirely positive that if you ever have a boy you'll name him Christopher, don't name a girl Christina when you give up hope on having a son, or vice versa. Accidents do happen.

DOUBLE TROUBLE

Twins offer a rare opportunity for parents to choose two related names at the same time, but also multiply the difficulties inherent in sibling names. With twins, it can be more tempting to use rhyme, sound play, and same-initial names, but in our opinion pairings like Eddie and Teddy, Faith and Charity, or Charles and Charlene should be relegated to a time capsule. While same-initial names that are clearly distinct from each other, such as Ross and Rachel, the twin children of Jane Pauley and Garry Trudeau, are okay, different-initial names that are consistent in style and tone are preferable.

Some celebrity examples that work: Cybill Shepherd's Ariel and Zack; Denzel Washington's Malcolm and Olivia; Ron Howard's Paige and Jocelyn. In all these cases, the names are distinct from each other yet make a harmonious pair—exactly what most parents would want for the twins themselves.

Two examples of twin names that don't work as well— Debby Boone's Gabrielle and Dustin, and Mia Farrow and André Previn's Matthew and Sascha—fall short for the same reason: Each set has one sexually distinct name and one unisex name. Based on the names alone, one would surmise that they were both boy-girl pairs. In fact, Gabrielle and Dustin are twin girls, and Matthew and Sascha are both boys.

Whatever the sex of the children, twin names should present a compatible image. As detailed in the discussion on sibling names, pairings like Gigi and Walter or Candida and Jennifer are too discordant. Gigi's twin would better be named, perhaps, Barnaby; Walter's sister might be Margaret; Candida's twin could conceivably be called Isabella; and Jennifer's obvious other half is—who else?—Jason.

WHOSE NAME IS IT, ANYWAY?

It is Thanksgiving. You and your sister-in-law, both newly pregnant, are sitting with the rest of the family around the table. The conversation turns to names.

"If we have a boy, of course he will be Richard the Third," says your sister-in-law, smiling sweetly at your father. Your brother, Richard, Jr., beams.

You, on the other hand, choke on your cranberry sauce. Ever since you were a little girl, you've wanted to name your first son Richard. Besides being your father's name, it's also your husband's father's name, your brother's name, and your favorite name for a boy in all the world.

"We were planning on Richard, too," you manage to sputter.

"You can't have it," booms your brother. "Clearly it's our name."

"There's room for two Richards in the family," you reason. "We'll just use different nicknames."

"That's stupid," your brother says. "Ricky and Richie?"

"Now, now," soothes your mother. "What if you both have girls?"·

"Amanda," you and your brother say in unison.

If you and your spouse have proliferating siblings, the issue of who gets to use which names is one you may have to face. And a difficult issue it is. Does a son have absolute dibs on the father's name? Is there room in a family for two cousins with the same name? Is there a pecking order for who gets traditional family names? Is·getting there first a good enough reason to usurp somebody else's name? Can you set claims on a name to begin with?

How you answered these questions depends a lot on your individual family. In some families, the oldest son has eternal right to his father's name, even if he never has a son of his own. In others, it's first-come, first-served, with the understanding that there will be no later duplications. And some families just play catch-as-catch-can, and worry later about how they'll deal with three cousins named, say, Eric.

If you anticipate some name-wrestling within your own family, keep the following tips in mind:

ANNOUNCE YOUR CHOICES EARLY ON: If you have an absolute favorite name you're sure you will use, don't make a secret of it. Planting it in everyone's mind as "your" name can help avoid problems later.

DON'T STEAL SOMEONE ELSE'S NAME: We're not talking about naming your baby Letitia, unaware that, on the same day in a different state, your sister is naming her baby Letitia. We're talking about naming your baby Letitia when your sister has been saying since she was fifteen that her fondest wish in life was to have a little girl named Letitia. And your sister is eight months pregnant. And knows she's having a girl.

AVOID CARBON COPIES: Two little Caroline Townsend Smiths in a close-knit family is one too many. If you want to use the same first and middle names that a sibling uses, can you live with a different nickname—Carrie, for instance? Or can you vary the middle name, so that, at least within the family, one cousin is called Caroline Townsend and the other, say, Caroline Louise? The only case in which two cousins named Caroline Townsend and called Caroline can work is if they have different last names.

HONOR FAMILY TRADITIONS: If the oldest child of the oldest child in your family is always named Taylor, don't break rank, unless your oldest sibling is a nun, priest, or gay rights organizer who has formally renounced rights to the name.

TAKE UNINTENTIONAL, UNIMPORTANT DUPLICATIONS IN STRIDE: We know two sisters-in-law, living across the country from each other, who were pregnant at the same time: Jane due in January, and Anne in April. During their annual Christmas Eve phone conversation, Jane said she was sure she'd have a boy, and that they were planning to name him Edward. "That's our name," gasped Anne. "Too bad," Jane said blithely. After a few minutes of intense anxiety, Anne decided Jane was right. Neither had officially "claimed" Edward, nor was it a name with any family significance. It would be as ridiculous to insist that Jane change her choice at the eleventh hour as it would be to deny her own son the name just so it wouldn't duplicate that of a cousin he'd see, at best, once a year. Besides, Jane favored the nickname Eddie, while Anne preferred Ted. P.S.: Due to mitigating circumstances, neither baby was named Edward. They ended up Juliet and Josephine.

THE NAME BECOMES THE CHILD

Finally comes the day when you hold on to your live child in your arms and make a final decision on a real live name. At that point, all the lists you've made, the considerations you've weighed, and the options you've juggled fall by the wayside and you and your child are left with your ultimate choice.

What happens then?

Well, on the one hand, the struggle over Miranda versus Molly seems less crucial in the face of three A.M. feedings, colic, and the high cost of diapers. And it doesn't take long for your baby's persona to dominate the name, for your baby to become his or her name. For the first two weeks, you may find yourself still calling little Miranda "It"; for the next few, you may feel self-conscious each time you pronounce the name; but a month later you'll find that when you say "Miranda" you don't hear the sound of the name but see instead your child's curved lips and dark curls.

On the other hand, once you've settled on a name, you deal with its myriad implications, often for the first time. You may discover, for instance, that your Aunt Elizabeth is not satisfied to be honored by a mere middle name, that people on the street do not necessarily assume Jordan is a girl, and that friends have to suppress a snicker when you tell them you've named your son Henry.

This may not be fun. This may cause you to retrieve your original lists of possibilities and say to your spouse in the middle of the night, "Maybe we should have named him Michael." And of course, it is possible to change a child's name two days or two months or even two years after you've given it, but it's not easy for many reasons and it's not what we're considering here.

Better than contemplating a name change would be to

mull over the fact that choosing one option—in names as in everything else—always means forgoing all others. That the name you've selected inevitably becomes influenced by reality, while the ones you've rejected remain fantasies, entirely pleasant because you alone control them. That in fact if you had chosen Michael, say, you might then be worrying about its ordinariness, and wishing in the middle of the night that you had gone with something more distinctive, like . . . Henry.

Obviously, much of the value of this book is that it helps you anticipate the real-world repercussions of a name. And much of the impetus for writing it came from our own experiences and those of our friends in choosing names for children and living with those choices.

One of our friends, for instance, has two children: Emily and Jeremy. "When Emily was born we were living in the country and it seemed like a really special, unusual name," she says. "Then when she was a few months old we moved to the city and I discovered that there were little Emilys everywhere. I felt terrible. I would listen in the playground for other kids named Emily, I would pore over nursery school class lists for other Emilys, and if she was the only Emily I'd feel so relieved. On one hand I feel badly because it seems as if the name is a cliché, but there also aren't so many Emilys as I'd originally feared."

Our friend pinpoints another reason why she was unaware of how widely used the name Emily was (and another reason we wrote this book): "Having a first child I didn't really know any other young parents. I had no idea what people were talking about when they named their kids or what the new style was. My idea of a trendy name was still Barbara or Sue."

What then of Jeremy's name? "That one I haven't had so many problems with," she says, "except that some people keep trying to call him Jerry."

Parents who've chosen less usual names talk of unanticipated problems with pronunciation and comprehension. A little girl named Leigh is sometimes called "Lay"; a child named Hannah is called Anna by some people. One of us has some regrets about calling her daughter Rory because the name is more often understood as Laurie, Corey, Tory, Dory, or even Gloria or Marie than its rightful self.

Then there's the issue of the child's name vis-à-vis his or her looks or personality. Many parents wait to make a name choice until they see which of their finalists best fits the child. This makes some sense, but you should be aware that a newborn is not necessarily representative of the five- or twelve-year-old he or she will become. The chubby, noisy infant daughter you name Casey may grow into a dainty, ultrafeminine ballet dancer, while the delicate baby who seems to be the quintessential Arabella may become, ten years later, goalie on the neighborhood boys' hockey team.

This brings us to the flip side of this issue: Children can irrevocably color our perceptions of their names. You undoubtedly have unique feelings about certain names based on the children you know who bear them, and so do we. When we disagreed about whether to include a particular name on a list here, it was usually because we each knew people who brought different things to it: a handsome and irreverent Ralph, for example, versus a boorish one; an adorable kid named Kermit versus the frog on TV.

Reading this book can help prepare you for some of a name's eventualities, then, but not for others. You wouldn't be surprised, as our friend was, that Emily is a fashionable name or that some people are bent on using undesirable nicknames. Neither will you be unaware of both the advantages and the complications of giving your child a popular or an unusual name, or that Cameron can also be a girl's name, or that Henry has an intellectual image and so can be perceived by some people as a bit nerdy.

But no one, including you, has ultimate control over the person your child turns out to be. A name can remind you of your hopes and fears way back when childbirth was a point on the horizon, but your child—the one who's laughing or crawling or walking across the room in his own special way—can remind you that Henry by any other name, be it Michael or Melchizedek, would still be your own sweet boy.

INDEX

BARNEY, 25, 124, 232
BARRA, 172
BARRI, 312
BARRY, 52, 63, 229, 233, 301
BART, 106, 266
BARTHELEMY, 282
BARTHÉLMY, 270
BARTHOLOMEW, 45, 46, 83,
    115, 124, 174, 310
BARTO, 286, 297
BARTOS, 286
BARUCH, 305
BAS, 266, 267
BASIA, 15, 284
BASIL, 19, 52, 115, 165, 277,
    310
BASILA, 275
BASILE, 270
BASÍLIO, 291
BASILIUS, 282
BASTIEN, 88, 270
BATHSHEBA, 15, 123, 303
BATHSIRA, 253
BAT-SHEVA, 303
BAUDIER, 270
BAY, 33, 37, 58
BAYLEE, 76, 79, 161, 214
BAYLEIGH, 76, 214
BAZIL, 297
BAZYLI, 286
BEA, 24
BEAH, 172
BEATA, 288
BEATRICE, 7, 18, 96, 119, 167,
    172, 185, 189, 200, 229, 308
BEATRIX, 200, 266, 288, 308
BEATRIZ, 288
BEAU, 82, 103, 106, 165, 176
BEAUREGARD, 97
BECAN, 312
BECCA, 24, 200
BECK, 9, 33
BECKETT, 9, 52, 98
BECKY, 24, 237
BEECH, 37
BELA/BÉLA, 95, 286
BELIA, 289

BELICIA, 289
BELINDA, 47, 123, 197
BELLAMY, 9, 58, 270
BELLE, 7, 24, 32, 33, 79, 91,
    95, 96, 97, 102, 113, 114,
    200
BEN, 24, 25, 82, 169, 301
BENAIAH, 305
BENEBA, 242
BENEDICK, 120
BENEDICT, 46, 81, 310
BENEDIKT, 266, 274, 282
BENEDIKTA, 280
BENEDIKTE, 189
BENEDYKT, 286
BENEVOLENT, 40
BENICIA, 289
BENITA, 200
BENJAMIN, 28, 57, 74, 85, 97,
    145, 173, 188, 208, 211, 225,
    237, 249, 301, 310
BENNO, 17, 165, 173, 274, 307,
    310
BENO, 258
BENOÎT, 270, 297
BENONI, 305
BENTLEY, 184
BENVOLIO, 120
BENZION, 305
BERGMAN, 13
BERIT, 280
BERNADETTE, 178, 200, 218,
    268
BERNADINE, 268
BERNARD, 65, 301
BERNARDO, 279
BERNICE, 61, 199, 204, 232
BERTHA, 65, 130
BERTHILDE, 268
BERTILLE, 268, 295
BERTITA, 272
BERTRAM, 65
BERTRAND, 310
BERYAN, 312
BESS, 24, 33, 172, 204, 228
BESSIE, 228
BETH, 136, 170, 204

MIATA, 251
MICA, 38
MICAH, 29, 166, 303
MICAYLA, 77
MICHA, 306
MICHAEL, 32, 54, 69, 73, 94,
    96, 101, 104, 130, 151, 164,
    191, 207, 208, 210, 211, 234,
    248, 249, 301
MICHAELA, 56, 70, 77, 79, 103,
    109, 162, 219
MICHEAL, 151, 263
MICHEL, 271
MICHELA, 88
MICHELINA, 309
MICHELINE, 269
MICHELLE, 56, 72, 87, 183,
    202, 219, 235, 238
MICK, 151, 229
MICKEY, 217, 232
MIGNON, 16, 269
MIGUEL, 76, 292, 298
MIGUELA, 290, 296
MIKA, 303
MIKAELA, 77, 103, 104
MIKALA, 77
MIKAYLA, 56, 70, 78, 79, 162
MIKE, 109, 160, 216
MIKHAIL, 287
MIKKEL, 283
MIKKO, 283
MIKLOS, 287
MIKOLAS, 287
MILAN, 22
MILDA, 285
MILDRED, 65, 157, 168, 204,
    206, 231
MILENA, 285, 290
MILES, 97, 108, 111, 176, 180,
    188
MILLICENT, 8
MILLIE, 25, 94
MILLY, 228
MILO, 30, 89, 104, 166, 180, 311
MILOS, 287
MILOSZ, 287
MILTON, 66, 300

MIM, 115
MIMBA, 243
MIMOSA, 38
MINA, 273
MINDWELL, 226
MINDY, 62, 236
MINERVA, 44, 49, 241
MINNA, 273
MINNIE, 8, 25, 64, 115, 142,
    172, 174, 228
MINTA, 164
MIPAM, 118
MIRABEL, 164
MIRABELLE, 16, 198, 269
MIRACLE, 41
MIRANDA, 58, 72, 77, 80, 107,
    111, 119, 164, 187, 202, 290
MIREILLE, 269
MIREYA, 77
MIRIAM, 142, 168, 206
MIRRA, 164
MIRYAM, 303
MISCHA, 166
MISERY, 245
MISHA, 287
MISHAYLA, 251
MISHIMA, 14
MISSIE, 198
MITCHELL, 104, 234, 301
MITZI, 25, 273
MOBY, 102
MODESTY, 26
MOE, 25, 59, 169
MOIRA, 19, 260, 296
MOISHE, 300
MOLINA, 11
MOLL, 173
MOLLY, 25, 88, 94, 111, 115,
    142, 187, 202, 228, 237, 301
MONA, 62, 168, 206
MONDAY, 39, 243
MONGO, 258
MONICA, 73, 202
MONIFA, 257
MONIKA, 273, 281
MONIQUE, 198, 269
MONROE, 14, 226

TAKE YOUR HEALTH INTO YOUR OWN HANDS

ORDER TODAY:

THE ARTHRITIS CURE
Jason Theodosakis, M.D., M.S., M.P.H., Brenda Adderly, M.H.A., and Barry Fox, Ph.D.
___96453-6 $6.50 U.S./$8.50 Can.

SECRETS OF SEROTONIN
Carol Hart
___96087-5 $5.99 U.S./$7.99 Can.

FOODS TO HEAL BY
Barry Fox, Ph.D.
___95987-7 $6.99 U.S./$8.99 Can.

NATURAL HEALING FOR CHILDREN
Winifred Conkling
___96044-1 $6.99 U.S./$8.99 Can.

TAKE THIS BOOK TO THE HOSPITAL WITH YOU
Charles B. Inlander and Ed Weiner
___96326-2 $5.99 U.S./$7.99 Can.

HEADACHES: 47 WAYS TO STOP THE PAIN
Charles B. Inlander and Porter Shimer
___96263-0 $4.99 U.S./$6.50 Can.

Publishers Book and Audio Mailing Service
P.O. Box 070059, Staten Island, NY 10307
Please send me the book(s) I have checked above. I am enclosing $_____ (please add $1.50 for the first book, and $.50 for each additional book to cover postage and handling. Send check or money order only—no CODs) or charge my VISA, MASTERCARD, DISCOVER or AMERICAN EXPRESS card.

Card Number_____

Expiration date_____Signature_____

Name_____

Address_____

City_____State/Zip _____
Please allow six weeks for delivery. Prices subject to change without notice. Payment in U.S. funds only. New York residents add applicable sales tax.   HH 12/97